DIALECTIC OF THE CHINESE REVOLUTION

From Utopianism to Hedonism

Dialectic of the Chinese Revolution

FROM UTOPIANISM TO HEDONISM

Jiwei Ci

Stanford University Press
Stanford, California 1994

Stanford University Press
Stanford, California
© 1994 by the Board of Trustees of the
Leland Stanford Junior University

CIP data appear at the end of the book

Printed and bound in Great Britain by
Marston Book Services Ltd, Oxfordshire

Stanford University Press publications are
distributed exclusively by
Stanford University Press within
the United States, Canada, Mexico,
and Central America

*In Memory of
My Grandmother*

For My Parents
and Shuang-shuang

Acknowledgments

I began work on this book as an Andrew W. Mellon Fellow at the Stanford Humanities Center for the 1990–91 academic year, and I wish to thank W. Bliss Carnochan and Charles Junkerman for making that year an unforgettable experience, both intellectual and personal. Having finished half the book under ideal conditions at Stanford, I had the further good fortune of being able to complete the second half at the National Humanities Center, thanks to funds provided by the John D. and Catherine T. MacArthur Foundation. The National Humanities Center, not least with its extraordinary library service, proved in every way to be a continuation of the wonderful things I had experienced at Stanford, and I am particularly indebted to W. Robert Connor and Kent Mulliken. For the opportunity to complete the final preparation of the manuscript, my thanks go to Jaegwon Kim for inviting me to be a Visiting Scholar at the Department of Philosophy, Brown University, for the 1992–93 academic year. I express my thanks to Tyrus Miller, Xiaomei Chen, Daniel Herwitz, and Debra Satz for commenting on an unpublished paper, parts of which have been incorporated into Chapter 1. I am indebted to David Konstan for commenting on ideas that went into Chapter 5. Although they have not read or commented on the manuscript, Nick Bunnin, Bliss Carnochan, Neil Cooper, Martha Nussbaum, and Sir Peter Strawson have helped me in important ways, and to all of them I am very grateful. I deeply appreciate the valuable comments of an anonymous reader for Stanford University Press on the first draft of the manuscript. My thanks go to X. Y. Wang for numerous helpful suggestions for improving the entire work. I have benefited enormously from the editorial help and advice of John Ziemer of Stanford University Press, who has seen the work through to publication with a wonderful combination of warm support and rigorous scrutiny. The last three people mentioned have done the most to make this a much better book than it would otherwise have been, though none of them, nor anybody else mentioned above, is to blame for the imperfections that remain. Finally, I wish to thank my sisters, Xiaohong and Xiaopei, for help and support, which I have always been able to count on.

J.C.

Contents

Introduction 1
1. The Detour on the Road to Capitalism 25
2. The Revenge of Memory 62
3. Teleology as Morality 102
4. The Ascetic Pursuit of Hedonism 134
5. Meaning and Fatigue 168
6. On the Far Side of the Future 207
   Conclusion 239

   Notes 247
   Works Cited 269
   Character List 275
   Index 277

DIALECTIC OF THE CHINESE REVOLUTION

From Utopianism to Hedonism

Introduction

There are many ways of writing about the past. The way that suggested itself to me, in the particular circumstances that led to the writing of this book, is what may perhaps be called the philosopher's way, and I have tried to bring it to bear upon the period of Chinese history that runs, for the most part, from 1949 to the present. In fact, there is not quite such a thing as the philosopher's way of approaching history, at least not in the same sense in which we can speak of the historian's way, with its well-established methods and readily recognizable results. History, after all, is not the philosopher's domain. By the philosopher's way, therefore, I mean to indicate that what is offered here is not a piece of historical research but rather an account of a particular period of Chinese history informed in one way or another by philosophy. Roughly, what this approach involves is not the intermingling of historical narrative and philosophical reflection but the presentation of the former in terms of the latter. There are certain intellectual endeavors to which a philosophical approach is particularly well suited, or so I believe, and these include an attempt to grasp certain vital things about human experience that are open more to introspection, even speculation, than to the observation and documentation of events. It seems worthwhile to enlist the help of philosophy in trying to make sense of a

2 Introduction

profoundly interesting period of Chinese history, if only as a supplement to historical scholarship.

The urge to do something like this first came to me amid the sadness, anger, and sense of futility in the wake of the suppression of the democracy movement in June 1989. The time had come, once again, a mere decade after Mao's death, for a major spiritual stocktaking and reorientation. As the nation's mood went from shock to despair and then, remarkably soon, from despair to business as usual, I sensed, in a way I had never quite done before, something profoundly wrong with the Chinese spirit, something whose nature and cause had to be sought at the deepest levels of the Chinese experience. Such a search was what I set out to pursue, however inadequately equipped I may have been for the task. My main object, it was clear to me from the start, was to reflect on history rather than to describe it, insofar as such a distinction could be maintained. Beyond that, it did not matter, then as now, whether what I was doing would be considered history or philosophy, or neither. To call it the philosopher's way of approaching history, as I did in the preceding paragraph, is merely an act of retrospective labeling, and a rather imprecise one at that, for the sake of orienting the reader.

Whatever the intellectual domain or domains from which I may have taken my basic categories, it is far more important that they should capture what is truly important about the period of Chinese history I cover. As I moved, in my mind, from concrete historical experience to the conceptual categories with which to comprehend it, I began to conceive, at a relatively high level of abstraction, the history of communist China in terms of the movement from utopianism to nihilism, where nihilism is to be understood not as an intellectual position but as a condition of existence (more of this later). As my thoughts on the subject matured, however, I found it even more crucial to view the experience of Chinese communism in terms of the movement from utopianism to hedonism, with hedonism both as an essential, though sublimated, component of utopianism and, in an overt form, as a sequel to nihilism. I had not expected to come to such a view of the history of Chinese communism, since on the surface Chinese utopianism was ascetic rather than hedonistic. The reader may initially experience some of the same surprise and doubt I felt. But at almost the same time as I was working out the hedonistic logic of utopianism on paper, that very same logic was unfolding itself in reality, as the whole Chinese nation threw itself into an unprecedented pursuit of wealth and pleasure.[1]

My task, then, as I eventually came to see it, was to give an account of how utopianism led, both historically and logically, first to nihilism and then, via nihilism, to hedonism. Since each of the six chapters that make up the main body of the book presents only a facet of this account, there is perhaps good reason to provide an overview here, both as a broad conceptual and historical context in which the individual chapters may be placed and as a relatively systematic complement to the messier and more nuanced picture contained in them.

Marx-inspired utopianism, first introduced into China as an ideal in the early decades of the twentieth century, became a possibility for practice after the victory of the communist-led revolution in 1949. And it did so under the most propitious of circumstances. Mao Zedong issued the call to build a communist society to a people whose political innocence and material poverty made them zealously responsive to the call of utopianism. To such a people, utopianism was at once tempting, as a quick way out of poverty, and tremendously exciting, because of its energizing newness, made all the more energizing by the charisma of the leader of the utopian project. Having never been tried in China, utopianism was burdened with no memory and no inhibitions. For a people accustomed to attach value to the past and not to think much beyond the present, utopianism enlarged the future in their consciousness and made it the purpose and meaning of their lives. In so doing, utopianism gave to their lives a heightened sense of meaning and purpose. Previously the absence of purpose had prevented radical change, but it had also helped them endure long and severe hardships. Now that someone with the power to command and the charisma to convince held out the prospect of an infinitely better future, that numbness of consciousness in which they had drowned their present misery was replaced by a heightened consciousness that eagerly, even impatiently, sought future happiness. In return for that future happiness, they were prepared as a people to believe, to obey, to strive, to sacrifice, and to expect—in ways unprecedented in Chinese history.

It is no exaggeration to say that this accentuation of the future, with its concomitant accentuation of consciousness and of meaning, totally transformed the traditional structure of experience. Stakes almost unknown when the future did not count so much came into being and introduced a new dynamic to temporal experience. The future envisioned in utopianism, like any future made the locus of an ambitious goal, brought with it the prospect of disappointment no less than of fulfillment. The heightening of consciousness that was part of the utopian project, even as it made voluntarism and social mobilization possible, threatened to undermine traditional patience and endurance, which had been so instrumental in maintaining the social fabric under circumstances of poverty and deprivation. And once utopianism had turned the awareness of meaning and the conscious search for meaning into deeply felt human needs, life not only was enlivened and enriched but also encountered a new and potentially devastating threat—the loss of meaning.

We now know that the future promised by utopianism did not materialize, that the meaning which had once so

Introduction 5

energized a people to search for collective well-being was lost, and that their heightened consciousness was left only to contemplate its degeneration into cynicism and resentment. To be sure, Mao Zedong's utopian project[2] accomplished much by standards that might fittingly be applied to China but for the utopian standards Mao himself introduced again and again. But equally, had it not been for the high hopes contained in these utopian standards, the Chinese people would not have sacrificed so much and demanded so little. Now that, with the waning of stamina and credulity after the expenditure of so much energy and trust, the time had come to sacrifice less and demand more, they faced a reality that both their utopianized consciousness and their sense of just deserts for their labor caused them to find wanting. At the point they expected the future to meet the present, meaning to become actuality, and heightened consciousness to register a sense of fulfillment, nothing happened. This gap between future and present, meaning and actuality, consciousness and fulfillment, which had been the locus of an energizing tension as long as people anticipated that the gap would one day be closed, became, once that anticipation evaporated through disappointment and loss of stamina, the very site of nihilism.[3]

Nihilism, then, as applied to China, refers to a situation in which reality and meaning have become so separated that the gap between them no longer seems to offer the possibility either for the meaningful interpretation of present reality or for hope-inspired action with a view to the future. In such a situation, it is possible to act but no longer to act meaningfully, possible to entertain abstract tenets of meaning but no longer to relate them to actual experience, so that hedonism seems the only way out. Nihilism is not an intellectual position that in leisurely contemplation one can choose to take or not; it is the product of a way of life — of thinking, feeling, hoping, and acting — having come to grief. Although it may require intellectual effort to raise this condition to the level of conscious reflection, it takes only the capacity for the acquisition and loss of meaning, which everyone has, to be open to the experience of nihilism. Indeed, an outstanding feature of the Chinese utopian project was its mobilization of an *entire* people, and insofar as utopianism, the psychological antecedent of nihilism, affected an entire people, so by the same token did its sequel, nihilism.[4]

Nihilism thus represents a disoriented condition of existence, one in which the connection between action and meaning is severed, but that condition may be experienced whether, and regardless of the degree to which, those involved have the ability or desire to raise it to the level of conscious reflection and appraisal. At the conscious level we may find nihilism articulated as a philosophical doctrine or critique, but this is neither a defining feature nor even a measure of nihilism. In the Chinese experience, it was rather a measure of the depths of nihilism that those experiencing it had, on their way from utopianism to nihilism, lost much of their capacity and even inclination for such reflection. It was therefore not consciously in terms of nihilism, as a philosophical distillation of experience, that most people perceived their actual situation of nihilism. Nihilism manifested itself rather in such non-intellectual symptoms as loss of idealism, relaxation of ideological austerity, cynicism or apathy, and even sheer bad temper — symptoms only some were able or inclined to explain as arising from the loss of meaning or the feeling of nothingness. More than any of these symptoms, hedonism, about which I shall say more later, represented one way of undergoing nihilism without raising it to the level of conscious reflection.

These symptoms of nihilism, including hedonism, emerged and worsened as the failure of the utopian project became increasingly obvious, particularly as the frenzy of the Cultural Revolution was replaced by sober disillusionment. It was in this context that the reform initiated by Deng Xiaoping became a new rallying point. Assuming the grand aims of the utopian project yet proposing to carry them out with more professionalism, while still appealing to the zeal and energy the utopian project had created, Deng's reform represented in its early stages a continuation of utopianism by other, more pragmatic means. In much of its old political and institutional context, utopianism thereby gained a new lease on life, and the progress of nihilism was slowed and even temporarily kept at bay. But with its gradual retreat from the idealistic rhetoric of the utopian project, its relaxation of ideological control, its new emphasis on the economy, and its open encouragement of consumerism, Deng's reform program not only showed an increasing readiness to compromise with nihilism but participated in its very progress.

In the gradual deepening of nihilism, two trends — hedonism and political liberalism — came to the fore. Nihilism, let us remind ourselves, is not merely the absence of meaning but the disappearance of meaning, a fall from a previous condition of meaningfulness. Itself a dynamic process, the fall from idealism into meaninglessness creates a dynamic and highly unstable situation, one that will remain so until some new meaning, and with it a new equilibrium, is found. It is in the nature of nihilism, however, that the fall from a condition of meaningfulness can give rise not only to the search for new meaning but also to a fear of meaning that comes from memory of the fall. In the Chinese case, the fall was from a height that only something as elevating as utopianism can enable a people to ascend, and the ensuing fear of heights — of idealism — was correspondingly overwhelming. In such circumstances hedonism emerged as a way of filling the void of nihilism without going through the ordeal of a new search for meaning. Deng's reform, indeed, was in part an attempt to overcome nihilism through hedonism. But the reform did not go far enough either in breaking with the repressive and ascetic practices of the utopian project or in creating opportunities for the hedonism it was encouraging. The result was the sublimation of hedonism, under circumstances of prolonged frustration, into a new ideology, namely, political liberalism.

Liberalism arose, then, in large part as the political ideology of hedonism, and in proportion as hedonism was thwarted, so liberalism, with its sublimated demands for freedom and democracy, captured the imagination of a society thoroughly disillusioned with utopianism but without, as yet, enough opportunities for escaping into hedonism. What I am saying here is not offered as a general explanation of political liberalism, nor even as an account of the *genesis* of liberal thought, in China. But there seems little doubt that the frustration of hedonism was a major cause of the growth of liberalism first into a popular sentiment and then, in 1989, into the popular democracy movement. It was highly indicative of the nature of the democracy movement that official corruption—the goods of hedonism unfairly enjoyed by some and denied to others—became a focal point of anti-government feeling that, even more than the slogans of freedom and democracy, transcended intellectual and political boundaries.

When the government crushed the democracy movement, what it sought to eradicate was not its underlying hedonism but only the political products of its sublimation. If political ideologies had kept the two sides apart, hedonism was soon to prove their common ground and their common escape from nihilism. But it had to take something as sobering as the Tiananmen massacre for both sides to bring their hedonism to the surface, each for its own reasons. It was not long before the movement from nihilism to hedonism, in which the government had until then participated only in an ambiguous fashion, acquired, with wholehearted official orchestration after the Tiananmen massacre, a new depth and a new breadth.

The two or three years after June 4, 1989, were thus pivotal in the history of post-Mao China, indeed in the history of communist China as a whole. These were the years in which the depths of nihilism were reached, bearing witness to the death of utopianism and leading in turn to the rapid growth of hedonism. It was in this crucial period of transition that the movement from utopianism to nihilism came to a definitive close and the movement from nihilism to hedonism assumed an altogether new momentum. It was in this period, too, in these two profound transitions, that the direct links between utopianism and hedonism stood fully revealed. There is a sense in which the entire trajectory of Chinese communism turned on nihilism, in that nihilism was both the effect of utopianism and the (partial) cause of hedonism.

It may seem a profound irony that the suppression of the democracy movement was, after a brief period of political terror, followed by unprecedented and officially encouraged opportunities for the pursuit of wealth and pleasure (for most people liberalism was merely the ideology of this pursuit). But if we look at the situation more closely, what we find in it is not irony but a profound revelation. The government, as if having understood the underlying hedonism of the democracy movement, set out to remove the causes that had made necessary the sublimation of hedonism into political liberalism. Unlike the political products of its sublimation, hedonism itself posed no threat to the government, unless the government was built upon principles opposed to hedonism. Of such principles, as opposed to superficial practices, the government did not have — had never had — any. And in its desperate effort to hold on to power, the government had no time for political superficialities. It had finally come to its senses, but it had yet to make its political enemies come to theirs.

The key, as the government soon divined, was the active encouragement of hedonism. What the government had denied, and continued to deny, the people at the political level, it now sought to give them at the sensual level. It thus came about that political control and economic asceticism, which had always been the twin vehicles of communist authoritarianism, were now allowed to grow apart. For the first time in four decades, even as political control was being tightened, private enterprise and consumerism, even foreign investment, were allowed to flourish — in the service of political control. Now that the Tiananmen massacre, an act of desperation, had demonstrated the limits of its power, the government realized that in the new circumstances of nihilism the only strategy that would keep it in power was not the repression of political liberalism but its de-sublimation into crude hedonism.

They were soon proved right. In proportion as people's sensual needs were satisfied, their political demands weakened and lost their relevance. Before the Tiananmen massacre, hedonism had been sublimated into political liberalism as a function of being forced through lack of satisfaction from sensual into idealistic, from economic into political channels. After the Tiananmen massacre, by exactly the reverse logic, political liberalism underwent a thorough de-sublimation as it was channeled away from idealism back to crude hedonism, from political dissent to economic prosperity. In the process, there was less and less need for heavy-handed political control, and as political control became less and less visible, political opposition to the government increasingly lost its urgency, even its relevance.

Even so, one cannot help being surprised, even shocked, by the swiftness and thoroughness with which the political opposition, after such sacrifice and bloodshed, was virtually maneuvered out of existence. But if the government's active encouragement of hedonism so soon after June 4 was an act of desperation, so was the nation's swift collective amnesia of June 4 amid new opportunities for material and sensual gratification. Earlier, with the failure of the utopian project, one massive search for meaning had come to grief. Now, with the disastrous outcome of reform and of the democ-

Introduction 11

racy movement, the search for meaning had squandered its new lease on life. And beneath the consciousness of these more recent failures was the collective memory of the demise of the Confucian tradition as a living source of meaning. Perhaps for the first time in modern China, certainly for the first time since 1949, there was the widespread sense — not always clearly articulated but unmistakably registered in the rampant growth of cynicism and apathy — that all worthwhile collective goals had been tried and found either wanting or beyond reach. This sense of futility came, moreover, for the nation as a whole, after an extraordinary amount of sacrifice and idealism over four long decades. Now that all this sacrifice and idealism had brought so much disappointment and turmoil, symbolized in a particularly chilling fashion by the Tiananmen massacre, no one had the stomach either for new sacrifice or for a new idealism.

The hedonism that soon enveloped China, pursued in the spirit of self-aggrandizement rather than collective prosperity, demanded neither sacrifice nor idealism but only respect for the political status quo. Such respect was first grudgingly and then willingly offered as fading memories of the democracy movement were overlaid with fresher comparisons, now to China's advantage, with what was happening in much of Eastern Europe and the former Soviet Union. In a world that seemed to offer fewer and fewer exciting possibilities for the human spirit, the Chinese had reason to feel lucky that at least their material life was flourishing. Indeed, now that they had lost the possibility of meaning and at least for now all interest in meaning, this material life was all they wanted to pursue. In hedonism, a spiritually exhausted people found a pursuit in which the spirit did not have to participate, an escape into meaninglessness that was at the same time an escape from meaninglessness. In hedonism also, those whose conflicting ideologies had led to June 4 could now find an ingenious compromise, one that each side for its own reasons could regard as a victory for itself. Not surprisingly, as nihilism gravitated toward hedonism, political conflict gave way to peaceful co-existence.

Hedonism, as I have tried to show, is a natural development of nihilism, a mode of life open and tempting to those for whom the possibility of values has been destroyed. But nihilism does not by itself lead to hedonism; it does so only through the crucial position that hedonism occupies in the logic of utopianism. If it is important for an understanding of how China in the past four decades has come to be what it is to see the causal links first between utopianism and nihilism and second between nihilism and hedonism, it is even more important to grasp the direct connections between utopianism and hedonism. Underlying, and making possible, the historical movement first from utopianism to nihilism and then from nihilism to hedonism is the logical movement from utopianism to hedonism.

The actual practice of Chinese utopianism was so ascetic and its rhetoric often so anti-hedonistic that it is easy to overlook the fact that, as a philosophy of human happiness, utopianism itself as conceived both by Marx and by his Chinese adherents is a species of hedonism. It would be an unnecessarily narrow understanding of hedonism, supported neither by usage nor by the history of ideas, if one were to restrict the application of hedonism to single-minded pleasure seeking in total disregard of morality and the long-term well-being of oneself and society. Needless to say, this is not what I have in mind in describing utopianism as a species of hedonism, although the hedonism that emerged from utopianism does come close to this characterization. In the context of Chinese utopianism, what I mean by hedonism — and this has much in common with the classical hedonism of Epicurus — is a conception of the ends of human life in terms of the satisfaction of what Marx, under no small influence from Epicurus, calls human "sensuous needs." The literature of Chinese communism, however rare its mentions of the concept of hedonism, abounds in descriptions of goals and ideals that fit this conception perfectly.

That Marx, as well as the Chinese communists, should place such a conception in the philosophical framework of materialism is entirely natural. In the philosophy that has guided the practice of Chinese communism, hedonism is to materialism what ethics is to ontology, although in each series the first term is not explicitly worked out but left to be implied by the second. If the concept of hedonism is seldom used in describing the normative or teleological substance of the Chinese utopian project, least of all by those involved in it, this is due in large part to the awkward position that ethics occupies in the utopian project. For one thing, just as in the works of Marx so in Chinese communism, ethics is the least developed part of the total philosophy, one important reason being that teleology has taken the place of ethics. One result of this neglect, at least for the Chinese Marxists, is a lack of theoretical understanding of the hedonistic character of the utopian project and its implications.

There is yet a more profound reason for the Chinese communists' blindness to the hedonistic nature of their project. Given the acute poverty with which the Chinese utopian project had to begin, ethics was caught in the tension between hedonism as the teleological substance of the utopian project and the actual conditions of life, in which hedonism was negated. Thus, in the ethics of the Chinese utopian project (which, contrary to Marx, was never shy of preaching morality) there was no point in prescribing hedonism as conduct. Rather, its very opposite, asceticism, was touted. Between hedonism and asceticism, however, there was no contradiction, since hedonism was the end and asceticism the means. Asceticism for now, hedonism later, so the logic went. In being postponed into the future, however, in being denied satisfaction here and now, hedonism underwent a radical transformation and emerged as utopianism. Accordingly, it was in its sublimated form, that is, in the form of utopianism, that hedonism was preached, which meant that it was not preached as hedonism.

It is in this context that we can speak of Chinese utopianism in terms of idealism. What I mean by idealism here is that hedonism exists in utopianism *in the form of* an idea or ideal rather than an actuality. In this context, then, idealism refers not to content but to form, and the idealistic or utopian form that hedonism takes is a function of its sublimation under the necessity of asceticism. As far as *content* is concerned, utopianism, or sublimated hedonism, is not idealist but materialist through and through. Mao Zedong's utopianism was an idealistic project with a materialist ontology, and because of this, the utopian project was destined to end up as hedonism, whether through success or through failure.

It was, in the event, through failure that utopianism was de-sublimated into hedonism. The utopian project had fallen far short of its original vision and yet had succeeded in significantly reducing the necessity of asceticism. Under these conditions, hedonism came to the fore both as actuality made possible by improved material conditions and as the non-sublimated desire for yet greater material gratification in the immediate future. If the logic of this process lies within utopianism itself in its original sublimation of hedonism, the agent of de-sublimation, as we saw above, was nihilism. At the start of the utopian project, the sublimation of hedonism as utopianism was made necessary by poverty and made possible by the belief, supplied by communism, that asceticism would through the products of its labor eventually make itself permanently unnecessary. With the failure of the utopian project, nihilism, the loss of belief in communism, made continuing sublimation impossible, and the improvement of material conditions brought about in part by the utopian project itself made asceticism less neces-

Introduction 15

sary, and some measure of actual hedonism possible. From the very beginning, there had been little in utopianism that was not hedonism postponed and sublimated. And so it was only natural that utopianism, once de-sublimated under conditions of nihilism, would degenerate into unalloyed hedonism.

It is the overriding importance of this logical movement from utopianism to hedonism that gives this book part of its title, with the role of nihilism, important though it is as the intermediate stage of this movement, implied rather than explicitly stated. Given this implication, the movement from utopianism to hedonism spans, both logically and historically, the two-stage movement first from utopianism to nihilism and then from nihilism to hedonism. Whereas the movement from utopianism to nihilism captures the loss of meaning caused by the failure of utopianism, and the movement from nihilism to hedonism the consequence of that loss of meaning, it is only the movement, direct as far as the logic of utopianism goes, from utopianism to hedonism that brings out the very nature of the meaning in utopianism and the mechanisms whereby that meaning was invented and destroyed.

This is a bird's-eye view of the story of the invention and loss of meaning that will unfold in these pages. But in the main body of the text I will not let it unfold quite in the way I have just done, that is, systematically and with one line of development from beginning to end. For it is a history not only with a main line of development, which I have just outlined, but also with many byways, which are as important and as interesting. It is only in these byways — that is, in the actual unfolding of the story in all its complexity and messiness — that history will come to life and show the outline just given to be merely a map that helps orient us for the journey but is not the journey itself.

If the movement from utopianism to hedonism is, as we

have seen, entirely logical, the historical process whereby this movement occurred was full of immanent reversals, unintended consequences, and self-defeating practices — characteristics we may quite fittingly describe as dialectical. Marxism, for example, proved to be China's tortuous road to capitalism, introducing the spirit of world-mastery into communist China but at the same time bringing along with it an independent teleology that hindered the very process of world-mastery. The forced crowding of Chinese memory with political doctrines and versions of history ended up creating a moral and intellectual vacuum that is being filled by the very things that "mnemonic engineering" was designed to crowd out. Indoctrination, in its very act of setting the mind in motion, proved to be at once an intentional attempt at mental enslavement and an unwitting promotion of enlightenment — so much so that we may even say that China's road from faith to cynicism was paved with indoctrination. The grounding of morality on political belief contributed in no small way to the undoing of both. Dialectical reversals such as these are numerous in China's journey from utopianism to hedonism. It is in order to capture such features of the historical process leading from utopianism to hedonism that I have chosen as part of the book's title "dialectic of the Chinese revolution."

Beyond a title to do justice to them, the complexities of this historical process, dialectical or otherwise, call in my view for a flexible approach. Accordingly, I have chosen not to proceed in such a way that a continuous account runs from one chapter to the next; rather, I have related what is fundamentally the same historical process six times in six chapters, each time focusing on a different aspect of the movement from utopianism to nihilism and hedonism. This somewhat fragmented approach applies to the structure of the individual chapters as well, so that within each chapter, in charting a byway of the historical process, I do not hesitate to explore paths branching off the byways.

Introduction 17

The result may appear to lack a historical structure holding the many strands of the work together. But my intention is not to produce a work of history but to offer a series of reflections on history that are informed primarily, though by no means only, by philosophy. Thus history is more often implied than presented in detail; the same may be said of the overall historical structure of the work. But if there is no explicit historical framework holding the narrative together, I have tried to offer in its place a broad philosophical-psychological structure consisting of the threefold movement, at once logical and historical, from utopianism to nihilism, from nihilism to hedonism, and, most important, from utopianism to hedonism. In addition to the schematic account of this threefold movement given above, a more substantial account can be found in Chapter 4, although the emphasis there is on the movement from utopianism to hedonism. The emphasis in Chapters 5 and 6 is on the movement from utopianism to nihilism, with some consideration of the movement from nihilism to hedonism in Chapter 5 but not in Chapter 6. Each of the three remaining chapters has a conceptual structure of its own, and each presents a facet of the broad philosophical-psychological structure that consists in the movement from utopianism via nihilism to hedonism. These chapters, theoretically less central but otherwise equally important, are placed first, so that the background and analysis they contain will lend the more theoretically central chapters both more clarity and more weight.

Within this relatively systematic conceptual structure, however, I have adopted a mode of writing that is often anything but systematic. As history, it tends to the episodic; as philosophy, it sometimes borders on the aphoristic — in both cases more so in some chapters than in others. I have therefore, for the most part, avoided summaries or conclusions so as not to do violence to this aspect of the work that comes precisely from its resistance to summary and highlighting. At an early stage in the germination of the project, I had contemplated, at one extreme, a work made up entirely of historical and philosophical fragments and, at the other, a study with the usual sort of structural and narrative coherence. The work I have produced is the result of a studied attempt to steer a middle course. With the somewhat fragmented character of the work, I have aimed at immediacy, flexibility, open-endedness, and room for tension and paradox. And with a loose narrative structure for each chapter (sometimes more, sometimes less), buttressed by a somewhat tighter conceptual structure, I have tried to do justice to the complementary aspects of historical experience, namely, movement, continuity, and causality. This balancing of the systematic and the fragmentary also reflects the nature of the task I have set myself. Notably in the Introduction, and to a lesser extent elsewhere in the book, I have from time to time taken the risk of presenting something of a total picture, if only for the sake of orientation. But for the most part my purpose is to offer illumination here and there, within a dotted, semi-luminous outline formed by the broad narrative and philosophical-psychological structure.

This philosophical-psychological structure entails a fairly high level of abstraction. The abstractness is in part a function of presenting history chiefly in terms of theoretical concepts (e.g., utopianism, nihilism, hedonism, the reactive mentality, the will to power, and consciousness of the future) rather than in terms that refer directly to individual historical events and actors, as historical writing typically does. Such concepts, which go naturally with broad descriptive terms (the utopian project, the Great Leap Forward, the Cultural Revolution, Mao's China, Deng's reform), are abstractions derived from concrete history with a view to their significance for historical understanding. As such they provide a more direct, though not necessarily a better, approach to the *interpretation* of history. Not that historical writing does not concern itself with interpretation or does not perform this task well. What historical writing usually does not attempt to do, however, and for its own good reasons, is, as a methodological principle, to sift all historical events through certain conceptual categories that have been worked out with a view to their significance for the interpretative task at hand.

One way of doing this is to adopt what I have called the philosophical-psychological approach. It would be misleading to regard this as the only means of access to what is important in history, but so would it be to insist that the only worthwhile approach to history is that of the historian. Indeed, every act of interpretation is an act of abstraction, and historical writing, with its unavoidable element of interpretation, is no exception. The abstraction inherent in historical writing is not obtrusive because its customary level of abstraction, shared to some extent by such well-established modes of writing as prose literature and journalism, has been made transparent through convention. But precisely because historical writing is our standard way of approaching history, there is the need from time to time to go both above and below its customary level of abstraction. For every level of abstraction from historical events and actors offers a unique kind of perspective on history. Every choice of the level of abstraction implies a view of what is important in and about the history being studied.

What I find important, although it is far from being the only thing important, in the period I discuss here is, for lack of a more precise yet compact expression, China's spiritual crisis. It is a spiritual crisis that existed *in potentia* in utopianism, came to a head in nihilism, and continues barely disguised in hedonism. It is both a symptom and a measure of the depths of this spiritual crisis that most of those caught up in it, now in hot pursuit of hedonism, do not know it for what it is, not the least because they do not want to. This situation, a crisis of the spirit that has gone largely undiagnosed by those involved in it, does not lend itself easily to the usual historical approach — or, for that matter, the relatively empirical approach typical of, say, sociology or political science. For it is the historian's strength to examine and piece together tangible records of the past, and as far as the human spirit is concerned, only what has occurred above the threshold of consciousness of the historical actors in question can leave the kind of tangible record the historian finds reliable enough to work on, with the rest probably assigned to the realm of speculation. Insofar as the rare historian sees fit to probe beneath the surface of clear consciousness by uncovering, say, the hidden or almost hidden energies and motives presupposed by events and states of mind that have occurred within full consciousness, the historian is already doing something perhaps most fruitfully and rigorously done with the aid of philosophy. Historical writing is not in the business of systematic extrapolation. The latter — the philosophical-psychological approach to history — is necessarily a riskier pursuit, prone in an especially high degree to the intellectual dangers that confront all attempts at historical understanding. But it is always a necessary pursuit, a necessary complement to historical writing, if we are to grasp that which is vitally and profoundly human in history.

My object is not the generically human but a specific period of Chinese history. With the philosophical-psychological approach and at the level of abstraction it entails, I have attempted to capture what is of vital importance in this stretch of Chinese history. This, however, is an act of inclusion, of what I find important about China, not an act of exclusion, of everything that is not specifically Chinese. I do not believe that Chinese history should be approached only in terms that apply to China alone, or that it should be approached in terms that necessarily transcend the Chinese experience and yield something of "universal" significance. My aim is to think about a specific period of Chinese history

Introduction   21

in a way that best sheds light upon it in its own right. But it is no accident that, in a human spectacle as rich in hope and tragedy and evil as Mao's China and its aftermath, I see also not only the story of twentieth-century communism insofar as it shares certain profound features with Chinese communism but also much that in an important sense is true or could be true of humanity as a whole. This consideration has also gone into my choice of a relatively high level of abstraction.

At this level of abstraction, I find I do not have to be shy of drawing on the thoughts of, say, Laozi, Nietzsche, Marx, Weber, Schopenhauer, and Adorno as they reflect on what in one obvious sense cannot but have been very different times and circumstances. But every time I cite them or others in agreement or disagreement, I do so with the sense that they are speaking, at a significant level of abstraction, of the same experience that I am trying to understand. Nietzsche, in particular, in his many insightful remarks on nihilism in its original Christian and then modern European contexts, gives me the feeling that it is the same humanity — the same human tragedy of the invention and loss of meaning — that I am writing about when I describe twentieth-century China's journey from utopianism to nihilism and hedonism.

I would resist the suggestion, however, that what I have produced is a discourse on Chinese history based, however selectively, on the Western philosophical tradition, still more the suggestion that this is somehow a Nietzschean reading of Chinese history. I have indeed drawn rather heavily on Western intellectual sources, Nietzsche in particular, but not to the same degree in the different chapters and, more important, not for the same reasons. In Chapter 1, for example, the fact that certain things of Western origin, Marxism and capitalism foremost among them, have become an intrinsic part of modern China's own problematic makes both natural and relevant my selective use of Western terms for dealing with them in the Chinese context.

The case is different with Chapter 5, where, in a way that is not intrinsically called for by the subject matter itself, I do draw upon a Western thinker—Nietzsche—in building a theoretical framework to examine the subject. But even here I bring in Nietzsche not as a thinker whose philosophy happens to provide a ready-made framework for making sense of Chinese history but, if you will, as an equal though especially insightful partner in the building of such a framework, as would anyone who wants to stand on the shoulders of past thinkers rather than at their feet. Nietzsche is only one among many Western thinkers or scholars whose ideas I find useful in Chapters 2, 4, and 6, and the use I make of them here is different from that in Chapters 1 and 5. In these three chapters, I use all intellectual sources, whether Chinese or Western, eclectically, for an insight here and an incisive formulation there. I believe this helps make the work richer and better, but these borrowings nonetheless are not central either to the conceptual structure or to the subject matter. In contrast, in Chapter 3, the conceptual structure is drawn entirely from the Chinese philosophical tradition, and even the incidental use of Western sources is minimal. This, in itself, does not make the chapter better or worse than the other chapters; it only testifies to the fact that there is no uniform strategy for what, and how much, use is to be made of Western or, for that matter, Chinese sources. The most relevant consideration for all the chapters is whether, and to what degree, I have shed light on Chinese history or have done violence to it, with or without the use of the Western intellectual tradition.

But like it or not, I cannot help but write as an "insider," as someone who has experienced, or at least seen at first hand, the utopianism and nihilism and hedonism described in these pages, someone who has the introspective knowledge—in this case the painfully introspective knowledge—that a patient has of how it feels to be sick, of what it means to be cured, but whose introspective knowledge is otherwise of no help — is no knowledge — in the search for a diagnosis and a possible cure. There is no royal road to these latter discoveries, either for the "insider" or for the "outsider." But the only insights that can be counted as true are those that do justice to the feel of experience, particularly since we are dealing with something as profoundly subjective as the experience of meaning and meaninglessness. Much of what I set out to describe I have personally experienced or witnessed; much else I have not. I have tried to do justice to how my experience — in its ineluctable uniqueness and its unavoidable limitations — feels to me, in the further hope that now and then I may also have succeeded, albeit at a theoretical level, in doing some justice to how an entire people's experience, whether or not registered in full consciousness, feels to them. The latter, much more than the former, is, after all, the task I have set myself. Except for a perspective that is unavoidably tinged with my personal experience and emotional involvement, the story that unfolds in these pages is not a personal story but that of an entire people. And I want to make sense of it as an act at once of understanding myself and of illuminating, with my very limited powers, an entire epoch.

If an atmosphere of futility and sadness envelops the story, I am also telling it with the hope that understanding this history may provide some of the resources necessary for facing and overcoming it. Hopefulness, under more propitious circumstances, ought to come from innocence, from the healthy instinct not to think and probe too deeply. The depth of China's spiritual and social crisis does not admit of this "superficial" remedy. If there is any genuine hopefulness to be had, it can come only from knowing the worst, if only so that whatever hope we may still be strong enough to feel — there is no guarantee that all of us or any one of us will find hope in this way — will not be dashed again in yet greater depths of nihilism.

CHAPTER ONE

The Detour on the Road to Capitalism

As the Chinese consciousness has moved from utopianism to hedonism, so at the same time and as part of the same historical process, China has been moving in its self-identity from would-be communism to capitalism. This profound transformation of self-identity and consciousness is the sequel to that even more profound transformation whereby China abandoned its age-old Confucian tradition in favor of the new and imported communism. China had first to let go of its old Confucian self-identity — under foreign pressure, as it happened — before it could embrace communism as its new self-identity. And then the communist project had to fail and China had to lose its respect for its communist identity before it could welcome back the capitalism that had dealt deathblows to its Confucian identity in the first place. It is only in the context of this tortuous detour from the Opium War of 1839–42 that we can make sense of the twists and turns of Chinese communism itself.

It is arguable that China might have developed capitalism on its own initiative, in which case what would have happened would not be perceived as Westernization, with its implications of cultural defeat and loss of self-identity. Be that as it may, China's actual transformation occurred under, if it was not exactly set in motion by, the Western impact (a hackneyed but still accurate description). It made a world of difference, both to the actual process of change and to the perception of its nature, that what might (or might not) have happened voluntarily happened under coercion, that what might (or might not) have occurred through the dynamic of domestic factors occurred under the overwhelming influence of foreign powers. Without such influence, China might well have "modernized" in one or more of the ways that this problematic term implies, but the history of modern Chinese consciousness would have taken a vastly different course, and this in turn could not but have made an enormous difference to the course of modern Chinese history itself. But for this history of consciousness, China's Marxist detour on the road to capitalism, as well as the conscious peripheralization of a formerly self-centered civilization, would hardly have happened.

In this light, the Opium War marked, both materially and symbolically, the birth of "modern" China.[1] It was a birth, however, that was to be recognized as such only when the effects of that violent encounter with the West, followed by more such encounters that ended in China's defeat, became clear and irreversible. One of the first such effects beyond the gradual territorial dismemberment of China by the Western powers was the division of a civilization the Chinese had hitherto viewed as *uniformly* excellent into the separate categories of value and technology, ends and means, culture and power. China could retain its sense of superiority only in the one but no longer in the other. Such a disjunction, with its traumatic acknowledgment of an alien culture as technologically superior and fitter for survival, had been totally absent from the Chinese way of viewing themselves and the world. And so had been the explicit formulation and rationale it was later to acquire in terms of *Zhongxue weiti, xixue weiyong* (Chinese learning as substance, Western learning as application), which proposed the opportunistic compromise of sticking to the Chinese way in what was supposedly important (*ti*) but adopting the

The Detour on the Road to Capitalism 27

Western way in what was necessary for self-preservation yet supposedly of merely practical significance (*yong*).[2] Implicit in the willingness even to contemplate such a compromise was an awareness, a slow and reluctant awareness, of something that had never happened to China before.

China had seen alien rulers on its throne, the latest being the Manchus of the Qing dynasty (1644–1911), who ruled China at the time of the Opium War. But each time the victor ended up assimilating to, rather than assimilating, China. The Manchus, who themselves first conquered and then assimilated to China, could not be expected to know without one painful lesson after another that the entrance of the European powers had changed the rules of the game. "Unlike the Manchus, modern Europeans had no need to assimilate to China. And the Chinese, unable to take them in, were just as unable to throw them out so long as the technological gap endured."[3] When the nature of this new situation finally began to sink in, however imperfectly, the fact that the West, which China regarded as culturally inferior, had repeatedly proved to be militarily and technologically superior took on a significance that earlier, superficially similar, events had never had. Where China had enjoyed a sense of uniform or integral superiority to the rest of the world, it now had to resort to what we may call the compartmentalization of superiority, with China still claiming superiority in cultural values but conceding superiority to the West in military might and technology.

It was, then, the function of the *ti-yong* formula to assign importance to the one realm and to deny it to the other. At a time when China had no choice but to adopt Western ways for the sake of self-preservation, the *ti-yong* rationale served conveniently, but only conceptually, to relegate those humiliating adoptions to the realm of cultural insignificance. The need for cultural change was thereby denied, and cultural pride seemingly preserved, in a desperate situation that imperiled nothing less than national survival. It

28 *The Detour on the Road to Capitalism*

had taken more than four decades following the Opium War, and no small amount of inventiveness, to arrive at a formula that allowed China to copy the West selectively with good conscience and at the same time ministered to China's cultural pride by finding a way of treating what China was copying as culturally irrelevant.

This was, understandably, the victim's way of retaining in theory the possibility of acting according to the dynamic of its own culture when that possibility had been destroyed in reality. The *ti-yong* formula was supposed to safeguard the integrity of the Chinese way of life by separating cultural essence from mere practicality, ends from means, what was really important from what was not. But the very need for such distinctions, whose absence had hitherto marked a culture completely sure of itself, bespoke the fact that the integrity of the Chinese order had been undermined and with it the possibility of continuing to evolve on its own terms and at its own pace. No longer able to operate in accordance with its own internal dynamic, which had become incompatible with self-preservation under circumstances of someone else's making, China was henceforth to be dragged along a course that it was for a long time either unwilling or unready to take. After the Opium War, China was no longer able to be the China it had always been (which in itself need not be a cause for regret), nor was it able to become quite like the West even when it wholeheartedly wanted to.

For what had happened between China and the West was at bottom a confrontation between cultures. The West, driven by the dynamic of capitalism, could not but come and knock on the doors of China. China, following the dictates of its largely subsistence economy, with equal predictability tried to keep its doors shut. And in the ensuing contests of military strength, of which the Opium War was only the first, there was no way in which China could avoid defeat. For it can hardly be a matter for doubt which kind of culture, once it comes to fruition, has not only a greater need but also a greater capacity for conquest. There was thus a certain inevitability, first, about the confrontation between China and the West because of capitalism's *need* for conquest (in the interest of market expansion) and, second, about China's defeat because of capitalism's *capacity* for conquest. From the military point of view, the victory was one of rifles and gunboats over more primitive weapons. But behind the West's military victory was its more fundamental cultural triumph — the triumph of capitalism over feudalism or the Asiatic mode of production (in Marxian terms) or the triumph of the principle of world-mastery over the principle of world-adjustment (in Weberian terms).

The triumph of the West was not, however, simply one of superior values. Who is to say that European civilization was superior to Chinese civilization, or vice versa, except in a de facto sense? The fact was that the West had won, and once the West had won, it was in a position to lay down, by maintaining a disparity in power, what was better.[4] Theodor Adorno, elaborating on an insight of Nietzsche's, remarks that "Victory was codified by the victor setting himself up as better." It is usually only a matter of time before the defeated accede to the code set up by the victor, when, again in the words of Adorno, "after a successful act of violence, the subjugated should believe that what survives has more right on its side than what perishes."[5] In a case like China's, this is also because the defeated can attain parity with the victor only by becoming like the victor — first superficially, then more and more fundamentally. The defeated otherwise will stay in the shape that caused their defeat in the first place, until they swallow their defeat as if it were their desert, accede to the code of the victor, and change themselves in the victor's image. This is indeed what was to happen to China in due course, but not before the

Chinese had realized that the West's victory was not merely one of military and technological superiority but one of the victor's cultural code as well.

Little did China know at the time that the Western technology capable of producing gunboats and rifles was itself the product, to use Marxian terms, of a different mode of production, with a unique level of productive forces and unique relations of production and, corresponding to the latter, unique social relations. Behind the rifles and gunboats was a whole history of social and economic development that the Chinese *ti-yong* reformers, armed with their magic *ti-yong* formula, ignored and tried to sidestep. What they wanted was only what they could see — rifles and gunboats — and they had only enough understanding of causality to know that the ability to produce rifles and gunboats required a certain level of productive forces. In their inability to extend the causal chain beyond mere technology, they could see no reason why it would not be possible to develop Western technology while holding fast to the traditional Chinese social relations and values.

Even so, they had come a long way from their erstwhile contempt for Western technology. They dropped their hostility to Western technology when they perceived that rifles and gunboats were essential for national survival but not before they had performed the psychological adjustment of assigning Western technology to the newly invented category of what was practically essential but culturally unimportant. Not surprisingly their naive belief that Western technology could be taken over without its corresponding institutions and values was matched by a lack of apprehension that the successful adoption of Western methods of production would give rise to new social relations and values that would challenge the Chinese cultural tradition. It was enough, as far as they were concerned, to invent a hierarchy of cultural realms, such as *ti* and *yong*; what they might otherwise have sensed as the incompatibility between preserving the Chinese tradition and adopting Western modes of production was hidden from their own fragile ego simply by assigning the incompatible to different, hierarchically ordered, and hence seemingly compatible realms.

This desperate psychological balancing act was, as we have seen, an adjustment to a reality that had never before confronted imperial China. Only in a situation of irreconcilable conflict between culture and survival — things that for obvious reasons should always go together — would some such distinction between *ti* and *yong*, ends and means, be improvised in order both to secure survival and to preserve a culture that no longer guaranteed survival. This was an unmistakable sign of a culture in crisis, a culture in which it was no longer possible to pursue what was essential for survival as culturally important. Indeed, when culture and basic human needs are in harmony, as they should be, ends accord with means. And when ends accord with means, they do not appear to human consciousness as hierarchically differentiated realms of pure ends and mere means but simply as one continuous space for human willing and acting. Means become reified as a cultural or political category when they apparently serve but actually violate the highest values. Ends become reified as a cultural or political category when they are perceived not as immanent in human activity but as its superimposed rationale or end product. Thus the disjunction of human activity into ends and means, pure intention and mere activity, self-sufficient value and subservient instrumentality, is a symptom of a profound cultural crisis, not its solution.

The mistake of the *ti-yong* reformers was precisely in thinking that it was a solution. In their blindness to the real nature of the conflict between culture and survival then facing China, all they managed to achieve with the *ti-yong* distinction was to shift a real conflict to an illusionary conceptual site. But there, in the new conceptual site, the conflict between Chinese tradition and national survival remained as acute as ever. In performing this conceptual trick upon reality and upon themselves, they committed two equally serious errors. One was to think that they could render something, in this case technological modernization, culturally unimportant simply by calling it so. The other, which was to prove of more immediate consequence, was to believe that they could make a success of something, the adoption of Western technology, even if they treated it as in some fundamental sense unimportant.

As it happened, the first error, that of underestimating the transforming effect of a new mode of production upon political and cultural values, was to be repeated more than a hundred years later, in the very different setting of post-Mao China, where little of substance remained of socialism after the increasing adoption of capitalism. In this case, as it were, *yong* got the better of *ti*. What began as the instrumental adoption of the market economy (*yong*), apparently in the interest of socialism (*ti*), ended up acquiring an independent momentum of its own that all but swept the old *ti* aside and put in its place a new *ti* that was socialist only because China's rulers chose to call it so.

The second error, that of underestimating the role of new political and cultural values in promoting a new mode of production and the role of old values in impeding it, had an immediate effect in imperial China. Technological modernization (*yong*) proceeded slowly because it was constantly reined in by traditional values and institutions (*ti*). In this case, it was *ti* that, so to speak, got the better of *yong* at a time when *yong* (technological and military modernization) was desperately needed for national survival. But there were special reasons why it was hard to let *ti* make way for *yong*.

It is hard for any people to give up their cultural tradition under outside pressure. What made it harder still for the

Chinese was their center mentality, their sense of their culture as the only "true" culture on earth. Painful as it was to give up the *substance* of the Chinese tradition, it was more traumatic still to part with the center mentality that went with it. It may be helpful here to distinguish self-identity and self-respect, although the two are closely related for cultures and individuals alike. In the Chinese case, to give up *gangchang mingjiao* (the rules of personal conduct and the doctrine of names) was to lose China's self-identity, the actual content that made Confucian culture what it was.[6] To part with the center mentality, on the other hand, meant losing China's self-respect, that is, a positive assessment of one's self-identity. What made China's self-respect doubly vulnerable — and this is true of all self-centered cultures — was that it depended not just on the secure possession of cultural self-identity but also on that self-identity being regarded by oneself and by others (or so one believes) as of higher worth than other cultural identities. For the Chinese, to lose their center mentality was to lose an integral part of their cultural self-identity.

What happened after the Opium War was the progressive disjunction of China's self-identity and self-respect, with its concomitant center mentality. In a desperate attempt to hold on to both, many Chinese labored under the illusion that as long as they could preserve their cultural self-identity in the shape of *ti*, they would also be able to maintain their self-respect and their center mentality, until *yong* one day restored China's power in the world. China's self-identity and center mentality, namely its self-respect, had always gone together. Every people with both cultural pride and political power likes to believe that cultural excellence is the cause of political might. The Chinese were no exception.

This same belief made it inevitable, however, that the new juxtaposition of Chinese tradition with prolonged national weakness after the Opium War would sooner or later make the Chinese blame their tradition for their plight, their self-identity for the loss of their self-respect. All that was needed, their center mentality being the stubborn thing it was, was the destruction of the geopolitical basis of their self-respect — China's erstwhile seemingly impregnable sovereignty, its acknowledged superiority to neighboring states, and its relative cultural isolation from the rest of the world — beyond a shadow of doubt. When this eventually happened, they saw that their *gangchang mingjiao* was just another cultural self-identity. And when they realized that this self-identity was no longer compatible with self-respect, indeed not even with self-preservation, they were quite prepared to give up their self-identity in order to regain their self-respect, and perhaps one day even their center mentality. By degrees, some of them even became prepared to refashion their cultural self-identity in the image of the West, whose cultural identity had given it power. As the vanquished finally accepted the code of the victor, the original code of the vanquished became the dumping ground to which a weak and sick people attributed and consigned their weakness and sickness and their debilitating memories so as to be strong and healthy again.

Thus, in the eyes of a new generation of Chinese, the technologically superior West came to be regarded as culturally superior; some even saw the West's technological and military superiority as but a symptom and effect of its cultural and political superiority. The separation of cultural realms into *ti* and *yong*, which had for a time helped sustain the nation's self-respect, finally broken down, but when the two realms were once again joined to form one scale of evaluation, it was China — this time not just one realm of China but the whole of the Chinese tradition — that was found wanting. The cultural crisis had entered a new stage. When China finally said no to its cultural self-identity, there

The Detour on the Road to Capitalism 35

came into being, for the very first time in Chinese history, the beginnings of what we may call the *periphery mentality*.

The periphery mentality represented the self-devaluation of China's cultural self-identity. As a product of the enforced disjunction of self-identity and self-respect, the periphery mentality saw China's own cultural self-identity as inferior to that of the West and hence, metaphorically speaking, as occupying the periphery. But China's new periphery mentality was not simply the product of occupying a peripheral position objectively or in the eyes of others. Even as negative self-consciousness, it reflected a mode of ethnocentric thinking whose categories of center and periphery had remained unchanged. What had changed was merely China's position. The periphery mentality represented the consciousness of this change within the unchanged categories of center and periphery. But as long as China retained consciousness of the category of center, it wanted to return to it. And what was this desire but the persistence of the center mentality barely beneath the periphery mentality? Thus even as China acquired its new periphery mentality, it betrayed a thwarted wish to remain at the center, that is, *thwarted ethnocentrism*.

China, the Middle Kingdom (*zhongguo*), had always been accustomed to positing a center.[7] Now that a new reality had forced China to see itself as the periphery, its old ethnocentric mode of thinking compelled China to posit a new center, even if it had to be a center other than the self. Thus *Euro*centrism struck a responsive chord in the Chinese consciousness. One world, one center—this had all along been China's view of the world. The same way of thinking that under different geopolitical circumstances had made China regard itself as the center now caused it, thanks to changed circumstances, to view the West as the new center. Paradoxically, China's own ethnocentrism helped a defeated

China to accede to the code of the victor. Long accustomed to universalizing from the center, it now, in defeat, assumed the new role of universalizing from the periphery, that is, universalizing the values of the West — first science and democracy and later Marxism.

To the values of the West, however, even the most antitraditional Chinese had only intellectual but little affective allegiance. No longer able to place its own cultural self-identity in the category of the center, China was prepared to fill in the category with the values of the West, but only intellectually. Given the damage the West had inflicted on China's self-respect, few Chinese were ready to do so emotionally. As long as the center thus remained empty as an affective category — and it did so for a long time — China's psychological equilibrium required that it be filled in with the shadow of its old center mentality. This disjunction of the intellectual and the affective, in regard both to the Chinese tradition and to the West, was a function of the forced separation of self-identity and the category of the center. The forced eviction from the category of the center, a cherished category of China's own making, was the most painful experience that had ever befallen China. Although the periphery mentality emerged in recognition of this eviction, the center mentality lingered on both as witness to the pain of the eviction and as its temporary relief through nostalgia. Indeed, in proportion as the periphery mentality grew in response to reality, the shadow of the center mentality enlarged in consciousness as psychological compensation. Until the wish to return to the center could be fulfilled in reality, it had constantly to be satisfied in consciousness.

Thus the periphery mentality and the center mentality came to co-exist in Chinese consciousness following the bankruptcy of the *ti-yong* rationale. The emergence of the periphery mentality against the background of the center mentality was indeed a further stage in that progressive loss of the cultural center of gravity whose first stage had been the disjunction of *ti* and *yong*. Once the center could no longer hold, all sorts of disjunctions and awkward conjunctions followed. If the ethnocentric mode of thinking served as the conceptual ground of both the center mentality and the periphery mentality, then the forced disjunction of self-identity and the category of the center constituted the historical condition for the *co*-existence of the two otherwise incompatible mentalities. Such a disjunction could be overcome only when China succeeded in making the West's self-identity its own, as Japan in its own way had done. Until that happened, China could only look on Western culture with a mixture of intellectual envy and emotional resentment as somebody else's self-identity. Just as earlier the introduction of Western technology had proved fruitless because of the inseparability of a mode of production and cultural values, so now, for exactly the same reasons, the wholesale transplantation of Western values and institutions had to await the slow evolution of the West's economic structure in China. In the meantime, China could no longer place its own self-identity in the category of the center, but it was equally unable to regard what it had placed in the category of the center — the West — as its own self-identity.

As long as this disjunction continued, neither the new periphery mentality nor the old center mentality could override the other to form a self-consistent assessment either of the self or of the West, in favor of the one or the other. The result was an ambivalent attitude toward both Chinese tradition and the West. Despite the separation between self-identity and self-respect, the Chinese tradition remained an object of love for being, and as long as it remained, the only self-identity that China had, but it was simultaneously an object of hate for its severance from the cherished category of the center. The West, on the other hand, became an awkward fixture in Chinese consciousness both as the new occupant of the center that China acknowledged as superior to itself and as the self-identity of a colonizer with which China could not affectively identify. In this way, the West, too, acquired a Janus-faced character as an object of simultaneous love and hatred, interacting in complex ways with the love and hate of the Chinese tradition.[8]

Given this twofold ambivalence, there was the potential, in roughly equal measure, for nationalism and xenophobia on the one hand and for anti-traditionalism and pro-Westernism on the other. As the climate of domestic politics and of China's relations with the West changed, the two tendencies manifested themselves as the alternating love and hatred of self and other. Now the one, now the other, nationalism and pro-Westernism, became the rallying point for cultural change or political mobilization. And by the same token, anti-traditionalism and xenophobia served, by turns, as the outlet for anger and resentment — the more so as neither the lingering Chinese tradition nor the introduction of Western values brought much improvement in China's desperate situation. As the Chinese tradition was being undermined through the propagation of Western values, the Western values were in turn being undercut through association with the actions of the West in China. In the process so much negative feeling accumulated around both the Chinese tradition itself and the imperialist West that a gaping void opened for a potential third value-system that could serve as a more palatable and more promising candidate for China's new self-identity. Never had China's psychological condition been so favorable to the introduction of a foreign import free of the bad memories associated with both the Chinese tradition and the imperialist West.

In due course, such a foreign import arrived in the shape of Marxism. Not only was it free of bad memories, it also held out the prospect of a speedier solution to China's desperate problems. For those whose impatience and frustration made them desire both radical and rapid change, Marxism represented a promise that, unlike any other promise, had already been made good — in the Soviet Union. It made a world of difference that it was the "booming cannons of the October Revolution" rather than the British Museum or even the Paris Commune that brought Marxism to China.

What the "booming cannons" signaled particularly loudly to China, in its semicolonial status, was the prospect of liberation from foreign imperialism. But since the Chinese tradition was already considered as oppressive as imperialism and even lumped together with imperialism as the twin culprits responsible for China's plight, Marxism offered the prospect of a double emancipation. Such a double emancipation would mean the acquisition of a new self-identity and a return to the category of the center.

In the meantime, China derived from Marxism, or Bolshevized Marxism to be more precise, an entirely new way of perceiving its peripheral status. According to this new way of thinking, the establishment of a communist political system in China would be a shortcut from the periphery to the center. Since an oppressed nation like China that was striving to bring about communism had the teleology of history on its side, or so the Chinese communists believed, it could drive Western capitalism not only from its occupation of Chinese territory but also from its occupation of the center. With the arrival of Marxism, China's peripheral status was no longer a cause for shame; rather, it was almost a cause for pride in the periphery's newfound claim to the center, as China eagerly joined the ranks of the oppressed peoples of the world. For the Chinese believers in Marxism, the periphery mentality was less the mentality of a victim and much more that of a future victor.

That future came about in 1949 when the communists founded a new republic on quasi-Marxist precepts and regained, for the first time since the Opium War, complete Chinese sovereignty over the mainland. Marxism, or communism, in its Chinese incarnation, became China's new self-identity, distinct both from China's Confucian past and from the capitalist West. The fact that Marxism came from the West did not matter, because it was not an *actualized* self-identity of the West. Since the capitalist West laid no claim to this potential self-identity, China considered itself free to appropriate it and make it its own. The establishment of the communist regime in 1949 marked the successful acquisition of Marxism as cultural self-identity, and China's possession of it became monopolistic after its ideological break with the Soviet Union in 1960.

With this new self-identity, backed up by new geopolitical power, China was once again able to lay claim to the center. Mao Zedong said that the communist victory gave back to the Chinese people their national pride, but what was really restored was the center mentality. For in the Chinese consciousness national pride signified, and had always signified, just this. But this new center mentality seemed a far cry from the hidebound sinocentrism of old. The basis of this new center mentality was no longer the old Confucian tradition but the new self-identity that China had acquired from Marxism. What Marxism, a product of the advanced capitalist West, gave to China was a self-identity that differed from the old Confucian tradition not only in being fresh and invigorating but also in being modern and cosmopolitan. The boundary between self and other was no longer drawn along geographical or even cultural lines but along lines of stages of historical development that were supposed to be universally valid. And so China's new center mentality took on the appearance no longer of parochial ethnocentrism but of broad-minded internationalism, very much in keeping with the spirit of Marxism itself.

As soon as China could feel good about itself again, thanks to its new self-identity derived from Marxism, it was able to extend, as if by contagion, its new pride to its old cultural tradition. This was also because the role of the tradition had undergone a fundamental change. As long as the Confucian tradition served as China's self-identity, it could not but be an object of resentment and even contempt as a cause of China's prolonged national weakness after the Opium War. Now that the tradition was no longer the basis of China's new self-identity, it was there to be both freely used and abused. In this malleable form, the tradition returned in response to the needs for cultural continuity and distinctiveness, needs as profound as those of modernization and cosmopolitanization. If the tradition, or what Mao Zedong called the bad part of it, came under fierce criticism after 1949, even more was it, or what Mao called the good part of it, appropriated to make China's new quasi-Marxist self-identity, which was already laudably cosmopolitan, also culturally distinctive and continuous with China's once glorious past.[9] This combination of the cosmopolitan and the culturally distinctive gave China a self-identity that could not belong to anybody else.

Far from undercutting China's new cosmopolitanism, the partial revival of the tradition served to strengthen it with roots that went deep into the Chinese cultural consciousness. Moving from Confucianism to Marxism was supposed to be a fundamental break with the Chinese tradition. But the break was possible in large part because of a profound continuity, for to move from Confucianism to Marxism was to move from one universalism to another. Along with the appropriation of China's old self-identity by the new, there also returned the old center mentality, which gave the new center mentality, in its as yet inexperienced cosmopolitan form, a self-confidence that could come only from a deep sense of tradition. It is a measure of Mao Zedong's political ingenuity that he was able to make the Chinese reject their tradition in favor of Marxism and at the same time to graft onto their quasi-Marxist self-identity the cultural pride that was the product of two millennia of being the Middle Kingdom. From these simultaneous moves there resulted a blend of nationalism and internationalism that China had never seen before.

What was new was the internationalism, and what was new about the internationalism was its teleology. Thanks to its new teleological underpinnings, the center mentality returned with a vengeance. China used to have the center mentality but no teleology and hence, in the further absence of the expansionist dynamic that marked capitalism, no global political project. Marxism, with its confident teleology, gave China a dynamic that the old Confucian center mentality had been unable to generate. For all the sense of rootedness that the tradition imparted to the new center mentality, it was not the tradition but Marxism that injected into the new center mentality the almost euphoric dynamism of the Mao era. The dynamic aspect of the new center mentality came entirely from Marxism.

Thus for the first time in its entire history China took upon itself a global political project, and at times the prospect of a new empire, a communist empire, beckoned from the horizon. Mao Zedong, now presiding over the Middle Kingdom like the old emperors, made himself busier still by constantly coming up with ways of making China the center of the world. At first the center of the true socialist countries, in contrast to the Soviet bloc, and the center of the Third World. Then the center, during the Cultural Revolution (1966–76), of part of the existing world and the whole of the future world; and during certain hallucinatory moments indeed the center of the whole world as it was. In this light, the Cultural Revolution may be seen as an attempt by Mao simultaneously to remain the center of China by means of domestic revolution and to become the center of the world by means of the projected global revolution. It is true that the idea of global revolution was often used to strengthen Mao's hand in domestic politics, but the amount of military and economic aid that China, itself a very poor country, shipped year after year to the "four corners of the earth" bore witness to the seriousness with which Mao took the idea of global revolution.

When Lin Biao, then defense minister, said in 1965 that "Comrade Mao Tse-tung's theory of the establishment of rural revolutionary base areas and the encirclement of the cities from the countryside is of outstanding and *universal* practical importance for the present revolutionary struggles of *all* the oppressed nations and peoples" (my italics),[10] it was the new center mentality speaking, and the treatment of the communist world as the "countryside" and hence in a way the periphery exhibited a confident analogy rather than an inferiority complex.

But this concern with global revolution, although it could not have arisen without the center mentality, also betrayed a lingering periphery mentality in its obsession with difference, with China's difference from the rest of the world, particularly the West. It was an obsession that China had not known before the Opium War. The imperial China of old knew, of course, that it was different from the rest of the world. But it quietly took this difference for granted as proof of its superiority. It did not see it as its business to make the rest of the world like China, even though China was the best; it preferred instead to let the barbarians copy the civilized ways of China if they had enough sense to do so. Still less did it see any need to make itself like the rest of the world in any respect, since China was already the best in every respect. China had been so securely ensconced in its sense of cultural superiority, its unalloyed center mentality, that it exuded a serene self-sufficiency, an indifference to difference.

This cultural self-sufficiency, progressively undermined since the Opium War, was totally lacking in the new center mentality that China regained after 1949. Admittedly, technology and trade, among other things, had in the meantime made the world a place where cultural self-sufficiency, in actuality or in perception, was increasingly a thing of the past. But in the case of China this erosion of self-sufficiency had occurred as part of an enforced process that also involved the loss of self-respect. In 1949 China regained its self-respect by regaining its sovereignty; it could not, however, after a century of struggling at the periphery quite regain that unalloyed center mentality that had always exhibited an indifference to China's difference from the rest of the world. Indifference was impossible not merely because of the changed material circumstances of China and the world but because of a new and profound psychological circumstance. Through its unprecedented experience as a victim of conquest by a totally alien power, China had acquired in the wake of the Opium War a qualitatively accentuated consciousness of the other (in the shape of the West) and with it a correspondingly accentuated consciousness of the self, in both cases either as superior or as inferior.[11] This accentuated consciousness of self and other led to the obsession with difference. Given the circumstances in which the accentuated consciousness was acquired, the obsession with difference was a reminder that Mao's China, even as it consciously looked upon itself as the center, had not completely exorcised the ghost of the periphery mentality.

The obsession with difference produced a certain dynamic, a tendency to types of action with a view to making the self like the other or the other like the self. Under Mao Zedong, China wanted for the most part to erase its difference from the rest of the world, particularly the West, by making the rest of the world like China, that is, by spreading communism to the entire world. Such action with a view to making the other like the self could not, in taking the self as the ground upon which differences would be erased, have been pursued without some sense of superiority. But it also betrayed an unease with difference that is characteristic not of a sense of superiority but of its absence or at least of uncertainty about its presence. A confident sense of superiority — that is, sheer pride in the difference of the self from the other — if disturbed from its indifference to difference, is compatible with the urge not to erase but rather to maintain the difference.[12] Trying to make the other like the self was for China an exaggerated way of asserting the center mentality in a way that admitted doubts about China's central status.

As it happened, China's uncertainty arose in large part from the fact that communist China, in a way reminiscent of its imperial forebear in the second half of the nineteenth century, could look upon itself as superior to the West only in its political self-identity but not yet in terms of productive forces. In the latter respect, China could erase its difference from the West only by making itself like the West, and this would amount to treating the difference as a cause not for pride but for a sense, however disguised, of inferiority. Even after China regained its center mentality with the aid of Marxism, the newly restored center mentality signified more of a potential than of an actuality. The future was thought to belong to communism and by the same token to China, but before that future arrived China had yet to "catch up with" the West in one fundamental respect, namely, productivity. Unlike the imperial China before its cultural confidence was undermined, communist China wanted to change itself, in at least one respect, in the image of the other. Clearly, the post–Opium War disjunction of *ti* and *yong*, that deep cultural scar, remained unhealed in a physically healed China.

But China, having just regained its national pride, was not about to relinquish it even in this limited fashion without psychological compensation. Given conditions that made it impossible for China to succeed in making the West like China (in political self-identity) but made it increasingly necessary for China to make itself like the West (in technology and armaments), all China could do to boost its center mentality was to emphasize its difference from the West. The more China saw itself as trying to make itself like the West in economic development, particularly when the West showed no comparable willingness to become like China in political self-identity, the more China felt compelled, for the sake of psychological equilibrium, to differentiate itself in a larger political and cultural context. Only in this larger context of differentiation could China assert its center mentality even as it was following, rather than leading, the West in that crucial Marxian category of economic development. Indeed, for China with its newly restored and fragile center mentality, the next best thing to making the other like the self (a hopeless project from the start as far as the more advanced West was concerned) was to emphasize its difference from the other and to treat that as what mattered most.

Thus by force of circumstance, difference, rather than similarity, became the locus of China's uncertain sense of superiority, its precarious center mentality. As long as it was impossible to erase the difference through the approximation of the other to the self, China's obsession with difference expressed itself as the urge to maintain the difference. Under these circumstances, the strategy of differentiation served as a psychological mechanism for keeping an at least latent inferiority complex at bay and as the intermediate stage between the humbling but necessary act of making the self like the other and the proud but impossible act of making the other like the self. To emphasize difference was China's only way of laying claim to the category of the center when the actual process of approximation was of the self to the other. It was a way of denying the superiority of the other and the inferiority of the self by denying the wish to imitate, to make the self like the other.

But China, as a self-proclaimed Marxist state, had to make itself like the West in productivity in order to have any chance of making the West like China in political self-identity, in order even to hold on to its precarious center mentality in a world where technology increasingly determined power. In this context, the *ti-yong* rationale returned in Mao's China in all but name: only this time the *ti* was no longer Chinese tradition but Mao's version of Marxism. Much as in imperial China of the nineteenth century, the maintaining of *ti* in Mao's China — although of course the idea of *ti* itself was not openly invoked — ministered to a center mentality under threat, and the willingness to copy the West in *yong* reflected a barely disguised inferiority complex characteristic of the periphery mentality.

The resultant twin obsessions with the West — as political adversary and as technological and military superior — came to occupy a major place in Chinese consciousness in the second half of the twentieth century just as they had in the second half of the nineteenth. The co-existence of these obsessions produced some awkward yet ingenious ideological acrobatics, chief among which was the idea of catching up with a West that was *behind* China. Indeed, the whole of Chinese Marxism was devoted to turning this self-contradiction into a paradox. The need to catch up (with the West in production) added a spur to the work ethic, whereas the idea of the West being behind China (supposedly in the teleological trajectory of history) served as a boost to the center mentality.

In its manifestations both as a sense of superiority to the West and as a sense of inferiority to the West, China's obsession with difference evinced a reactive mentality.[13] The history of modern China, from the Opium War to the communist movement, was a history of reactions, and much of modern Chinese thought the attempt to supply a rationale for these reactions.[14] Under Mao Zedong, as under the late Qing emperors, China did not simply act, as it were, did not simply do what its own culture valued most. Instead, it had to react to what was different in the other. Thus the source of action, the center of gravity, was not in the self but in the other, even when the other was ostensibly considered inferior. Reaction, as a sustained way of behaving, always presupposes a force more powerful than the self.[15]

Symptomatic, if only as one instance, of this reactive instinct was Mao's tendency to situate domestic political struggle in a context that assigned a predominant, albeit negative, role to foreign influence. It was more than a matter of tactics or propaganda that in the Maoist classification enemies came in the order of *di-xiu-fan*, of which the first two referred, respectively, to the Western "imperialists" and Soviet "revisionists" and only the last to humble domestic "counterrevolutionaries." There were enemies at home (*fan*), the implied logic went, only because there were enemies far away (*di* and/or *xiu*). Domestic enemies were always perceived as puppets of foreign enemies, who were somehow pulling the strings. And because these enemies existed, one needed to know who they were and how bad they were. Hence the "raising of class consciousness" — a constantly recurring theme in Maoist ideology. But class consciousness, in this vulgarized version, was precisely the consciousness of a hostile *and* superior force, first and foremost a superior foreign force, in relation to which China gained its political identity and its aim. In the things to negate, by way of self-definition, China instinctively found its center in the West.

But in setting itself in opposition to the West, Mao's China helped to keep the West alive in the Chinese imagination — as a time bomb — and thereby to make possible the later transition from communism to capitalism, from trying to make the West like China to trying to make China like the West. Mao's China, seemingly proud of itself and contemptuous of the West, turned out to be more successful at forgetting its own past than at forgetting the West. Even after China regained its sovereignty and a measure of its old center mentality, the West remained a bittersweet object that China could not digest, until its stomach changed thanks in large part to Marxism.

When Marxism triumphed in China, as we have seen, it gave China a new self-identity distinct both from the Chinese tradition, though with a shared universalism, and from Western capitalism. But this was only one side of the coin. For Marxism also stamped China's new self-identity with something of fundamental importance that Marxism shares with capitalism, both having grown, in large measure, out of the problematic of the European Enlightenment. To use Max Weber's distinctions, we might say that Marxism shares with capitalism the spirit of world-mastery as opposed to the spirit of world-adjustment, the latter marking the cultural paradigm of traditional China.[16] Although Mao Zedong's "application" of Marxism to Chinese reality was in many ways very superficial, the adoption of the outlook of world-mastery ran very deep. China's abandonment of world-adjustment in favor of the Western cultural paradigm of world-mastery proved to be one of China's most fundamental paradigm-shifts; from this many other important transformations, including China's later move from communism to capitalism, were to follow.

It is not hard to see why it was relatively easy, all things considered, for China to move from world-adjustment to world-mastery, on the level of worldview if not yet fully on that of its implementation. For one thing, the relative ease with which China accomplished this paradigm-shift suggests that the practice, even the ideal, of mastery may not have been alien to Chinese culture: only the mastery was not of nature but of something else, be it of the self in the realm of self-cultivation (Confucianism) or of others in the realm of social domination (Legalism and Confucianism). The traditional Chinese idea of adjustment or harmony applied more to the human relationship with nature than to human relations, where harmony was both established and maintained through mastery and domination. Thus within the Chinese culture of world-adjustment, the idea of mastery, though more of human beings than of nature, occupied an important place. When the time came for China to move from world-adjustment to world-mastery, it was only necessary, once nature (*tian*) had been demystified, to move from one type of mastery to another.

The move was made easier still by one strain in the traditional Chinese conception of nature. The ethical-metaphysical conception of nature (*tian* or *ziran*), as represented by Mencius, Dong Zhongshu, and the Song dynasty Neo-Confucianists (Cheng Hao and Cheng Yi in particular), served for the most part as a conservative ideology, with its conception of *tian* as the embodiment of cosmic moral force and with its equation of that cosmic moral force with the will of imperial rulers. But there was also what we may call the naturalist conception, as variously developed by Laozi, Zhuangzi, Xunzi, Wang Chong, Zhang Zai, and others, which treated nature as a material realm independent of morality and human will. This naturalist conception was more double-edged in its social implications: although it helped to engender an attitude of world-adjustment (*shunying ziran*), it also contained the potential for generating an attitude of world-mastery, or world-adjustment through world-mastery. In its second dimension, the naturalist conception of nature was but a step away from the modern European outlook characterized by world-mastery and the conquest of nature. After all, love of nature can equal love of science (as the best way to understand nature), and love of science can in turn equal conquest of nature. Both equations came to be deeply ingrained in modern Chinese consciousness, not least through the introduction of the spirit of world-mastery via Marxism.[17]

But it was one thing to import the outlook of world-mastery, and quite another to adopt its rationalized mode of implementation, namely, what is commonly referred to as instrumental rationality. As far as the latter was concerned, Marxism proved to be a hindrance rather than help. In this connection, the fate of Marxism in Europe, its place of birth, is instructive. Although Marx the political economist showed extraordinary insight into the workings of capital and although Marx the materialist refused to see morality and human volition as the prime movers of history, Marx the Hegelian nevertheless attempted rather idealistically to defeat or supersede capitalism by superimposing upon it, albeit in a manner apparently independent of human will, a teleology that culminates in communism and by positing a Hegelian Spirit in the proletariat as the vehicle of that teleology. This in effect injected idealism, dressed in a scientific instead of a utopian garb, into the materialistic movement of capitalist society and inserted into the non-teleological operation of capitalism what capitalism had already left behind on its way to, and as a condition of, its success.

Instrumental rationality matured in the capitalist economic order precisely because that order was able to shed its original teleology after the latter, as one among many factors, had helped to set it in motion.[18] Capitalism became the instrumentally rationalized system that it is by sweeping out of its way every independent human motive that impeded its progress. Once the capitalist system had been properly set in motion, all the extraneous teleologies or ideals were eliminated or, what amounted to the same thing, subordinated to the non-teleological proliferation of capital itself. It was because all other concerns — the happiness of the worker or even of the capitalist, the usefulness, as distinct from the consumability and hence profitability, of the products for human needs, etc. — had been removed that the economic machine came to operate with such relentless efficiency. Capitalism took a qualitative leap precisely at the moment when, in practice if not in ideology, it did away with the difference between ends and means, between purpose and action — when, as Wallerstein puts it,

"One accumulates capital in order to accumulate more capital,"[19] or when, as Weber puts it, natural science (which in this regard is representative of instrumental rationality as a whole), in the process of "giv[ing] us an answer to the question of what we must do if we wish to master life technically," "leaves quite aside, or assumes for its purposes, whether we should and do wish to master life technically and whether it ultimately makes sense to do so."[20] Once this had happened, it was only a matter of time before the capitalist economic order became efficient enough and thereby equitable enough for the proletariat, as much a product of the materialistic operation of capitalism as the bourgeoisie, to enjoy a big enough share of the surplus profit to want no more of teleologies or utopian ideals — least of all the Hegelian Spirit of Marxism.

No longer needed by the proletariat in its place of origin, Marxism emigrated to the "backward" countries, where no self-sufficient economic order made the Marxist teleology superfluous. It was precisely because these countries, China among them, were "backward" that they had a use for what the more developed West had happily dispensed with. Marxism appealed to China because China, having lost faith in its Confucian tradition, was badly in need of a new belief system to make its society go round. Under these circumstances, a utopian vision that had been proved to work (in Russia, another relatively "backward" country) was a most timely godsend. But the teleological outlook that made Marxism, after due sinification, so effective in making the communist revolution a success is precisely what was to make it so ineffective in developing China's economy after the success of the revolution.

It is thus a profound irony that Marxism helped to introduce the spirit of world-mastery into China but at the same time brought with it an independent teleology that hindered the process of world-mastery. What made the West technologically advanced was precisely what Marx the Hege-

The Detour on the Road to Capitalism 53

lian rejected and what China, following Marx, resisted—namely, the self-sufficient principle of capital, or the autonomous operation of the market. China resisted it first through its own tradition, then through Marxism. With his outlook of world-mastery, one that he shared with capitalism, Marx made the development of productive forces one of Mao's overwhelming obsessions. But, with his quasi-Hegelian teleology, Marx also taught Mao what turned out in the long run to be the least effective way of going about it. Having made possible communist China's first major step toward capitalism, Marxism was to cause a long delay in the process.

Mao Zedong, at heart a romantic believer in sheer human will, above all his own will, accentuated the idealistic side of Marxism into a wild voluntarism, while leaving the supposedly scientific and deterministic side of Marxism to serve as a confidence-enhancing background. At the hands of Mao Zedong, the Marxian teleology came to be separated into the realm of belief, which was dominated by the supposedly scientifically based (and hence *necessitarian*) conviction that communism was bound to triumph over capitalism, and the realm of action, which was to be organized on the principle of revolutionary *voluntarism*. With his deterministic belief system and his voluntaristic social program, Mao thought he would in the long run have the edge over the capitalist West, which had neither China's teleology nor China's voluntarism, in the development of productive forces and thereby in the right to claim the center of the world. In the short term, Mao's voluntaristic strategy did work and even worked what the outside world considered "wonders," for a teleology was needed to launch the economic effort and the utopian vision was best suited to the Chinese conditions of material poverty and spiritual fatigue.

Things began to go wrong not because they had been set in motion by the teleology or teleologically inspired voluntarism, but rather because they had to be kept in motion that way. Things could not be kept in motion that way, given the irrational and sporadic character of voluntarism and the independence of the teleology behind the voluntarism from the operation of the economy. Because of its irrational character, voluntarism could not be effectively channeled. Because of its sporadic character and its moral limits, voluntarism could not be regularly sustained. Because of its independence, teleology, or what Mao called "revolution" (*geming*), constantly interfered with the operation of the economy, or what Mao called "production" (*shengchan*), much as in the imperial reforms after the Opium War *ti* had made a failure of *yong*. It is hard to see how social production, as long as it is burdened with an independent teleology, can long maintain that relentless economic efficiency that goes together not with the accentuation but with the automation, and hence the virtual eradication, of human agency, just as it is hard to see, as shown earlier, how social production, once made autonomous and self-proliferating, can once again take on any independent teleology or ideal. If the second is the lesson of the West, the first is the lesson of Mao's China.

But already, in a manner true both to his quasi-Marxist credentials and to the spirit of the modern times, Mao assigned much greater weight to the *yong* side of the equation than the imperial reformers had ever done. Whereas the *ti-yong* reformers unequivocally set *ti* above *yong*, there was an intrinsic ambiguity in Mao's understanding of the relationship between "revolution" and "production." And appropriately so, since in (sinified) Marxism "revolution" and "production" belong to a dialectic in which it is impossible, if not downright erroneous, to distinguish between ends and means. It is difficult to imagine that Mao Zedong would have set such great store by "revolution" if he had believed that it would impede rather than promote "production." Nor, of course, did he attach so much value to "production" — and at times he didn't — once he suspected that making "production" important allowed the technocrats to steal the show from Mao, the undisputed master of "revolution." The Great Leap Forward of 1958–60 was in large part an attempt to squeeze centuries of capitalist history into a few socialist years. One of the most important guiding slogans of the Cultural Revolution, which many think of as partly directed against the technocratic emphasis on production, was "Grasp revolution, promote production." This slogan exhibits a profoundly symptomatic ambiguity as to which was the end and which the means, if these were to be distinguished at all.[21] Indeed, the Cultural Revolution witnessed more "production campaigns" than the previous seventeen years of communist China, and these were not merely a passive response to the threat of economic breakdown but an active, indeed ecstatic, endeavor to propel China to the forefront of economic and political power in the world.[22]

As such campaigns failed one after another, the balance tipped, in consciousness if not to the same degree in reality, more and more in favor of the economy. And accordingly, China's attitude to the West became more and more one of identification rather than differentiation. This occurred not only by design but also as the outcome of a process in which China had trapped itself unawares. From the first, China's ambivalent relationship with the West had given rise, under Mao Zedong much as a century earlier, to the idea of "accepting the best of Western culture while rejecting its worst" (*quqi jinghua, quqi zaopo*). In this process the humiliating idea of imitation transformed itself into the much more dignified idea of selective *appropriation* (*yang wei zhong yong*). And the idea of appropriation was made even more palatable when it was further narrowed down to the appropriation of means as opposed to the adoption of ends, which served as the ground of differentiation. But in the process of means-appropriation, China had one foot trapped in the Eurocentric global economic structure, the other foot being caught in Marxist teleology. And that indeed accounts for China's limp on its march to modernity. By virtue of the almost irresistible momentum of the growth of instrumental rationality, there gradually began in communist China the familiar reversal of means and ends, much as in the European "dialectic of enlightenment." Before long, what had started off as means-appropriation merged into ends-appropriation, whereby China again had one foot caught—thanks in no small part to Marxism—in Eurocentric ideology (e.g., scientism and econocentrism), the other foot again caught in Marxist teleology. Eventually, in a desperate move driven by the psychological need for differentiation, ends were distinguished into practical, earthly ends (the all-around modernization of China) and quasi-metaphysical, essentially otherworldly ends (the increasingly ethereal idea of communism). The former were hardly distinguishable from Western ends. The latter, though superficially distinct from their Western counterparts, were not much more than a functional equivalent of Western religion after it had been displaced from the center of human activity. Thus the locus of differentiation from the West was removed further and further from the practical realm—into thin air, which has always been the abode of theo-ideology. So Marxism made its way to heaven, and down on earth China was poised, with the timely departure of Mao Zedong, to welcome the triumphant return of capitalism.[23]

So once again China was prepared, step by step, in reality if not fully in name, to give up its self-identity—this time its Marxist self-identity. With China's devaluation of its new self-identity, the disjunction of self-identity and self-respect, which had first happened to China in the wake of the Opium War and had later been overcome with the aid of Marxism, returned in a new form. But whereas the earlier disjunction had been caused by foreign intervention, the

The Detour on the Road to Capitalism 57

more recent one was the result of the failure of China's own chosen agenda. China could no longer value its Marxist self-identity because, having failed either to make the other like the self in terms of political system or to make the self like the other in terms of production, Marxism could no longer sustain China's self-respect, still less its claim to the center. As the ground of difference from the capitalist West, China's Marxist self-identity ceased to be a source of pride, however precarious, and became instead a cause for unmitigated self-depreciation and embarrassment. In the heyday of Mao's rule, Marxism had restored to China not only its self-respect but also its center mentality. Now, with Mao gone and with the mess he left behind, Marxism served only to remind those still in power in its name of China's peripheral status in a changed world.

Not surprisingly, it proved easier to give up Marxism than it had been to let go of the Confucian tradition. Although Marxism in its Maoist form pervaded Chinese life and Chinese consciousness, even the Chinese language, there remained a sense in which Marxism — imported from Europe in the first place and then serving as China's self-identity for only three short decades (by the time of Mao's death) — did not quite define Chineseness. Marxism, transplanted rather than homegrown, imposed rather than inherited, had all along assumed a conspicuous instrumental dimension, which, unlike Confucianism, could never quite merge with its less obtrusive role as China's new self-identity. Now that China no longer valued Marxism as self-identity, its relationship with Marxism, which had served both as the all-important vessel of self-identity and as the contingent instrument of national and personal advantage, became purely instrumental.

And for the majority of Chinese, Marxism was no more prized as instrument than it was valued as self-identity. It was only because Marxism was still useful to some, particularly those in power, that it was kept on the pedestal, in name more than in reality, and in reality only to the extent necessary for the preservation of those vested interests that were still parasitic on Marxism. It was a sign of the growing cynicism toward Marxism that just as those defending Marxism in name had no qualms about compromising Marxism in reality, so those opposing Marxism in reality were prepared at least from time to time to pay homage to Marxism in name. Even for those loudest in defense of Marxism, their link with Marxism was no longer a matter of positive self-identity worthy of courageous allegiance in hard times. Rather, the stakes had come down to vested interests or power or sheer habit — to the fear that some particular advantage which in more idealistic and less self-conscious days they had enjoyed as a byproduct of their Marxist self-identity would disappear along with Marxism. Marxism, no longer valued as self-identity, had died; what managed to survive were only the powers that Marxism had helped to bring into being. Other than as a life-sustaining machine for those powers, Marxism was left with no further role to play. In these awkward times of mutation, China emerged as a hybrid that was taking on more and more features of capitalism but insisted on calling itself socialist.

What had happened in China's relationship with the West in the meantime helped to make China all the more willing to exchange Marxism for capitalism. When Marxism had won the heart of China with its sympathy for the oppressed nations, capitalism had been showing its ugly face with its colonization and plunder. By the time China began to abandon Marxism and to grope for a new self-identity, however, its relationship with the West had already changed. If memories of the West's brutal subjugation of China had not been erased, the passage of time had removed some of the bitterness. Perhaps even more important was the new face the West was presenting to its former colonies and semicolonies.

At the same time that sinified Marxism had gradually exhausted, or rather displayed (as some would see it), its potential in China and was made to take on, in the Cultural Revolution and in retrospect much earlier, an aspect as ugly as that of capitalism at an earlier time, capitalism had changed, thanks not least to the way in which its thorough success at colonization had made naked colonization unnecessary, from the evil military conqueror and colonizer to a benign trade partner and even kindly provider of assistance. The time finally came for Marxism and capitalism to change places in Chinese consciousness, in China's economic order, and increasingly, though at a slower pace, in China's political self-identity. Marxism and capitalism, though the latter under semicolonial conditions, had each failed once in China, but Marxism had the disadvantage of being a more recent failure, a disadvantage made all the more glaring by the West's new image and new prosperity. Moreover, just as the successful October Revolution in Russia had convinced China to take the path of communism, so the "economic leap" of Taiwan, South Korea, and other formerly backward societies gave China the incentive to have another go at capitalism.

But this meant giving up the only self-identity China had, other than a vague sense of Chineseness that lingered from the Confucian tradition, and valuing a self-identity that did not yet belong to China and could only do so through an act of imitation. So China found itself suspended between two identities, Marxism and capitalism, of which China could not value the one it had and could not yet have the one it valued. Something similar had happened to China before, when China jettisoned its homegrown cultural tradition to embrace the imported self-identity of Marxism. But this time there was a big difference, since this time China wanted to appropriate something that was already, unlike Marxism, the *actualized* self-identity of the West. It took a total loss of self-respect for China, always known for its cultural pride, to want to do for its self-identity something as imitative as this.[24] But the way had already been paved by Marxism not only through the low esteem in which it as China's self-identity ended up being held but also thanks to the education it had provided in cosmopolitanism. Marxism itself, after all, had been for China an imported self-identity.

No longer taking pride in its own self-identity but envying the self-identity of the West, China no longer cared to maintain, through its Marxist self-identity, the ground of its difference from the West. China no longer enjoyed the conjunction of self-identity and self-respect with which to pride itself on its difference from the other, to try to make the other like the self, and to proclaim itself the center. Instead, China was prepared, indeed eager, to make itself like the West, this time in all respects, not just in technology. It no longer wanted to be different from the West in any significant respect whatsoever, apart from a vague sense of Chineseness. Once self-identity could no longer command self-respect, difference was a cause no longer for pride but for shame, to be overcome by making the self like the other.

Without pride, there could be no more laying claim to the center, except that China could still maintain, particularly for those in the government, a modicum of its center mentality by virtue of its geopolitical importance and sheer size. Other than this geopolitically defined remnant of its center mentality, China, for the first time in its history, was prepared willingly — that is, by force of circumstance rather than coercion — to accept a peripheral status and to remake itself entirely in the image of the actualized self-identity of another culture. Thus for the first time since the reactive mentality came into being, first in the wake of the Opium War and then in another form under Mao Zedong, it had shed its aggressive side, the side that both reflected and sustained China's precarious center mentality. As never before, China was naked in its periphery mentality.

The Detour on the Road to Capitalism 61

The momentous significance of all this must not be lost on us. For China's new assessment of self and other means that the disjunction of the Chinese cultural consciousness into *ti* and *yong*, value and technology, ends and means — a disjunction that first occurred in the wake of the Opium War and continued to beset China even under Mao Zedong, has finally been healed. It has been healed, however, not through the conjunction of self-identity and self-respect, but through their complete — for the first time complete — disjunction. A China that has suffered from chronic disjunctions of consciousness since the Opium War has at long last let go of its insistence on having its own cultural self-identity and opted for what it considered the only remedy that could bring the cure — wholesale Westernization.[25] If there is any tension or conflict left, it is between those who have come to their senses and those who have equally come to their senses but whose vested interests prevent them from acting accordingly. What will happen from now on, for quite some time to come, will decidedly be anticlimactic.

CHAPTER TWO

The Revenge of Memory

The social order set up in China in 1949 has in essence all but collapsed in one of the two places where a social order can stand—in people's minds. And it has collapsed there in the only way a social order can collapse in the mental world—under the weight of bad memories. When Mao Zedong, in founding the People's Republic of China in 1949, replaced the old regime with the new on the land of China, he had yet to do the same in the minds of the Chinese people. A huge load of old memories had yet to be removed and new memories put in their place before a change of political regime could result in a change of the whole social order. Part of that task had already been accomplished by the triumph of the popular revolution. The communists' success in ending a century of chaos and humiliation that began with the Opium War spurred a miraculous feat of national forgetting: the forgetting of collective weakness and a concomitant remembering of national strength and pride. The history of modern China, until then a haphazard series of national disasters, was made to exhibit in retrospect a heartening teleology, culminating in the advent of socialism in China and presaging yet better things to come. Under the new sky, history took on a different and altogether brighter aspect: "As flowers turn toward the sun, by dint of a secret heliotropism the past strives to turn toward that sun which is rising in the sky of history."[1] Indeed, the past was not alone in turning toward the rising sun of the new regime; the people did so with a tremendous outburst of energy and enthusiasm that had lain dormant for decades.

Something like this, though not always quite so impressive, had happened at the founding of other regimes or dynasties, both Chinese and foreign. But loyalty and enthusiasm based solely on the excitement of the new and on the perception of immediate well-being were, as some rulers soon learned, only skin-deep. Mao Zedong wanted much more: he wanted to place his social order in the hearts and minds of his people, and he wanted his people to have only one heart and one mind — one heart beating at his chosen rhythm and one mind fashioned in the image of his own. In this ambition, Mao found both the greatest help and the greatest hindrance in the old Confucian order, which had collapsed on the visible political stage but not quite in the inner world of consciousness and still less in the unconscious. Mao Zedong had no desire to rid his people of the Confucian virtues of self-denial and compliance, but he wanted to replace Confucianism with himself and his own thought — Mao Zedong Thought — as the object and beneficiary of these virtues. And he wanted these virtues to be known, not as new versions of old Confucian virtues but as brand-new communist virtues to be exercised in a brand-new social order. Thus the Confucian order was to be forgotten and remembered at the same time. The Confucian virtues were to be remembered, but both their origin and their old object of allegiance were to be forgotten. Indeed, the effective remembering of the one depended crucially on the thorough forgetting of the other. The more people lost conscious remembrance of the Confucian tradition, the freer Mao was to shape and manipulate their unconscious remembrance in ways that those manipulated would not be able to recognize. Mao Zedong knew, as profoundly as any truly creative founder of a new social order, that "the knowledge of political foundation is the art of political amnesia."[2]

Symptomatic of, and instrumental in maintaining, the inequality of power in the new social order was the ingeniously created inequality of memory, with Mao Zedong devouring the classics as a rich source of statecraft and the people taught to despise them as a repository of "lingering poisons of feudalism" (*fengjian yidu*). This inequality of memory was brought about in ways both subtle and crude. Among the cruder was "forced forgetting," a method used so pervasively that Mao's China would undoubtedly count as "an era of forced forgetting."[3] The archetype of forced forgetting in Chinese history was created by Qin Shihuang (r. 221–210 B.C.), the first emperor of China, when he ordered the wholesale burning of books and the burying alive of (mostly Confucian) scholars. This drastic measure demonstrated both the rationale and the limits of forced forgetting. Forced forgetting cannot be effectively carried out unless the repositories of memories — minds and books (but not only these) — are physically destroyed. Qin Shihuang failed, as it turned out, not because he went too far but because he did not go far enough. But can we imagine him going far enough when what had to be destroyed existed in so many minds and when there was no absolutely reliable way of telling which minds harbored undesirable thoughts? The limits of forced forgetting inevitably prove, as in the case of Qin Shihuang, to be its undoing.

There is thus a sense in which forgetting, unlike remembering, cannot be forced. Memories fade with the passage of time and with the loss of relevance, and one can hasten this process by removing the physical and verbal reminders of a memory or by making a memory useless in a new order of life. But any attempt to erase a memory by force before amnesia has run its "natural" course will, short of doing physical violence to the brain, only serve to lodge the memory more firmly in the mind, even though negative associations may grow around a memory as a result of the physical or psychological pain to which the rememberer is subjected in the process of being made to forget. Precisely through such negative associations, however, people can be made, by the more or less subtle application of force, to forget (that is, to give up) a certain attitude to a memory, to forget a certain past as heretofore remembered. This is very real forgetting, for a change of attitude toward the past is the forgetting of that past. It is this kind of forgetting — *affective* as opposed to *cognitive* forgetting — that the art of political amnesia can be realistically designed to bring about.

Qin Shihuang, who had no time for the art of affective forgetting, went in for a more thorough cognitive forgetting. His sole success was to create indelible memories of his violence. After the first emperor's death, these memories served precisely to promote the remembering of the Confucian legacy, which had only partially been destroyed. Mao Zedong was both ruthless enough to resort to cognitive forgetting and subtle enough, as we shall see, to devise some of the most ingenious means of affective forgetting. The repeated political campaigns launched by Mao Zedong after 1949 destroyed millions of people in order to destroy their minds and memories. These same campaigns, backed up by ongoing "political education," also changed the minds and memories of even more people while leaving their physical selves more or less intact. Mao's methods of affective forgetting clearly worked in his lifetime, but much of their effectiveness did not long survive Mao's death. Affective forgetting, as well as affective remembering, always requires an emotional and moral bond between the ruler and the ruled that transcends simple fear and sheer prudence. Mao's death ruptured that affective ambience, much of which had already evaporated under exposure to the repeated outbreaks of organized violence in the interest of cognitive forgetting. And when a few years later Mao died yet another death — in the minds of his people — that ambience disintegrated, and with it much of the affective forgetting sustained by that ambience.

It will be neither possible nor necessary, however, to completely recover what was cognitively and affectively forgotten under Mao Zedong's mnemonic tyranny. The undoing of affective forgetfulness is not proportional to the regaining of either cognitive or affective remembrance. But a partial recovery is both necessary, in order at once to learn from the past and not to be unconsciously enslaved by it, and possible — possible not only because cognitive forgetfulness was not and could not have been complete, but also because affective forgetting actually aids, in its own way, cognitive remembrance. For every affective forgetting involves a cognitive remembering, although the cognitive remembering is shaped by the affective forgetting and hence not purely cognitive. Affective forgetting, like that carried out under Mao Zedong, is aimed at the discrediting of old values, but in order for them to be discredited these values have to be named, and the very naming acts as a mnemonic reinforcement rather than a mnemonic weakening.

It is not without irony that both the Confucian tradition and a whole stock of Western ideas have been kept alive in this fashion, as targets of criticism or as aids to the understanding of Marxism. It was also in this way that millions of people, particularly those born after 1949, made their first acquaintance with ideas and traditions of which in the normal course of their lives under the new political system they would otherwise have probably remained ignorant. This mnemonic reinforcement was allowed to occur only at the cognitive level, so that memories of undesirable things, although they retained their cognitive content, had been emptied of their old affective force.

Most of the time Mao seemed to find this partial forgetting good enough for his needs. And to a great extent he was right. For memory of the past impinges on the politics of the present less because it is a store of knowledge and more because it is a repository of affects. A new ruler who tries to transform his people's relation to the past does so because he wants to change or remove the affective forces contained in memories of the past. To this end affective forgetting is indeed sufficient, except for those whose memories openly and stubbornly resist change. But through cognitive remembering, the old values subjected to affective forgetting are nevertheless preserved, although for the time being rendered politically harmless.

Cognitive remembrance is a stubborn thing. There is much more room for the exercise of reason and prudence in affective forgetting than in cognitive forgetting. Self-interest, particularly when not consciously perceived as such, may lead to a change of attitude to what is remembered, but it cannot, short of converting memory into hysteria (which is only another form of memory), easily make one cognitively forget even what it is against one's interest to remember. Unmoved by self-interest, cognitive memory requires no courage, because punishment, "the most powerful aid to mnemonics,"[4] is by the same token the most powerful enemy of amnesia. Those who genuinely want to forget end up remembering with guilt, and those who do not want to forget but who are forced to act as if they did end up remembering with fear or hatred. That forced forgetting may in these and other ways affect emotions and even change personalities is testimony at once to its enormous impact on the human psyche and to its inability to remove cognitive remembrance. The tenacity of cognitive remembrance adds to our suffering under oppression, but it also makes us resist in spite of ourselves.

As long as we are in possession of our cognitive memory, this separation of the affective and the cognitive aspects of our memories can last only as long as the regime that had enough affective power to bring about that separation. Once this affective power or, as I called it earlier, affective ambience is lost, as happened not long after Mao's death, the affective forgetting dissipates. For the duration that certain values are rendered powerless by affective forgetfulness, these same values are nevertheless kept alive by cognitive remembering, as it were, for future use. If, as Walter Benjamin says, "every image of the past that is not recognized by the present as one of its own concerns threatens to disappear irretrievably,"[5] then criticism, even criticism aimed at the destruction of certain images of the past, is certainly one way of recognizing these images of the past as concerns of the present. And so long as cognitive remembrance is not destroyed, it can serve as the basis for affective remembrance — or, as perhaps happens more often, affective reconstruction — when the time comes, as it certainly did after Mao's death. Forced forgetting, unless we take it to mean either the forced removal of physical and other reminders of the past or the narrower sense of forgetting which I have called affective forgetting, goes against the very nature of human memory. In the narrower sense of affective forgetting, forced amnesia is often politically expedient, but even here it obeys a logic that constantly threatens to be its own undoing. For those who live under a mnemonic tyranny and fear the permanent loss of their cultural memories, it is heartening to know that political violence to memory, both cognitive and affective, obeys a logic that sooner or later renders it counterproductive. The tragedy is that for millions of people this does not happen soon enough.

The kind of affective forgetting just described, though more subtle than cognitive forgetting, still involves the use of coercion and thus belongs with cognitive forgetting under the rubric of forced forgetting. There are means of more "natural" forgetting that can do the work left undone by forced forgetting. Although "natural" here presents a convenient contrast with "forced," it is in fact not quite precise to describe such processes of forgetting as natural. A more fitting description would be *indirect forgetting*, where "indirect" points to the most crucial feature of such processes of forgetting: that, unlike forced forgetting of either the cognitive or the affective kind, they bypass cognitive remembering. Except for this sense of naturalness, there is nothing at all natural about indirect forgetting, for it too involves design, even the use of force, and differs from affective forgetting only in the cunning with which it avoids cognitive remembrance.

One of the most durable ways of removing values from public memory is to remove the linguistic medium that alone affords access to them. In the late 1910's the New Culture Movement's campaign to replace classical Chinese (*guwen*, *wenyanwen*) with modern Chinese (*baihua*) marked a turning point in the evolution of Chinese consciousness and memory whose importance cannot be overestimated. For over two thousand years the Chinese cultural tradition had been inseparable from its linguistic embodiment in classical Chinese — so much so that the marginalization and mummification of classical Chinese meant nothing less than the marginalization and mummification of the cultural tradition as a resource accessible to consciousness. The impact of this transformation took many years to by fully felt, because for a long time the two forms of Chinese, classical and modern, existed side by side and most educated people were versed in both and able to live in both thought-worlds. Since 1949 classical Chinese, though still part of a normal education, has dwindled in importance, both as an educational requirement and still more as a medium of communication, to the point where we can say without exaggeration that it has been forgotten by the vast majority even of the intelligentsia. And with it has been forgotten a very large part of the Chinese intellectual and moral tradition. A thought-world has disappeared with a linguistic world.

I am far from crying over spilled milk: indeed it is not

hard to think of reasons why the tradition deserves to be at least partially forgotten — partially but *really* forgotten, that is, discarded from the texture of our lives and not just from the surface of our consciousness. Nor am I suggesting that Confucianism is just an intellectual tradition embodied in a certain set of texts, a certain type of scholar(-official), and a certain number of visible institutions. Confucianism also represents a way of life, and as such it is embodied in the habits of doing and thinking of the illiterate peasant no less than it is in the conscious adherence to the Confucian canon on the part of the scholar-official. But with the forgetting of classical Chinese, the only conscious and reflective access to the tradition is removed, and with the removal of this access our relationship to the tradition becomes unconscious and passive. Insofar as we are unconscious of the tradition, we are at its mercy, because it is still in us; and we are even more at the mercy of those who, without our knowing it, draw on the resources of the tradition to control and enslave us, as Mao Zedong knew extremely well how to do.[6] It is precisely because the tradition is forgotten by the many that it can be so effectively used by the few. Thus when I say that a thought-world has disappeared with a linguistic world, I do not mean the disappearance of the thought-world from our whole way of life but only its disappearance from our consciousness and hence from our control.

Even though the forgetting of classical Chinese did not mean the total forgetting of a way of life, it did open up a linguistic-mnemonic space, and what has since been put in that space is of the utmost importance. The forgetting of classical Chinese is important as much because of the entry to one thought-world it opened as because of the entry to another it closed. Mao Zedong's linguistic revolution, already active for quite some time before 1949 within the revolutionary army and in "liberated areas," could not have assumed full momentum at a more opportune time. In

1949, not only was classical Chinese almost moribund as a cultural force, but the new form of Chinese known as *baihua* had not had much time to develop and consolidate itself. It was thus too weak and plastic to resist the transformation it too was soon forced to undergo as part of a wholesale social transformation. Before long, the modern Chinese that had begun replacing classical Chinese some three decades before was in turn replaced by, or reshaped into, Maoist Chinese, which has since monopolized the linguistic and hence a very large part of the mnemonic universe. Of course, the tendency toward reification and hence toward the impoverishment of the potential range of experience is inherent in language as such by virtue of its very social character. Quite predictably, nearly all the linguistic features of Maoist Chinese as well as their stultifying effects can be found to varying degrees in any language. And these in turn can be traced to every society's needs for control, for solidarity, for exclusion, as well as to the common human craving for economy of effort and for certainty. A listing of the linguistic features of Maoist Chinese and their effects, however pronounced and flagrant in comparison to other languages, will therefore not shed much light. What gives the Chinese process of linguistic reification its distinctive character is, rather, a combination of social and political circumstances usually not found together.

The Maoist state, through its total control of education and the media, has all but monopolized the resources to shape the written and, to a barely lesser extent, the spoken word. As a result, what would occur relatively slowly and moderately in the course of "natural" reification is made to occur quickly and pervasively in the process of what may be called "enforced reification." Enforced reification creates a homogeneous linguistic world, and in the absence of other perspectives that world soon becomes naturalized, just as in the absence of competition it soon becomes stabilized as well. The coupling of the state's control of language with an extreme collectivistic ethos has greatly strengthened the tendency toward uniformity that is already strong in the social institution of language as such. Moreover, Mao Zedong's brand of anti-intellectualism, deeply rooted in the origins and aims of the revolution, has accentuated the inherent tendency of language toward the simplification of experience by discouraging all forms of intellectual complexity and, above all, complexity of human character and motivation. Almost to an equal degree, Mao's attempt to politicize the whole of Chinese life has accentuated simplification in yet another way — by casting all experience in the stark terms of "revolution" and "counterrevolution." If these features are common to many totalistic societies, at least two further features have marked the Chinese situation. The first, shared with "backward" totalistic societies, is a high level of illiteracy, which makes people receptive or at least amenable to linguistic control, and which in itself is a force on the side of anti-intellectualism and simplification. The second feature, to which I have already referred, is probably unique to China; namely, the process of enforced reification started at a time when modern Chinese was barely thirty years old and hence particularly amenable to attempts to reshape it.

Out of this unique blend of circumstances has grown Maoist Chinese — cliché-ridden, heavy-handedly political, intellectually crude, emotionally shallow, aggressively judgmental, blindly self-confident — in a word, a linguistic medium supremely conducive to uniform and complacent stupidity. Precisely such a language is the only language known by the vast majority of Chinese; what cannot be expressed in that language is naturally debarred from consciousness and conscious memory. In the shade of each language are what Mary Douglas calls its "unthinkables and unmemorables, events that we can note at the same time as we observe them slipping beyond recall."[7] As the path of least resistance to what can be thought, conventional language (as opposed, to some extent, to "poetic" language) is a culture's golden means of indirect and unconscious forgetting. A culture forgets thoroughly when it does not even know (as it would know in any forgetting that involves cognitive remembering) what it has forgotten. "Institutions" — of which language is one of the most important — "create shadowed places in which nothing can be seen and no questions asked."[8] As each generation of Chinese born after 1949 has acquired basic literacy, it has entered the prison house of Maoist Chinese, beyond whose walls all is oblivion.

We must not forget that the new language was formed at the same time as a new reality — a whole new way of life — was created. Both were constructed within the narrow limits set by the political aims of the new ruler, who was able to set a whole new world in motion from the Archimedean point at the conjunction of past victory and future promise. At the same time that an impoverished and heavily politicized way of life developed, an equally impoverished and heavily politicized language developed to reflect it and to inscribe it in the public memory. The new language in turn helped to make the new way of life possible — constituting it, naturalizing it, and making unnatural and inaccessible to thought all that lay beyond its scope. This impoverished way of life, too, once naturalized in this way, served as an aid to indirect forgetting. Forced forgetting occurs when objects of memory are singled out to be consigned to (affective) oblivion. But a ruler does not always have to resort to this crude method of collective forgetting. A new political system, a new way of life, a new set of institutions — once set in motion by means including forced forgetting — create by their own momentum a new ordering of things, and the new ordering in itself will in time bring about a reordering of memory. A large part of socialization consists precisely in becoming accustomed to the social ordering of values and in acquiring a mnemonic structure in keeping with the social order, a mnemonic structure that tells you instinctively what kind of memory rewards and what kind of memory hurts.

Linguistic reification and the reification of experience thus go hand in hand, supporting each other and hiding each other. It is this mutual impoverishment and politicization of language and a way of life that makes it so hard to escape the prison which they together make up and hard even to realize that the prison exists. The remembering of Maoist Chinese means the remembering of an ideology and a whole way of life, a remembering that is the more insidious and powerful because it is indirect and unconscious. The ideology and the way of life remembered in this way will not be forgotten until the language permeated with these values is forgotten. But how difficult it is to forget a language! Until then, we can say of Mao Zedong what Nietzsche says of God: "I am afraid we are not rid of God because we still have faith in grammar."[9]

Forgetfulness would seem to imply prior remembrance, the existence of something in the mind that is then somehow removed. This need not always be the case. There is forgetting in the sense that an individual mind forgets, cognitively or affectively, what it used to remember, but there is also forgetting in the sense that a memory fails to be passed on from one mind to another, most significantly from the collective consciousness of one generation to that of the next. Both types of forgetting have played a part in Mao's organized political amnesia. The first type of forgetting, which we may call *mnemonic erasure*, is much harder to bring about, since this process may not easily be amenable to indirect forgetting, particularly when a memory is strong in the first place, and may thus require forced forgetting, with all its potentially counterproductive side effects. The second type of forgetting, *failure of mnemonic transmission*, occurs, not within one mind, but across separate minds, usually of different generations. A large part of the education of the young since 1949 has been designed to put a stop to the mnemonic transmission of the Confucian tradition. Meanwhile, those already burdened with undesirable memories have been subjected again and again to forced forgetting, the only kind of forgetting that can work for them. Even if, as is to be expected, forced forgetting has not always caused amnesia within individual minds, it has done much to keep quiet those who might otherwise have acted as agents of mnemonic transmission.

But much more important, there can be no genuine transmission of cultural memories unless there is at the same time an underlying continuity of the culture itself. The creation of a new social order in 1949 broke the cultural and experiential continuity that alone could have supported the continuity of memory from one generation to the next. The new experience — that is, a new way of life embodied in a new language — has been the mold within which the memories of the young have been shaped. Memory and amnesia depend, not so much on the success or failure of intellectual transmission, as on "a mnemonic system that is the whole social order."[10]

It is in the twofold continuity of experience and memory since 1949 that the new regime has found its psychological source of legitimacy. But the shape of that memory has been the result, not only of the remembrance of new experience, but also — and to an almost equal degree — of the organized amnesia of that very same experience. Every political authority accumulates memories, good and bad, and there can come a point when government means the governing of memories. Regimes fall — first in the minds of the people and then in the visible world — when they have created too many bad memories and do not know how to get rid of them.

Mao Zedong's regime soon ran into this problem. As time passed, not the forgetting of the Confucian past, but the forgetting of its own, much shorter past became the chief preoccupation of Mao's mnemonic engineering. Bad things that could not be hidden were either given good names or else attributed to those who were dead. Bad things done behind closed doors were conveniently kept there, safe from public scrutiny and public memory. Through a combination of ignorance of bad things and gratitude for good ones, the Chinese people showed a remarkable capacity for amnesia. And amnesia breeds obedience. It was thanks to this forgetfulness — and to the alchemy that so often turned bad memories into good ones (the Great Leap Forward of 1958–60 being the prime example) — that the regime could keep itself afloat in the minds of its people under the weight of so many bad memories accumulated so fast. Censorship, indoctrination, monopoly of the media, all have been used in the service of amnesia, and they are used frantically, as after the suppression of the democracy movement in 1989, whenever memory and forgetfulness are matters of life and death.

But political alchemy cannot long convert into golden amnesia a mountain of bad memories that is still growing. The passage of time brings amnesia, but it also brings more to forget. And every new bad memory threatens to reactivate all the bad memories that have been temporarily suspended and to reveal yet more bad memories where political alchemy used to do its trick. Meanwhile, political gratitude, feeding on memories of deeds long since past, dies of malnutrition for lack of new deeds worthy of remembrance and feelings of indebtedness. Despite all that has been hidden from public memory, more than enough memories based on the openly known have accumulated in the collective consciousness to make up a mnemonic version of history, a history in the mind that no official history books can dislodge. Maurice Halbwachs's statement "So long as a remembrance continues to exist, it is useless to set it down in writing or otherwise fix it in memory"[11] ought to be a lesson to politicians, too. Not long after Mao's death, memory undid history—that is, unofficial memory undid official history. From the perspective of the newly liberated memory, the history of China after 1949 was re-remembered by many, though not entirely accurately, as a nightmare of madness, folly, and disaster. Memory recovered a formerly repressed perspective from which it was now possible to discern a devil where the eye had heretofore been accustomed to see an angel. At this point, forced forgetting—even of the purely affective kind—became difficult and useless, and those in power had to make do with forced silence—a silence not of amnesia but a silence in spite of memory.

The official recourse to forced silence amounts to an acknowledgment of the existence of indestructible mental resistance. This resistance, in more subterranean forms, has in fact existed all along, even in the heyday of Mao's rule. The Cultural Revolution (1966–76), which has been described as an outbreak of madness, was to a large extent just that. But its roots went much deeper than the power struggle between Mao and his political opponents. Far from being merely Mao's brainchild, the Cultural Revolution satisfied a deep psychological need. After nearly three decades of the "socialist" kind of "surplus repression,"[12] only intermittently relieved by political campaigns of relatively short duration, the people needed a holiday, a really long and exciting holiday. In Mao Zedong's China, political movements represented an exciting cessation of routine and afforded in an otherwise unbroken ascetic regime the only legitimate outlet for hedonistic and destructive impulses, serving as the functional equivalent of wars, carnivals, and witch hunts in other times and places. Mao's belief that China needed a major turmoil every seven or eight years grew not only from his doctrine of continuous revolution but also from the nature of the highly ascetic regime, which would become intolerable without regular opportunities for release. In launching a political campaign every few years, Mao was not only manipulating the crowd, he was also keeping the crowd—as well as himself—entertained. The Cultural Revolution stood out from other political campaigns only in the length and excitement of the holiday.

After 1949 there soon developed, on the basis of traditional practices and new doctrines, an authoritarian structure that encompassed all social relations, between superior and subordinate, between teacher and pupil, between parent and child—a Maoist variation on the old Confucian theme of "three *gang*" as codified by the Han dynasty Confucian Dong Zhongshu. The sense of oppression caused by inequalities of power was compounded by the envy that resulted from equally obvious inequalities in income and prestige, with eight grades of rank and income for factory workers, twelve for university teachers, and as many as twenty-four for administrative personnel. Each increase in rank brought new opportunities in housing, medical care, and even travel. Mao's China was never the egalitarian society it was so widely taken to be. These were only symptoms of the general condition of alienated labor, whose repressive character was not in the least altered but only disguised by the state ownership of the means of production. For those at the lower end of the scale of power and income—and these people formed the majority (a source of some comfort no doubt)—there existed few opportunities for leisure and distraction to ease the pain of envy, powerlessness, and an only half-willingly endured ascetic daily routine of work and edification. Nor was there freedom of speech to serve as an outlet for emotional tensions. Rather, a vague feeling of unhappiness was prevented from becoming fully conscious and the potential for widespread social discontent was kept in check largely by a stringent morality in which collectivism demanded the subordination of the individual to society and altruism called for the sacrifice of the self for the sake of others. The mental life of large sectors of the population was dominated by the tension between personal unhappiness of whose nature they were often not fully conscious and moral demands that they consciously believed in and conscientiously tried to live up to.

There thus gradually opened up a breach between what Vološinov, adapting Freud, calls the "official conscious" and the "unofficial conscious."[13] The year 1957 saw both the most outspoken expression of the unofficial conscious and its ruthless suppression in the Anti-Rightist movement. Thereafter the unofficial conscious apparently ceased to exist, for it did not lead to the emergence of a political underground. It was not until the Cultural Revolution that it became clear in retrospect that the unofficial conscious, or a large part of it, had turned into the unconscious. The evidence came in the form of an unprecedented display of destructive energy that was as amenable to political manipulation as it was in itself without political direction. After the Anti-Rightist movement there had apparently occurred a gradual separation of substance and affects within the unofficial conscious. The substance or content of the unofficial conscious had apparently been eliminated, and the affects, once deprived of their conscious content, had naturally found their way into the unconscious, becoming thereby a blind force that could surface in ways unrelated to the original unofficial conscious.[14] In this sense, the fanaticism of the Cultural Revolution, as George Santayana says of Hebraic fanaticism, consisted precisely in "redoubling your efforts when you have forgotten your aim."[15] Even before the Cultural Revolution, when political dissent had been wiped out, all was not well with the official conscious, if only because the enlargement of the unconscious "bespeak[s] the disintegration of the unity and integrity of the [ruling ideology] and ... the emergent disintegration if not of the class as a whole then of certain of its groups."[16]

In launching the Cultural Revolution, Mao Zedong appealed neither to the then existing official conscious, which

Mao wanted to destroy, nor to the unofficial conscious, which had ceased to exist after 1957. Mao appealed rather to the unconscious, whose pent-up energy was crying out for release. What Mao did was to ignite all that energy in a way that would burn his enemies but neither himself nor his realm. And he did so in a way that worked upon emotions that lay close to the surface of consciousness. When Mao called on the "masses" to attack those whose ideology was wrong, the masses were able to identify the "capitalist roaders" in much more tangible ways; their sense of powerlessness and envy pointed almost invariably to those with more power or money than themselves.

Not surprisingly, it turned out to be much easier to detonate the mass of repressed affects than to control the manner or duration of the explosion. Once released from the unconscious, the energy took much longer to expend itself, and expended itself in more violent ways, than was useful for Mao's purposes. Lest the overflow of destructive energy wreak too much external havoc, Mao Zedong ingeniously channeled it inward by shifting, as the catchphrase (*linghun shenchu naogeming*) has it, the site of revolution to the depths of the soul.[17] It was not long after the start of the Cultural Revolution, originally aimed narrowly at Mao's enemies in high places, that Mao brought to the fore his superbly cathartic version of the Christian confession known as *dousi*, which can be literally rendered as "combating selfishness" but more aptly translated as "combating the self." Thereafter conjoined with *pixiu* ("criticizing revisionism," a euphemism for other-directed persecution) both in formulation and in practice, the institution of self-persecution turned people into wolves and sheep at the same time. And when Mao eventually wanted them to be sheep alone, they became sheep.

But in time they also became something else. Because the Cultural Revolution allowed for the most thorough discharge of affects, its aftermath witnessed an unprecedented sobriety. Once the unconscious had emptied itself of its accumulated affects, it did not take long for the conscious to acquire sufficient sobriety to develop a new unofficial conscious. And to the great discomfort of Mao's successors, the new unofficial conscious, despite its recent suppression, has developed to a point of self-consciousness where it is difficult to imagine it turning again into the unconscious, as it did after the 1957 Anti-Rightist movement.[18] This time, political suppression could drive memory into silence but no further.

Precisely because memory can take refuge in silence, it is best countered not by amnesia but by another memory. In the collective mind there is perhaps no "net" forgetfulness, particularly affective forgetfulness; rather, there is the replacement of one affectively charged memory by another. Affective forgetting endures only when it is accompanied by affective remembering, the remembering of something new that guards the entrance to the place formerly occupied by what has been affectively forgotten. Organized forgetting, whether forced or indirect, is designed to create a mnemonic space through the eviction of old memories, but that space, unless filled with something else, is in constant danger of being reoccupied by what has been cleared away. Not only must it be filled with something else, but something that has a stronger appeal and leaves a deeper impression. In this sense, every sustained forgetting involves an even more sustained remembering, not in the sense discussed earlier that affective forgetting involves cognitive remembering, but in the sense that every affective forgetting needs to be completed by an affective remembering. Indeed, the only dependable way of making people affectively forget one thing without the aid of natural amnesia is to make them remember another with greater affects. Thus the art of political amnesia always goes hand in hand with the art of political remembrance. The shaping of political remembrance, like the engineering of political amnesia, has naturally enlisted the service of history (that is, history writing). As an instrument of those in power, history is an institution for the social regulation—or sanitation—of memory. But memory requires sanitation only because it contains a record of too many soiled deeds. Official history covering events within living memory is an artificial weapon against natural memory. It is counter-memory.

History has been used, first of all, in the service of historical determinism, which has in turn served to provide political legitimation. Those who are in power are there not because of historical accidents but through the operation of laws of history—Is there any educated Chinese who does not know the term *lishi guilü* (laws of historical development)? Yet, in a move whose self-contradiction few have dared to expose, those in power claim full credit for being able to discern and act in accordance with the laws of history. Thus their being in power is both inevitable, because of historical laws, and deserved, because of their wisdom. The history of modern China and of the Communist party in particular has been written in such a way as to show how the conjunction of historical laws and political wisdom brought the party to victory.

If the Communist party won power for itself through insight into historical laws, the beneficiaries of this wisdom are the entire Chinese people. Modern Chinese history has therefore been written so as to maximize the gratitude due the party. So written, history serves as a record of debts, the debts owed by the ruled to their rulers. Alongside this kind of history, there has developed the practice known as *yiku sitian*, that is, recalling the bitterness of the past so as to appreciate the sweetness of the present. Each reading of history or participation in *yiku sitian* is expected to renew and redouble the memory of debts and the readiness to act as debtors. The debts are to be repaid with the currency of loyalty and obedience. But the debts are piling up with each

The Revenge of Memory 83

passing day, for the party never stops doing good deeds for the People, who can only hope to repay a fraction of those debts and must pass the remainder, and a fitting sense of indebtedness, to the next generation. In this way political obligation takes on the tangible and sentimental character of interpersonal ethics.

This debtor-creditor relationship is felt to be perfectly reasonable despite the party's insistence that it is the servant of the People (*renmin de qinwuyuan*). The People take precedence over the party — but only the People as understood in the abstract and hence in their nonexistence. Peoplehood, unlike the purely descriptive concept "humanness," is not a birthright but a political and moral category. Real men and women qualify as members of the People only when the party confers that qualification, which it is the party's to grant as well as to take away.[19] In this way the party ends up in the best of all places — impregnably situated between the People and the people, between a fiction of which the party can only be not the servant but the master and a reality whose value depends upon its approximation to the fiction. The party humbly places itself below the People, but not the people, whose qualification as People is conditional precisely upon their behaving *not* as People, that is, as masters of the party, but as mere people, as debtors of the party.

Indebtedness to the party is only one side of the coin. The other side is hatred of the Enemy, that is, all those whom the party has refused admission to the ranks of the People. Indeed, the party has put the People in its debt precisely because it has defeated the Enemy, who oppressed and exploited the People before the party came along and who would still be doing this if the People were not protected by the party. Love of the one is inspired by fear of the other. The party stands to lose the love if the People lose their fear. But the fear is not easily exhausted. As long as there are poverty, misery, and injustice, someone must be to blame. That someone is the Enemy, and enemies are to be identified by their opposition to the party. If the party occasionally seems to let the People down, that is also because of the "interference" of the Enemy. This is therefore no reason to distrust the party and all the more reason to feel greater hatred toward the Enemy. History books devote much space to the evil thoughts and deeds of the Enemy. Political campaigns and criminal trials give everyone the opportunity to see the Enemy in the flesh. The Enemy will eventually be vanquished, because historical laws operate against the Enemy and there is the party, which will see to it. In the meantime, trust historical laws and love the party — and be patient.

The political culture thus openly teaches love and hate at the same time — love of the party and hatred of the Enemy — and in roughly equal measure. Lack of hatred toward the Enemy is as much a sin as deficiency in love of the party. The intensity of the one emotion mirrors that of the other; the two contrary feelings are linked in a mutual cause-and-effect relationship. Neither those who teach this love-hate mixture nor those who pick it up as part of their moral and political education, however, see or feel any contradiction in the coexistence within the mind of these contrary emotions. This is because both love and hate are made to spring from the same source, namely, a particular form of utility calculus that we may call the calculus of debts. In the realm of feeling, benefit is to be returned with love and harm with hatred. And in the realm of action, benefit (from those in power) is to be repaid with obedience and harm with revenge. The psychological ground of the calculus, carefully disguised, is self-interest, which alone divides debts into benefits and harms to be discharged accordingly. Love is thus nothing more than a sense of indebtedness, hate a sense of indebtedness inverted, and conscience a sense of unease from failing to discharge a debt of either kind. In this context, we can indeed say with the *Laozi*, taking slight liberty of interpretation: "How much difference is there between 'good' and 'evil'?"[20] Not surprisingly, today's object of love can easily turn into tomorrow's object of hate, for the ground of the calculus — the perception of self-interest — constantly shifts. After decades of the instruction in this calculus of debts, love not narrowly based on self-interest is all but forgotten, and the habit of hating is easily excited long after most of its original targets are forgotten.

Debts cannot be paid quickly enough, but the debtors must not be too quick to ask for more. Patience is required — particularly in the matter of improving the material aspects of everyday life — because the people in their ignorance and ingratitude tend to want too much too soon. Here history comes to the aid of the party by showing what a poor start the party had, what a sorry shape the country was in when the party took over. In this regard, memory, rather than amnesia, may indeed be on the side of the party. With their memories of pre-communist China selectively refreshed or, in the case of the younger generations, with their rash hopes tempered with a sense of proportion, the people learn to see speediness of progress where they might otherwise see slowness, to see moderate well-being where they might see poverty, and they learn to be grateful for what their improved perspective and sense of proportion enable them *now* to see. The debtor must be made to remember the contracting of his first debt. Debtors have a shorter memory than creditors, and history allows the creditor to redress this natural mnemonic asymmetry between debtor and creditor.

It is not only as debtors but also as creators of a future utopia that the people are instructed in the history of their nation's past. In moments of both supreme confidence and barely disguised pessimism, China's rulers are wont to tell the people that there is still a long way to go, a message with different meanings in different national moods. But this forward-looking message, whether delivered as a goad to greater effort or offered as a euphemistic warning of harder times to come (and as a half-hearted rationalization of the slowness of progress under socialism), is always backed up with the resounding declaration that we have already come a long way. Not only a long way, but also against overwhelming odds (historical determinism is temporarily forgotten). Official history serves the future, or the present when there is no future, by recounting how the Chinese people have come such a long way and what a long way it has been, always with the implication that they can go further if they follow the Communist party and work as hard as they did in the past.[21] There is no more awe-inspiring event connecting past, present, and future than the Red Army's extremely arduous strategic Long March of 1934–35 — testimony to, and a symbol of, both the formidable odds against victory and the invincibility of the human spirit nourished by faith in communism. The Long March is both warning and stimulant, and for the faithful the warning serves only to add to the stimulant. To this *stimulative* function has been added, as a natural consequence of the profoundly collectivist character of action in Mao's China, a no less important *normative* function: the heroes, dead or living, who fill the pages of stimulative history take on the additional status of officially sanctioned norms to which the citizenry are expected to conform. Official history is used at once to inspire greatness and to make it the only greatness there is.

History in its stimulative function and even in its normative function implies strength, which it is the role of history to inspire and to regulate. Weakness calls for a different kind of history, history that serves to give strength and pride to a people who need reminders of the past greatness of their nation in order to compensate for their present weakness and self-doubt. This *compensatory* function of history is not easily distinguishable, at the level of the substance of history it presents, from the stimulative function. Past greatness can be used as much to call forth present greatness as to make up for its absence, and we can determine the intended effect of history on the present only by determining the mood of the present. But since the mood of the present is seldom purely one of hope or despair, of strength or weakness, official history often performs its stimulative and compensatory functions at the same time. And once compensatory history has done its job, stimulative history can take over. Although stimulative history and compensatory history tend to go hand in hand, the emphasis placed on one or the other is highly indicative of the mentality and standing of China's rulers. Stimulative history comes to the fore when they are confident and ambitious, out to achieve some grand goal, rather than merely hanging on to power. The emphasis shifts to compensatory history, with a view to arousing patriotism, when they are on the defensive, when the exhaustion of their ideological resources drives them into their last refuge — the logic that equates xenophobia with patriotism and patriotism with love of the ruler.

Weakness also calls for critical history, history that explains the weakness and shows the way to strength. In official Chinese historiography, critical history is almost always used to criticize somebody else in order to vindicate oneself or to criticize the past in order to vindicate the present. Criticism is directed first and foremost at the party's enemies, past and present. Insofar as the party finds it necessary to be self-critical, the targets of its criticism are usually its past leaders. And insofar as the party finds it in itself to admit its present errors, that admission serves only to regulate criticism by setting limits on discussion of the party. For a regime that believes itself to be in the right at each present moment, there is no place for genuine critical history, history that is critical of the past as part of the self and part of the present so as to make a radically new beginning. For Nietzsche the practice of critical history stems from a sense of crisis, so much so that "men and ages which serve life by judging and destroying a past are always . . . endangered men and ages."[22] When China's rulers feel endangered, history is an occasion not for self-criticism but for redoubled self-glorification.

These and other functions that history has been made to serve give official Chinese historiography a number of distinctive features: objectivism, whereby history is viewed as a completely scientific enterprise (ours is the only correct version of history); moralism, which sees history as a struggle between good and evil, typically viewed in terms of classes (we are the forces of good); historical determinism combined with a teleology of progress (we are bound to triumph and make the world a better place); and voluntarism, which modifies historical determinism and allows for the exercise of human agency, exhibited as wisdom on the part of the leaders and as the willingness to follow on the part of the "masses" (if we work together, we giving orders, you carrying them out to the best of your abilities, we can make happen sooner what historical laws would make happen later).

Within the parameters of these spoken or unspoken metahistorical dogmas, history has been constantly rewritten, with changes in the cast of heroes and villains, in the timetable of history, in the apportioning of wisdom and folly, and in the reading of entire periods of history. To bring history up to date is to bring it in line with the ruler's political needs of the moment. But history, to be effective as ideology, can be rewritten only so often. Official tampering with history has long since passed that limit. The very rewriting of history undercuts objectivism and betrays the self-serving opportunism of those in power. The perception of opportunism undermines moralism, which is made still less credible by the constant recasting of heroes and villains in the light of the outcome of the latest "class struggle." The constant postponement of the goals of secular eschatology creates not enthusiastic voluntarism but cynical fatalism and makes a mockery of historical determinism, which, if one still believes it exists, seems more and more to be operating in favor of capitalism rather than communism as the "goal of history." The mutual cancellation of different versions of history leaves a moral and intellectual vacuum in what is otherwise an overcrowded mnemonic space, because the constant juxtaposition of contradictory memories takes away belief, leaving memory nothing to rest on. It is no wonder that Chinese have increasingly been turning toward the West for histories of contemporary China, even for biographies of Mao Zedong. It is a profound irony that the communist regime monopolized the writing of modern and contemporary Chinese history only to lose almost all credence to its ideological adversary. By a logic that few could have foreseen, brainwashing by a domestic tyranny ended up as a major cause of mental colonization by a foreign ideology.

To this outcome political campaigns and persecutions have contributed greatly, but they have also done much more. Political movements are essentially punitive in character, dividing the people into those who punish and those who are punished, giving the former the pleasure of persecution and self-righteousness and breaking down the latter with fear of persecution and guilt. But in reality nobody but the Leader is spared fear and guilt. For everyone may do or say something wrong and end up in the ranks of the persecuted. Thus every political movement is a reign of fear, even for those who happen to be temporarily on the giving end. Fear of being wrong is equivalent to fear of punishment, for every political wrong brings punishment in the form of persecution. And by the same token the urge to be right derives from the same motive as the urge to mete out rather than to receive punishment. To be right is to have the right to persecute. Small wonder that one remembers certain political dogmas as one remembers laws prohibiting theft and murder.

Fear, however, does not by itself make one identify the punishable with the wrong. Only guilt can do that. Not surprisingly, within every political movement there flourishes, alongside persecutions, the organized practice of confession known as *dousi*. By the impossibly high standards of political correctness and moral virtue set by the Communist party, nobody is perfect and everybody ought to feel guilty. One can be made to feel guilty for having done or said something wrong, for having contemplated doing or saying something wrong, for not doing anything when catching somebody else in the act of doing or saying something wrong, for not thinking often enough about one's wrong, and for being not quick enough in correcting one's wrong. If all this does not make one's burden of guilt heavy enough, one can be made to feel guilty simply for not feeling guilty enough.

The institution of confession is built upon a cynical insight. Perhaps most people who look into their hearts see there infinitely greater potential for evil (as well as perhaps for good) than will ever be actualized. Confession depends not just on one's knowledge of one's actual deeds and thoughts but also, and even more profoundly, on an awareness of one's potential for evil, to be grasped by imagining its actualization under the most conducive circumstances. This awareness, even when it amounts to nothing more than vague glimpses, is a far more formidable source of guilt. Having looked into his own soul and hiding what he sees there from public view, the Leader invites his people to take a deep look into their souls *and* to put the results of that soul-searching on public display. The people, for their part, out of their psychological need to believe in the ruler's perfection, are reluctant, even unwilling, to make the same inference about the Leader. That is how the Leader became God and how the people came to need him to give them moral guidance and to relieve them of their guilt. In this way fear of the punishable is made identical with fear of the wrong, and prudence with virtue. Punishment results, not just in a "heightening of prudence,"[23] but also in a heightening of "virtue," for one now believes in the justice of the punishment.

Not everyone does, of course, but those who do not are no less effectively tamed through a heightening of prudence alone. Within the institution of confession, incorrect thoughts and memories cannot be kept private without psychological cost. "Honor the magistrates and obey them — even the crooked magistrates. Good sleep demands it."[24] If one confesses, one receives a publicly administered dose of guilt, and the conditional pardon each confession brings serves only to increase the sense of indebtedness. On the other hand, if one does not confess, one may suffer an additional sense of guilt for hiding one's sins. Those who do not feel burdened with either guilt or indebtedness because they can see through the institution do not fare much better, for they too are caught in a dilemma. If they protest against the institution, they will end up having their voice silenced. If out of fear they keep their protest entirely to themselves, however, they suffer from a loss of vitality and self-esteem caused by the constant effort to maintain the appearance of outward submission. Their self-esteem partly returns only when outward submission is no longer an effort but merely a habit. But by then they will have sunk deep in cynicism, which causes a further loss of vitality. It is indeed as Nietzsche says:" 'Injury makes one prudent,' says the proverb: insofar as it makes one prudent it also makes one bad. Fortunately, it frequently makes people stupid."[25]

Fortunately indeed — for badness (cynicism in this case) is a worse and less curable sickness than stupidity (blind belief) — except that stupidity tends to be succeeded by badness. While Mao had the Chinese people under his spell, his political campaigns induced the willing remembrance of Maoist values. The combination of charisma and punishment made people stupid, and stupidity made them willing.

But the stupid belief in the Leader was conditional, depending as it did on the secrecy of the Leader's soul and on the expectation of the Leader's fulfillment of his eschatological promises. The secrecy eventually broke down, and the promised paradise never descended upon earth. So people ceased to be stupid, at least in the way they had been stupid before, but the punishments were still in place and made people prudent. What began as willing remembrance took on the character of forced memory as soon as it was uncoupled from belief. Henceforth the psychological basis of power shifted from the stupidity of the people to their prudence, and power became as precarious as prudence.

Meanwhile, prudence has meant more than just the avoidance of punishment. Side by side with the institution of punishment, there has developed a system for meting out rewards and promotions that is openly political and that is no less powerful an aid to political mnemonics. When certain values have behind them the power both to punish and to reward, they become for many people hard to resist. And when, furthermore, these values appeal simultaneously to virtue and to self-interest, it becomes unnecessary to resist them, for one can promote one's self-interest and at the same time have the comfort of believing oneself to be acting out of virtue. It is only when the two are out of step that people start questioning one or the other. Even then it is far easier to question values when they do not promote one's self-interest than to question one's self-interest when it comes into conflict with one's conscience, whose voice must be very faint indeed when official approval and self-interest go conveniently together. In the long run, utility begets memory and forgetfulness.[26]

In the meantime certain ideas have to be instilled into not always receptive minds. The totality of these ideas we may call the canon, whether they take the form of philosophy, literature and art, or political tracts. At the core of this canon are the works of Marx, Lenin, and, above all, Mao Zedong. Parts of this core-canon, up to entire volumes, have from time to time been made mandatory objects of study for the entire literate population. If some of these objects of study, particularly the works of Marx, lie beyond even the most superficial comprehension of most, as those who prescribed them must have known, the situation is far from being as ridiculous or pointless as it seems. Apart from certain cardinal commandments to be found in a few of Mao's very brief and readable works, the canon, even the core-canon, is there not so much to be intelligently understood as to monopolize the thought-world and in so doing to deny all other ideas, particularly the heterodox and the dangerous, the right of entry. Moreover, the very institution of mandatory political indoctrination, in which people are told what to read, how to read, and have to read what has been prescribed for them regardless of their interest or inclination — this institution in and of itself offers highly effective training in submission and conformism. This training reached its most rigorous stage during the Cultural Revolution when in many places people were required to memorize selected works of Mao Zedong running to dozens of pages. It is hard to think of greater deference that could be accorded the thoughts of a mortal being. The deference is that due to a sage, just as the submissiveness is that due to a ruler. Here, political legitimacy and intellectual legitimacy are made, in a manner characteristic of the Confucian tradition, to go hand in hand.

If there is a canon to be both cognitively and affectively remembered, there is also a counter-canon that is to be affectively forgotten. But to be so forgotten, it has to be named, with the unavoidable yet undesirable consequence of consigning the object of forgetfulness to only affective, and hence partial and probably temporary, oblivion. Those in power would certainly have preferred to let sleeping dogs lie, but the dogs in question — "feudalism" (chiefly the Confucian tradition), capitalism, and revisionism (anything that was heterodox within the Marxist tradition) — happened to be awake and barking. Thus the counter-canon is what it is because it is seen as a threat to the canon unless it is constantly discredited. But in terms of cognitive salience, and we know what that can do, the counter-canon has acquired in this way a canonical status second only to the canon and constantly endangers it.

If the counter-canon is to be deprived of influence, it must be cognitively forgotten as well. It must, in other words, cease to be a counter-canon at all. In this regard, the Confucian tradition, beginning with Dong Zhongshu's proposal to "ban the Hundred Schools and worship Confucianism alone," was much more successful, making Mao Zedong akin to Qin Shihuang, whose failure to eradicate cognitive memory of Confucianism made it possible for Confucianism to be affectively remembered by the succeeding dynasty.

Once a canon is established, the last thing it can afford is flexibility. Both the Confucians and Mao Zedong knew this very well. But they also knew that doctrinal inflexibility need not entail inflexibility in practical affairs. Just as the Confucian rulers quietly incorporated into their political practice, but not into their doctrinal canon, elements of Legalism (a school of extremist authoritarianism that flourished during the third century B.C.), so Mao Zedong did the same with both Confucianism and Legalism. Deng Xiaoping, who had opposed Mao's doctrinal inflexibility with the pragmatic idea that cats, white or black, are good cats as long as they can catch mice, had the sound instinct, as soon as he became China's top ruler, to be seen to uphold the Maoist canon, suitably adapted, almost as rigidly as Mao himself had done. But like Mao before him, Deng did not let canonical rigidity tie his hands, introducing without qualm capitalist practices that at the level of doctrine still belonged to the counter-canon. From the ruler's point of view, the more he departs from the canon in practice, the more he needs to be seen to uphold the canon as doctrine. The canon provides political authority with a center of gravity that comes not from the canon's flexibility and practical usefulness but from its immunity to time and change. Memory of the canon, with all the submissiveness and conformism it has fostered and all the political-intellectual legitimacy it has created, is too valuable an asset to squander.

But even better remembered than the verbally transmitted canon are certain corporeal practices, things done to form bodily habits that are more than bodily habits. Because they do not enter consciousness as overtly political values, these corporeal practices bypass consciousness and in so doing avoid conscious resistance. Individualism is subdued and uniformity in thought and action fostered, for example, through uniformity in clothing. Even though things have changed greatly in this regard, reflecting changes in habits of thought and conduct, there is still a lingering timidity in matters of dress on the part of people (myself included) who see no good reason for this timidity. Intellectually, these people may be among the least conservative and the least conventional, but their conservativeness in clothing betrays years of training in uniformity and fear of public opinion, which they have overcome in thought but not in action and which therefore they have not really overcome even in thought.

Physical labor, around which has been built a highly effective cluster of corporeal practices, has also fostered habits that die hard. As a painful necessity, physical labor (particularly hard physical labor) is a double-edged political weapon. Because it is necessary, physical labor can easily be shown to have a moral value that goes beyond its necessity. Because it is painful, physical labor is a natural means of punishment. In combination, the moral and punitive aspects of labor form a powerful political weapon. It can be used to make those occupationally engaged in physical labor happy and proud to do what they have no choice but to do, and it can no less effectively be used to make those professionally engaged in thinking think timidly for fear of being made to do physical labor as a form of punishment. The punitive use of physical labor has been applied to intellectuals with an effectiveness that may long outlast that of political campaigns and persecutions. The attachment of great moral value to physical labor makes it a form of punishment and taming that intellectuals have no moral grounds for resisting. But to be morally willing to engage in hard physical labor as a way of moral re-education is already to have gone through a profound self-devaluation. And the process of this moral re-education greatly reinforces that self-devaluation. In doing something to which they have learned to attach great moral value but which they do poorly, intellectuals are made humble. In doing something to which they have learned to attach great moral value but which they dislike, they are made guilt-ridden. And in doing something that they find physically painful, they are made aware of the punitive aspect of physical labor, which teaches a lesson in prudence even to those who do not see physical labor as filled with great moral value. In time many intellectuals learn to be good at physical labor and to enjoy it, and thus they lose awareness of its punitive aspect. But when this happens, they have already undergone a profound change — into "docile bodies" and timid minds.

The remembering of pain and punishment — undergone not only in labor reforms but also in political campaigns and persecutions — has caused the forgetting of courage.[27] Few still believe in the values that their past mnemonic training directly teaches. But the memory of those painful experiences is sedimented in the body as a lack of vigor and sedimented in the mind as cynicism and prudence. One no longer believes, but one acts as if one still did. At the same time, memory of the constant political changes makes one prudent for a different reason, since active support for one leadership may well get one into trouble with the next. Thus prudence both manifests itself as lack of active opposition and cautions against active participation. Paul Connerton observes: "Every group . . . will entrust to bodily automatisms the values and categories which they are most anxious to conserve. They will know how well the past can be kept in mind by a habitual memory sedimented in the body."[28] In this fashion the same way of life is preserved, with the same authority presiding over it, not by what people have been taught to remember, but by what they — their bodies no less than their minds — are unable to forget.

If the body has been the site of taming, it has also been the locus of resistance. For the body is forever sensitive to pain, and pain dictates its own laws of memory and forgetfulness. It is not true, *pace* Habermas, that "the integration of inner nature does not run up against absolute barriers."[29] The body recognizes limits beyond which pain cannot be perceived as pleasure, as goodness, or as truth. Beyond those limits the body resists — or dies. The body does not know what is moral, but it knows what is not. Every brainwashing is a denial of the body, an attempt to make one believe the opposite of what the body says. But the body has its own way of fighting back. Its silence is merely a sign that it does not find the pain intolerable. When pain is past endurance, whether in intensity or in duration, the body withdraws all the credence that the mind has given to years of apparently successful brainwashing. The body receives input from the mind too, for every rise in expectations raises the threshold of pain. The threshold has been raised again and again in China in recent years, but the rise in levels of pleasure has not caught up with this politically dangerous change.

Within its limits, however, the body's endurance translates into the mind's timidity. Within those limits is the wide-open field of political engineering, in particular of memory and forgetfulness. But even the mind acts on behalf of the body, constantly demanding pleasures, if not for now, then in the future. Not far behind asceticism lurks hedonism. The Leader promises these pleasures and much more, and on that promise has rested the Leader's ability to undertake and the people's willingness to submit to the remaking of Chinese memory. With the dashing of that promise begins the unraveling of the mnemonic tapestry woven over four decades.

But what has been accomplished through indirect, including bodily, forgetting and remembering is not easily undone. It is hard even to know what has been remembered and what has been forgotten in this way. What has been forgotten cannot easily be retrieved because we cannot begin to regain what we do not even know we have lost. By the same token, what has been remembered cannot easily be forgotten, for it cannot occur to us to rid ourselves of memories that, through our habits, through our institutions, and through our entire way of life, we carry around with us unawares.[30] Memory takes its worst revenge upon us through our ignorance of it, so that our inability to retrieve our past fully and digest it is like a poison that spreads the sense of meaninglessness from past to present and future. Undigested memories of utopianism make up the nihilism that negates the past still in us.

In this connection, Aristotle's distinction between remembering, conceived as affection or pathos and hence passive, and recollecting, conceived as an active undertaking, proves highly illuminating.[31] If we extend Aristotle's concept of remembering to include indirect and bodily remembering, we may indeed say, using Aristotle's distinction, that very often we remember precisely because we cannot recollect.

Aristotle's distinction takes on more than just intellectual significance in the case of patients suffering from hysteria, because, as we have learned from Freud and his colleague Josef Breuer, symptoms of hysteria result precisely from the somatic remembrance of traumatic experiences that lie beyond conscious recollection. There is reason to believe that what is true of hysterical patients can be true also of a society suffering from its "unknown memories."[32] This is the thesis not only of Freud, who sees a profound correspondence between ontogeny and phylogeny, but also of Nietzsche, who regards both cultures and individuals unable to will properly as behaving like a dyspeptic who "cannot 'have done' with anything"[33] and who therefore cannot begin and will anew. Thus a society trapped in nihilism is somewhat like a hysterical patient unable to escape the imprisonment of a mental disorder. Both are victims of past experiences they cannot begin to master because they are unconscious of these experiences. Nietzsche's genealogy seeks, in a manner somewhat analogous to psychotherapy, to bring to a culture's conscious awareness the ways in which its past has undermined its present, so that the culture will not only recognize its malaise for what it is but also understand that the malaise, being a product of historically contingent circumstances, is not necessary and is therefore curable. Just as in psychotherapy, we remember (recollect) in order to forget.

But unlike psychotherapy, in which, if we are to trust the findings of Breuer and Freud, "each individual hysterical symptom immediately and permanently disappeared when we had succeeded in bringing clearly to light the memory of the event by which it was provoked and in arousing its accompanying affect, and when the patient had described that event in the greatest possible detail and had put the affect into words,"[34] a society's "sickness" does not automatically disappear when the heretofore unknown causes of the sickness are brought into full consciousness. There is an important sense in which a hysterical patient suffers only from the past, because his traumatic experience is not, but for the unconscious reminiscences, part of his present life. A society in psychological crisis, however, never suffers from the past alone; it always suffers from the present, too, in that there is something wrong not just with its present memories, conscious or unconscious, but also with its present way of life. Genealogy — the tracing of causes — can at best bring to light and thereby place within the range of possible cure those debilitating memories that the body has remembered but the mind cannot recollect.

It is a profound paradox that these memories both impede the creation of a new way of life and require for their removal precisely such a creation. The building of a new form of life is at once the condition and the consequence of genuine forgetfulness, short of which amnesia can be no more than repression, the very undoing of genealogy. The paradox seems therefore to be a circle without an exit. Indeed it is, unless we "know" how to unconsciously forget (really forget, not just repress), just as we "know" — often to our detriment — how to unconsciously remember; unless we have in ourselves "the shears with which you cut away what you cannot use,"[35] which is how Kierkegaard characterizes forgetting. Thus by a logic not unlike that behind Spinoza's statement that "no one rejoices in blessedness, because he has controlled his lusts, but contrariwise, his power of controlling his lusts arises from this blessedness itself,"[36] so we can say that we have the strength to begin anew not because we are able to forget, but because our ability to forget comes precisely from our strength.

It is only when we are able to forget (that is, not to be incapacitated by our memories) that we can afford the luxury of remembering (that is, recollecting experiences that no longer hurt). That luxury is also a necessity, because, as George Santayana's well-worn yet still insightful maxim cautions us, "Those who cannot remember the past are condemned to repeat it,"[37] and because the forces working for repetition are formidable not only, as Freud tells us,[38] on the level of individual instinctual behavior but also, for essentially the same reasons that account for the repetition compulsion, on the level of social action. That which caused us to act in a certain way in the past will, being part of our inherently conservative psychical economy, cause us to act again in the same way, unless we bring it into consciousness, where we may have some hope of modifying its causal power. In social action as in individual instinctual behavior, "the compulsion to repeat" is a function of the failure of "the impulsion to remember."[39] If forgetfulness gives us back our childhood again, remembrance will help us grow into a new and better adulthood. For from forgetfulness come innocence and strength, and from remembrance wisdom. It is in this sense also that we can understand Kierkegaard when he says, albeit in a context different from ours: "When we say that we *consign* something to oblivion, we suggest simultaneously that it is to be forgotten and yet also remembered."[40]

CHAPTER THREE

Teleology as Morality

The abrupt end to the Mao era, with its teleologically grounded political order, was accompanied by the equally abrupt disintegration of a moral order whose imperatives of collectivism and altruism had in their day been as much practiced as they had been merely preached. Within a few years, what had been fostered and enforced for four decades was swept away, and pure selfishness came back with a vengeance, undisciplined, knowing no scruples, no sense of fairness, often not even its own good. Impulses that had undergone little unobtrusive regulation but much ostentatious sublimation in the name of a political project soon became, with the failure of that project, de-sublimated and refused to be disciplined. All this occurred as part of a larger transition from utopianism to hedonism, a newly liberated hedonism that has yet to learn how to discipline itself through instrumental rationality. Until this happens, China is morally very much between two worlds — one dead, the other in prolonged birth pangs caused by the nature and manner of the death of the first.

My main object is to explain the nature and consequences of the breakdown of the Maoist moral order in China. But there are at least two reasons why this account must begin with traditional morality. As we shall see, Maoist morality was, on the one hand, in some aspects a con-

Teleology as Morality 103

tinuation of traditional morality but, on the other hand, in its logic or structure, a radical departure from the same morality.

By "traditional morality" I refer not to the totality of the various conceptual positions — Confucian, Daoist, Mohist, Legalist, and so on — handed down from pre-Qin times and continued or discontinued (as the case may be) in the imperial period but to a doctrine, or a set of doctrines, that has exerted a predominant influence both on traditional moral consciousness and traditional moral practice. Given this focus, we can take traditional Chinese morality to mean Confucian morality. This is already a considerable simplification, but even more simplification is needed. For reasons that will soon become clear, I single out one version of Confucian morality — not Confucius' own — as its most comprehensive formulation. This is Dong Zhongshu's explicit formulation, not so much his original invention, of *sangang* (three bonds) and *wuchang* (five rules), which, as further spelled out in the *Baihu tongyi*, became from the Han dynasty on the frame of reference for the subsequent development of Confucian morality.[1]

Dong Zhongshu's *sangang wuchang* is of interest here not so much for its comprehensiveness as ordinarily understood as for the comprehensive three-level logic or structure that can be extrapolated from his formulation. This structure consists of *li* (ritual), *ren* (benevolence), and *tian* (heaven); *li* and *ren* represent two of the five *chang*, and *tian*, though not included in the *sangang wuchang*, is figured in the "heavenly" number *wu* (five — the five elements). This is spelled out more explicitly in Dong Zhongshu's famous treatise *Chunqiu fanlu* (Luxuriant gems of the *Spring and Autumn Annals*). *Li* and *ren* were key components of Confucian morality before Dong Zhongshu, but it was Dong Zhongshu's accentuation of *tian* as the cosmological ground of *li* and *ren* that gave his formulation of Confucian morality the comprehensiveness so important for understanding the logical structure of Confucian morality and, by contrast, the logical structure of the morality Mao was to develop.

Corresponding to each of the three levels of this comprehensive structure is a moral code, with *li* representing the code of conduct, *ren* the code of virtue, and *tian* the code of belief. These three moral codes, to which the remaining elements of the *sangang wuchang* can be assigned, can in turn be seen as constituting the grand and all-encompassing system of Confucian morality.

A closer look at the functions of each code and particularly at the connections between the three codes will help clarify the rationale or logical structure of Confucian morality. The code of conduct serves as a direct guide to behavior since it consists of explicit rules that can be directly translated into action. Thus one distinguishing feature of this code is that it lies close to embodiment, that is, to being acted upon. If the code of conduct were sufficient by itself to make people follow it, there would be no need for the other two codes, at least for the purpose of creating and maintaining civic order. But the code of conduct, while closest to embodiment, lies furthest from self-sufficiency. People obey rules of conduct only when they see good reason to do so, and one such reason has to do with the kind of person one ought to be. Hence the code of virtue, whose function is to give meaning to, and to induce practice of, the code of conduct. The moral teachings of Confucius himself more or less stop here, with *li* as the embodiment of *ren* and *ren* as the meaning of *li* and indeed as the be-all and end-all of moral life. Although the idea of *tian* figures occasionally in the *Analects*, it is not made out to be either the source or the foundation of *ren*, which requires no meaning or justification beyond itself. The same is true of Mencius, whose *siduan* (four beginnings) already make up four of the five rules of Dong Zhongshu. Dong Zhongshu's radical innovation was not to invent the idea of *tian* but rather to move the

Teleology as Morality   105

foundation of moral order beyond *ren* and to locate it in the idea of *tian*. This in itself is to deny and undermine what Confucius and Mencius see as the self-sufficiency of *ren* and in so doing to make necessary the introduction of a further code, namely the code of belief (in *tian*), whose function it is to ground both the code of conduct and the code of virtue.

Now, the need for a code of belief is not a good sign; nor is the need for a code of virtue; nor, indeed, is the need for more than one code. Since the code of conduct is insufficient, a code of virtue is required to justify it and make it meaningful. Since both codes are required, it is evident that the code of virtue, though functioning as the basis of the code of conduct, is not self-sufficient either. To be more precise, the code of virtue is self-sufficient with regard to meaning or justification, but not with regard to embodiment. And it is this lack of self-sufficiency that renders the code of conduct necessary. The combination of the two codes amounts to an acknowledgment that it is possible to follow the code of conduct without seeing any moral significance in the process, that it is possible to follow the code of virtue without acting on it, and that it is impossible to follow the code of virtue spontaneously. Thus both codes are devoid of independent moral value — devoid, to put it more poignantly, of authenticity. Dong Zhongshu's introduction of a code of belief in the shape of *tian* moves the ground of justification and, more important, the ground of motivation to a realm even further removed from embodiment. Because it is needed to ground *ren*, it denies that *ren* is sufficient, in terms of justification and motivation, to bring about good behavior. In so doing, it brings into the moral order elements of coercion and prudence. Thus the creation of the code of belief is proof of even more inauthenticity and opens up even greater possibilities for disembodiment.

The *Dao de jing* says, moving step by step from the loss of the *dao* to the emergence of *li*: "When righteousness is lost, only then does the doctrine of propriety [*li*] arise. Now, propriety is a superficial expression of loyalty and faithfulness."[2] This shows what can be inferred from the need for *li*, from the emergence of a code of conduct. It makes equal sense to draw the converse inference from the need for *ren*, from the emergence of a code of virtue: only when authentic *li* — *li* that is, so to speak, self-authenticating — is lost does the need for *ren* arise. For *ren* is not immanent in *li* but something independently established to give to *li* the authenticity it lacks. The need for *tian*, in turn, indicates the loss not only of *li* but also of *ren*. We are concerned here not with temporal causality but with logical inference, and from this point of view the need for, and the co-presence of, the three codes bespeaks the loss of all three as authentic modes of moral experience.

Fortunately for the Confucian moral order, this logic was never quite fully actualized. The *Dao de jing* goes on, in the same passage, to say that propriety is "the beginning of disorder." This may be so from the Daoist point of view, but not quite the case by the standards of Confucian morality. Indeed, for some two thousand years Confucian morality showed remarkable resilience and stability, something one could hardly infer from the logic of Dong Zhongshu's formulation of Confucian morality. Although all three codes influenced the Confucian moral order, the code of belief (the code of *tian*) was seldom allowed, with the notable exception of Dong Zhongshu, to take ontological or psychological precedence over the code of virtue (the code of *ren*). Just as *ren* was paramount, before Dong Zhongshu, in Confucius and Mencius, so the code of virtue again took pride of place, after Dong Zhongshu, in the hands of the Song and Ming dynasty Confucians, who re-anchored morality in the realm of *ren* ("humanity," one of the two closely related meanings of *ren*, the other being benevolence) as opposed to *tian*. This is not to say that Dong Zhongshu's introduction of the code of belief was redundant or nonsensical: it imparted awe and grandeur to the

Confucian moral order, and in that role it subsequently turned out to have served Confucian morality as the ladder rather than as the bedrock. Thereafter *tian* maintained a low profile — enough to lend its vague aura to the other two codes but never so much as to take the center of gravity away from them. Thus for most of the history of Confucian China the center of gravity was firmly situated somewhere between the code of conduct and the code of virtue. The high-sounding code of virtue made possible a lot of hypocrisy, but the habit-enforcing code of conduct helped bring about a good deal of embodiment.

In the crucial role of the code of conduct lies much of the secret of the durability of the Confucian moral order. Long before Confucius the code of conduct had already acquired the considerable measure of independence it was to maintain for over two thousand years after Confucius. Although the code of conduct required the code of virtue (and sometimes the code of belief) as a source of meaning and justification, it nevertheless displayed a remarkable capacity for keeping, or reifying, the meaning it thus received — so much so that the code of virtue did for the code of conduct much of what the code of belief did for the two lower-level codes. Once the code of virtue had imparted meaning to the code of conduct, it receded into the background of official doctrine and lip service, and the code of conduct emerged into the real foreground that was daily practice. Relatively little meaning accumulated around the code of belief. For this reason, unlike the code of virtue or the code of conduct, it was open to fundamental questioning by later Confucianists who wanted to place essentially the same codes of conduct and virtue, namely, the *sangang wuchang*, on metaphysical rather than cosmological foundations. By contrast, an intricate web of meaning formed around the code of virtue, but much of this meaning was not independent and could only be channeled through the code of conduct. By thus serving as the indispensable channel for much of the code of virtue, the code of conduct became the site where moral significance congealed and reified itself, until the code of conduct partook of the character of, though it could never entirely dispense with, the code of virtue. And because the code of conduct as the primary site of reification was also the site closest to embodiment, this reification contributed enormously to the stability and durability of the Confucian moral order.

The secret of Confucianism's durability, then, is the minimization of moral consciousness through its reification at the closest possible level to embodiment. Indeed, the Legalists of the Warring States period (475–221 B.C.), Shang Yang and Han Fei in particular, had no less clear a perception of the potentially detrimental effects of moral consciousness. Where they went astray was in believing that a code of conduct—in this case *fa* (law) instead of *li*—could be enforced through the threat of punishment alone without even a modicum of moral consciousness or willingness. The Confucianists knew what the Legalists knew, but they also knew that a code of conduct was more effective if obeyed willingly. Confucius was not quite right when he said: "Lead the people with governmental measures and regulate them by law and punishment, and they will avoid wrongdoing but will have no sense of honor and shame,"[3] for people do not avoid wrongdoing under pain of punishment alone. Confucius was more nearly right when he went on to say: "Lead them with virtue and regulate them by rules of propriety [*li*], and they will have a sense of shame and, moreover, set themselves right."[4] He would indeed be describing the secret behind the success of the Confucian moral order if he had found a place for *fa* in his art of rulership; those who ruled in his name did succeed in doing this.

The function of the code of virtue was precisely to induce a willingness to follow the code of conduct: to follow *li* willingly was already to follow *li* with what Confucius would consider the right spirit. Of *ren* and *li*, there was no doubt which was the end and which the means—so much so that in a famous saying in the *Analects* Confucius even defines *ren* in terms of *li*. "To master oneself and return to propriety [*li*]," says Confucius, "*is* humanity."[5] And elsewhere in the *Analects*: "Yu Tzu said, 'Among the functions of propriety [*li*] the most valuable is that it establishes harmony. The excellence of the ways of ancient kings consists of this. It is the guiding principle of all things great and small. If things go amiss, and you, understanding harmony, try to achieve it without regulating it by the rules of propriety, they will still go amiss.'"[6] Harmony is the end, the code of conduct is the means, and the code of virtue is the means of the means.

To treat *ren* as the end is not sensible if only because it is not possible—"ought" implies "can"—and Confucius reveals much about the place of *ren* in his moral doctrine when he acknowledges that "I have never seen one who really loves humanity or one who really hates inhumanity. . . . Is there any one who has devoted his strength to humanity for as long as a single day?"[7] The kind of *ren* that *is* within human reach is the *practice* of *ren*, that is, *ren* as temporally delimited action, something whose transitory quality is well reflected in another well-known Confucius saying: "Is humanity far away? As soon as I want it, there it is right by me."[8] The unattainability of *ren* as a permanent virtue, however, is no reason for abandoning *ren*. For although *ren* is unattainable as an end, it is indispensable as a means of inducing a willingness to follow *li*, which is the more direct path to harmony. Provided *li* is followed willingly, there is no need to opine that the willingness does not come from wholehearted *ren* or even from genuine understanding of *ren*. "Confucius said, 'The common people may be made to follow it [the Way] but may not be made to understand it.'"[9] "Confucius replied, '. . . The character of a ruler is like wind and that of the people is like grass.

In whatever direction the wind blows, the grass always bends.' "[10] This is possible only because of the distinction between *li* and *ren*; only the former can be practiced without understanding.

By his own logic, then, Confucius should not be at odds with Laozi when the latter argues from the existence of *li* to the loss of *dao*. If Laozi shows more blunt insight, Confucius exhibits more mature wisdom. For once the *dao* is lost (supposing it ever existed), it is no use, as Laozi advocates, trying to regain it through the elimination of moral consciousness. The only thing that can be done is to try approximating to the *dao* by cultivating enough moral consciousness to follow *li*; only in this way can *dao* find such visible embodiment as mortals are capable of. The *dao* that is thereby approached is not the authentic *dao*, and this Confucius comes close to acknowledging in his sayings about the unattainability of humanity. The greatness of Laozi is to have demonstrated this; the greatness of Confucius is to have made the best of it.

The best was best, of course, only within the framework of the Confucian social order itself. For a complex variety of reasons, that social order, after enduring for some two thousand years, crumbled in the early years of the twentieth century. Once the framework that had held everything together burst asunder, the code of belief was found to be absurd, the code of virtue hypocritical, and the code of conduct repressive. And in their place arose, first in communist-controlled areas and then in the whole of the mainland when the Communist party swept to power, a new trio of codes, with which Mao Zedong was to found a new morality as part of a new society.[11]

The structure of this new morality was shaped above all by its evolution as the morality of an army fighting a protracted and ideologically inspired war. Only after the war was won in 1949 did what began as the morality of the

Teleology as Morality 111

communist army expand to become the morality of an entire people. The product of war was made to function in peace, however, without any fundamental change in its structure. Not only did wartime habits die hard, but more important, as we shall see, the structure of the wartime morality was to prove well suited to Mao's peacetime needs as the leader no longer of a military but of a continuing ideological war.

A strict code of conduct is indispensable to war, and because the Communist party was in charge of an army rather than a civilian population, its code of conduct took the form of military discipline. In contrast to the Confucian code of conduct, that of the Communist party had a simplicity dictated by military discipline. Since the communist army was drawn mostly from poor peasants with a high level of illiteracy, simplicity was a necessity. As it happened, this code of conduct consisted of only "three major rules and eight points of attention" (*sanda jilü baxiang zhuyi*) — a code whose simplicity also served to underline its importance and strictness.

No less important was a code of belief to justify the code of conduct and to sustain morale under conditions of extreme danger and deprivation — the more so since the communist army was not a professional army but an army fighting for an ideal. Just as the Taipings in rebelling against an all-pervasive Confucian order had taken their code of belief in part from Christianity, so Mao Zedong in trying to bring about a radical transformation of Chinese society adopted his code of belief from another foreign source — this time, Marxist communism. Communism was ideal both as a rich store of meaning to justify the code of conduct and as an inspiring vision to give heart and courage to those fighting a protracted war. The communist code of belief derived its power from its teleological, indeed eschatological, character. This teleological character had, in turn, the far-reaching effect of inflating the code of belief into a huge and elaborate structure. For to make this teleology convincing, it was deemed necessary, given the ethos of scientism following the May Fourth movement of 1919, to show that it was scientific; to show it was scientific required nothing less than what purported to be a science itself. Thus, all the while the fighting was going on, a huge and elaborate code of belief gradually took shape around what had begun as a fairly simple belief in liberation from oppression.

Not surprisingly, there was little room or need for a code of virtue. An army needed only discipline and morale. Discipline came from the code of conduct, and morale came from the code of belief. And such meaning and justification as the code of conduct required were amply supplied by the elaborate code of belief. If a code of virtue could be said to exist, its content, such as altruism and courage, was more or less supplied by the other two codes. The thinness of the code of virtue was both effect and cause of the elaborateness of the code of belief.

Such a morality is distinguished by a top-heavy structure — top-heavy in the sense that the most developed level of morality, the code of belief, is the level most removed from embodiment. Thus one obvious drawback of a morality with such a structure is the high likelihood of disembodiment. The communist wartime morality, however, did not suffer this drawback despite its top-heavy structure. The communist army was made up entirely of volunteers, people who joined its ranks because the conditions of their lives predisposed them to embrace the code of belief that they were instructed to see as the very aim they were fighting for. Once they were made to see communism as the sole and assured solution to their misery, that misery already prefigured the embodiment of their code of belief. It was the function of the code of belief precisely to drive home this link, and in this it was remarkably successful, helped by China's prevalent hunger and poverty as well as by the gradually brightening prospects of the revolution.

Teleology as Morality 113

This set of moral codes proved enormously effective for purposes of inspiring and disciplining the army, whose military success eventually brought the Communist party to power.[12] But when applied to a civilian population, under conditions that made embodiment more difficult and elusive, the same set of moral codes revealed all the drawbacks of a top-heavy morality. Under wartime conditions the Communist party did not develop, and had no need to develop, a comprehensive code of conduct. A civilian population may need such a code of conduct, but an army requires only a much simpler military code of discipline. But when the Communist party began to preside over a state and not just an army, it did little to set up a comprehensive code of conduct, and in this the Communist party was truly anti-Confucian. True, the wartime code of conduct was adapted for peacetime purposes, but it could hardly do for a huge civilian population what it had done for an army. Thus a huge vacuum opened up where Confucian China had had an elaborate code of conduct. The vacuum was all the greater since little attempt was made, either before or after 1949, to construct a comprehensive code of virtue. If the wartime code of conduct was simple, the wartime code of virtue was even simpler. A few items were added to it after 1949, but it never developed beyond a bare skeleton. In a radical break with the structure of Confucian morality, the Communist party shrunk the code of conduct and the code of virtue and enormously expanded the code of belief.

Thus the single most distinctive overarching feature of morality in Mao's China was the subordination, one might even say the reduction, of virtue to belief, along with the total politicization of belief. Accordingly, moral goodness was a function of holding, and preferably also practicing (more of this later), certain beliefs that were openly part of a political program. Virtue was what promoted the political program and vice what hindered it. Opponents of the program were therefore not just politically unsound but morally reprehensible. They were, as the awesome term had it, counterrevolutionaries, and counterrevolution was, politically and legally, the most heinous of crimes. The formula "The end justifies the means," though seldom openly invoked in Chinese politics and morals, nevertheless expressed a mentality and even a practice common in Maoist China. The subordination of means to ends was nothing other than the subordination of virtue to political belief or, worse still, the reduction of the former to the latter. The inconspicuousness of the formula itself was symptomatic not of the absence of the mentality and practice it articulated but, quite the contrary, of its status as the morally obvious. The belief that moral wrongness was a matter not of using inappropriate means but of pursuing incorrect ends was so deeply embedded in the Maoist moral consciousness that the need for justifying the means never arose, until the time came to call into question Maoism in its entirety.

Along with this conception of morality went a moral psychology according to which, as Mao Zedong put it, "There is in the world neither love without cause nor hate without cause," the cause in question always being one's membership in and emotional attachment to a class. Love actuated by wrong class membership and attachment was not a virtue, just as hate that sprang from the right class membership and attachment was not a vice. Lei Feng, that well-known paragon of virtue who had thoroughly absorbed these sentiments, wrote in his diary: "One should be as warm as spring to one's comrades and as cold as winter to one's enemies." Here comrades and enemies were identified politically, that is, largely according to belief. Not surprisingly, it was customary in Mao's China to attach to virtues the epithets "proletarian" or "revolutionary" and to vices the epithets "bourgeois" or "counterrevolutionary," proletarian humanitarianism and revolutionary heroism being examples of the one, and bourgeois egoism and bourgeois hypocrisy examples of the other. Strictly speaking these epithets were redundant; according to the rationale at work here, to call a virtue proletarian or a vice bourgeois was a tautology, just as to call a virtue bourgeois or a vice proletarian was a self-contradiction. The use of these epithets served only to guide those not yet clearheaded enough to see the obvious.

The result of this education, systematically conducted from 1949 with only a few interruptions, was the building of morality on the most shifting of foundations. Political programs fail easily, and political beliefs sacrosanct today can look ridiculous tomorrow. People act on a politically grounded morality only when they subscribe to certain political beliefs, and these beliefs command allegiance only when the political program of which they are a part is thriving. It was thus a source of potential disaster that Mao's China relied on a morality that could last only as long as Mao and his political program lasted. We should not be surprised that Mao's death was followed by the gradual worsening of the moral climate. What had preceded this moral decline, however, was not the flourishing of morality but the success of politics; the subsequent moral paralysis was nothing more than the consequence of the failure of the political project. The political project was everything; its collapse naturally caused everything, including morality, to collapse with it. When Mao's successors tell the Chinese people that only the Communist party can give China stability, they are not just making a threat but stating a stark fact — a fact of their own making — about the nature of the Chinese moral and social order since 1949.

The political beliefs one had to hold in order to qualify as morally good varied slightly in content and number over the years. But their substance remained the same, just as the vested interests and the stakes remained the same. That substance was well encapsulated in the relatively recent formulation "four fundamental principles," namely, Marxism–

Leninism–Mao Zedong Thought, the socialist system, the leadership of the Communist party, and the dictatorship of the proletariat (alternatively called the democratic dictatorship of the people). Since in the official interpretation each of the four principles entailed the other three, one may wonder why one principle was not allowed to suffice. Apparently all four were included to encompass all important aspects of what was seen as a totality so as, in a manner characteristic of the employment of key political axioms, to leave no loophole for incorrect interpretation. These four principles, written into the state constitution, were seen as necessary conditions of virtue. One sometimes gets the impression that they were regarded as sufficient conditions as well. It is not hard to see the rationale behind this way of joining virtue and political belief, a rational we may easily capture in the form of something like a syllogism. A virtuous Chinese person, so the syllogism goes, desires the well-being of China and its people (end); only the four principles can ensure the well-being of China and its people (means); therefore a virtuous person embraces the four principles (since anyone who sincerely desires the end must necessarily desire the necessary means for achieving that end). The minor premise, which serves as the link in this chain of reasoning, was taken as proved beyond all possible doubt and as having been proved once and for all.

The cardinal status of the four principles is the paradigmatic instance in China of the subordination of the moral to the political. But to speak of the four principles is to speak in political rather than ethical terms. When we cross over the nominal boundary between politics and morals, we find a slightly different mode of discourse in which it is customary to translate the belief in the four principles into the belief in, and the readiness to act in accordance with, communism, which thereby becomes the cornerstone of the whole moral edifice in China. But communism differs from

Teleology as Morality   117

the four principles only in having two official faces, one political and one moral, and that only goes to show that morality does not even have a face of its own.

In its role as the foundation of morality, communism was first and foremost a goal, and the two things that need to be demonstrated about a goal are that it is good and that it is feasible. That communism was good was seen, quite wisely, as requiring no proof. But people who contemplated years of hardship in order to realize it needed reassurance that communism was feasible, and what could better demonstrate its feasibility than science. The science called upon to play this role was China's version of Marxism,[13] which had served as the intellectual source of Chinese communism in the first place. Unless we grasp this crucial role of Marxism, we would not even begin to understand why those in power were so concerned to demonstrate that Marxism was a science — the science of all sciences. The status of Marxism as science or non-science was the battleground. The Chinese believers in Marx had not gone beyond scientism, but neither had most of their opponents.

The scientific pretensions of Marxism were helped, not hindered, by its complexity. For lay people the dignity and grandeur of science lie not just in its practical usefulness but much more in its mind-boggling incomprehensibility (combined, of course, with its practical usefulness). The same was true of Marxism in China as long as it was believed to be a science. In this light, it no longer appears absurd that an intellectual system as daunting and complex as Marxism was, as the governing ideology, made the object of nationwide study in a country with a high level of illiteracy and a small college-educated population. One was made to study Marxism not so much to understand as to be awestruck and to be made submissive. One follows when one is charmed, and one is charmed by what one does not quite understand. Thus an ideology is stable in inverse proportion to people's knowledge of it. Ideology thrives on ignorance; not complete ignorance, to be sure, but ignorance in the sense of slight or vague knowledge.

To be more precise, we need to distinguish two levels of ideology: on the one hand, the theoretical or intellectual part of an ideology (which may or may not have started off as ideology); and on the other hand, a simplified version of the ideology. The first level of ideology is the preserve of theorists, those who may be aptly called experts. The second level of ideology is for mass consumption. My earlier remark that the stability of an ideology requires a certain degree of ignorance may more accurately be expressed as follows: an ideology thrives when ordinary citizens are allowed only a hazy knowledge of the first level but as precise as possible a knowledge of the second level, which for this reason needs to be simple and accessible.

There are good reasons, moreover, for having an ideology in the first sense that is forbiddingly difficult and complex. First, the sheer difficulty and complexity of such an ideology can command respect and even awe, doing for an ideology what charisma does for a political leader. Complexity can easily create a sense of mystery, which can, though it need not, be a drawback. Marxism, however, does not suffer from this drawback, since its believers generally accept it as scientific. Second, the sheer difficulty and complexity of the first-level ideology make interpretation necessary before it can become second-level ideology. The very need for interpretation confers flexibility on the ideological apparatus, for the first-level ideology can be given different interpretations in the light of changing needs and circumstances. Such flexibility, unless it is exercised too often or too blatantly, need not undermine the stability of the ideological apparatus, since different interpretations are seen as interpretations of the *same* first-level ideology. It is possible, as has often been demonstrated, to condemn past interpretations, or somebody else's present interpretations, of the first-level ideology without thereby undermining the first-

Teleology as Morality 119

level ideology itself. The interpretations thus dismissed can simply be treated as distortions of the first-level ideology, which in itself remains holy and pure. Those who win politically always win ideologically. And they win with the aid of those officially appointed interpreters of the first-level ideology, whose job it is to mediate between the first and the second levels of the ideology and to prove that the politically powerful are the ideologically correct.

A further source of flexibility is that Marx himself did not lay down any system of moral rules in opposition to the bourgeois morality he so scathingly exposed, just as he did not propose in detail any practical methods for the attainment of the political goals he so eloquently set forth. Thus, unlike Confucianism, Marxism contains neither a ready-made moral code nor a ready-made statecraft. These absences facilitate the severance of means from ends and give wide scope to the choice of morality and to the exercise of statecraft. It was as if Marx had given Mao Zedong a book of blank checks on which Mao could write any amount provided it could be shown — and this was easy — that the checks were made out to the order of communism. The checks were blank precisely because, to put it in the terms used earlier, they had printed on them an elaborate but ethereal code of belief that could be interpreted any way Mao wanted.

This represents nothing less than a reversal of the logic that governs the relationship among the three codes of Confucian morality. There the code of conduct is primary, the code of virtue serves as its source of meaning and justification, and the code of belief, insofar as it exists, serves in turn to ground the other two codes. The underlying process of derivation, the actual order of importance, runs from the code of conduct through the code of virtue to the code of belief, although ostensibly the process could also be reversed. In Maoist morality, the process of derivation does move the other way, with the code of belief as primary and with the other two codes derivable from it. It is therefore not just the case that the code of conduct and the code of virtue are thinner than their counterparts in Confucian morality; it is more importantly the case that these codes, the code of conduct in particular, perform a very different structural role and function according to a very different understanding of how best to govern.

That understanding, in a nutshell, is that flexibility matters more than stability. Mao Zedong needed the flexibility not only as poet-dictator but also, if we are to take his words at face value, in order to maintain revolutionary momentum. Flexibility is a function of the distance from embodiment. The code of belief, by virtue of being situated furthest from embodiment, is thus most conducive to flexibility. This is not to say that Mao had no concern for stability and embodiment; what he wanted was a stability that would not hamper his flexibility. A large measure of such stability can be achieved through some kind of reification, provided reification occurs at a considerable distance from the level of embodiment. For this purpose the code of belief is the ideal site. Reification need not curtail flexibility, not only because this kind of ideological reification is open to a great deal of fine-tuning before it reaches the level of embodiment, but also because, as we shall see, within the code of belief flexibility can exist side by side with reification. Even more remarkable, such flexibility need not prevent embodiment. Although the code of belief lies furthest from embodiment, it can also be very effective in bringing about embodiment, provided it is sincerely believed. For subscription to a code of belief induces a readiness to obey commands coming from the authority that presides over the code of belief. Thus the authority need not be equipped with a comprehensive code of conduct — that would only be a burdensome constraint; all it needs to do is to establish a code of belief upon the most secure foundations possible,

Teleology as Morality 121

thereby ensuring its own legitimacy and the credence of the people. The people will then be ready to embody what they are told to embody, but that — and this is the essence of the flexibility — will be neither the code of belief nor any ready-made code of conduct but the will of the ruler.

Psychologically what this manner of governing involves is, to put it in terms of a stark contrast, the organization of impulses through highly conscious sublimation rather than through subliminal regulation. It is not that sublimation and regulation exclude each other, but in the case of socially organized sublimation the regulation of narcissistic and aggressive impulses is made heavily and consciously dependent upon the internalization of some socially imposed goal or ideal that serves as the raison d'être of sublimation in the first place. If socially imposed goals that form part of a political program are often unstable, their internalization is even more so, being contingent on confidence in the future success of the political program and on constant perception of oneself as an actual or potential beneficiary. And the more conscious the goal, the more contingent the sublimation, so that once the goal is no longer valued this change of consciousness alone can result in the rapid de-sublimation of hitherto apparently well-regulated impulses.

But the precariousness of such socially organized sublimation was of no concern in Mao's brand of radical politics. What mattered in such politics, which believed in its own indefinite continuation or did not care about the social consequences of its possible failure, was the flexibility that some such means of psychological control afforded for social mobilization. Every time Mao issued a call for social action, the masses responded with an unrestrained passion and a total disregard of convention that would have been made impossible by respect for a stable and comprehensive code of conduct. Total mobilization meant allowing no energy to be held back by habit. Small wonder, then, that Mao had no use for a comprehensive code of conduct. Insofar as a code of conduct could be said to exist in Mao's China, it contained only one imperative: Do as you are told. As long as the code of belief sustained Mao's legitimacy, the code of conduct served as an open space into which he could insert any directive that happened to suit his political needs at the moment.[14] For such a moral order only two constants were essential: communism as the code of belief, and, as we shall see presently, collectivism and altruism as a bridge from the code of belief to that open space which in Confucian morality is occupied by a rigid code of conduct.

Being far removed from practical conduct, the code of belief in and of itself gives as much flexibility of conduct to the ruled as to the ruler. Something is needed, therefore, to preserve the flexibility for the ruler and deny it to the ruled. Nothing can do this better than collectivism, which serves for the elaborate and ethereal code of belief the twin purposes of simplification and concretization. Collectivism simplifies the elaborate code of belief to the point where everybody can grasp it and allows the new ideology to take nourishment from the traditional collectivism whose roots lie deep in the collective unconscious. Collectivism brings the ethereal code of belief down to earth as the concrete imperative to obey the collective, just as in Confucianism the moral imperative was to defer to sovereign, father, and husband. But what is the collective but the new patriarchs who run it? The code of belief is the alchemy, characteristic of all religion, that transforms the work of man (usually powerful men) into the work of God or Truth.

At the hands of Mao Zedong this alchemy was used above all to transform submission into the appearance of mastership, authoritarianism into democracy, but freedom into egoism. Much of the alchemy was effected by mixing communism and collectivism. It is not hard to see how collectivism can be derived from communism. For communism itself is collectivist, understood as an ideal that is embraced

Teleology as Morality 123

by all (who move along with, rather than against, the march of history), that is in the interests of all, and that requires for its realization the efforts of all (but the counterrevolutionaries). Nor is it difficult, in an alternative conception, to see how communism can be grafted onto collectivism. For activist collectivism, by nature goal-oriented, finds in communism a goal that can justify and sustain collectivism in times both of war and of peace in a way that is not possible with, say, cultural loyalty, which furnished the chief goal of traditional collectivism. In this alternative conception, collectivism is viewed as the real end of politics, for which communism serves both as an expression and as a justification. By the logic of either conception, collectivism bonded with communism means, as a moral imperative, contributing to the collective cause of communism in a collective way. Since the cause of communism is the one goal in pursuit of which all should act in unison, there can no longer be any conflict of goals, nor by implication any conflict of interests, between individuals and the state, or among communism-loving individuals. What is left is the struggle between good and evil, revolution and counterrevolution.

As a natural extension of this line of reasoning, there developed a number of assumptions that formed an important part of Chinese political consciousness under Mao Zedong. One interesting feature of these assumptions is that all can be, and sometimes actually were, construed in such a way that they cast a more favorable light on democracy (or what is called "democratic centralism") than on freedom (understood as negative freedom).

With the overthrow of the exploiting classes in 1949, it is assumed, people who had formerly been their "slaves" now became "masters" of the socialist state. Freedom is a reasonable aspiration when it is interpreted as freedom from oppression and exploitation. But once oppression and exploitation are eliminated, the demand for freedom ceases to make sense, because with the advent of socialism freedom has necessarily become a reality. Freedom is viewed here as part and parcel, not only in theory but equally in practice, of the socialist system, such that once the socialist system is established, freedom is simultaneously achieved in its entirety and the demand *for more* arises necessarily from egoism or a pernicious ideology or even evil intentions.

A somewhat different logic applies to democracy. As a matter of political principle, so the logic goes, the working class and its allies, as masters of the socialist state, naturally and necessarily have the right to political participation. Socialism alone makes the genuine exercise of this right possible. But as a matter of political method, so the logic continues, democracy takes time and experience to mature and to be perfected. When the two parts of the logic are taken together, it makes perfect sense to demand greater democracy, provided that it is democracy of the right kind (i.e., socialist democracy) and provided that those demanding greater democracy concede that democracy must be combined with the necessary centralization of authority to yield what is called democratic centralism.

No comparable two-tier logic is applied to freedom. Freedom is treated not as a matter of the scope of activity of the individual versus that of the state but as a question of sovereignty or mastership, which is in turn treated as a function of the nature of a given political system. At this level of abstraction, mastership, and hence also freedom, is naturally viewed as an all-or-nothing matter. Of course, mastership may not be perfectly exercised, but that is a matter that pertains to the methodological level of democracy. Thus once the working class and its allies have become masters of the socialist state, the question of freedom is solved, and there is no more to be said about freedom than pointing to its actual realization under socialism. This kind of reasoning works by not distinguishing those who wield actual authority from those whose authority (or mastership) is the mere product of a certain conception. When such a distinc-

Teleology as Morality 125

tion is drawn, as it has been drawn by people with poor judgment or bad intentions, its implications can be canceled by a second assumption.

And that is to assume, as we have seen, that there is a fundamental identity of goals, and hence also of interests, between individuals and the state and by implication also among individuals. Indeed, it is impossible to deny, without at once putting oneself in an awkward position, that the objectives set forth by the leadership are also the aspirations of the people, and that the leadership and the people are united in the march along the road toward communism. Freedom, construed as negative freedom, thrives on individualism, which regards the choice of goals as the province of individuals and which therefore views the interests of individuals, and by implication of individuals and the state, as necessarily conflicting up to a point. Collectivism is opposed not so much to freedom as to individualism. By substituting individualism's assumption of conflict of interests with its assumption of identity of interests, collectivism obviates the very raison d'être of freedom.

But even where conflicts of interests — short-term interests, of course — between individuals and the state are acknowledged, there is the further assumption, which has a democratic ring to it, that individual interests ought to give way to collective interests, and local interests to state interests. This formula can be seen as quite compatible with democracy, inasmuch as democracy is majority rule. Freedom, on the other hand, pertains only to the individual and as such can be seen as the enemy of the collective and hence of democracy. There is thus an all-important difference between democracy and freedom, with the one pertaining to the collective and the other to the individual. Since democracy pertains to the collective, it is legitimate and up to the collective to bring it about. Since freedom pertains to the individual, it is illegitimate and up to the collective to fight against it. As soon as democracy is viewed as pertaining to the individual, that is, individual political rights, it ceases to be legitimate democracy and becomes subversive freedom, which must be suppressed.

Yet another difference separates democracy and freedom, a difference that may be described in terms of means and ends. This difference has two aspects. First, although it is perfectly plausible to treat freedom (particularly in the senses of feeling free and being a free person) as an end in itself, it would be more difficult to treat democracy in like fashion. Unlike modern Western morality, which consists of constraints on means, Chinese morality is end-oriented, where the end for the short term is the all-around modernization of China within the framework of socialism and for the long term is communism, when everyone will enjoy positive freedom. Clearly, treating freedom as an end would interfere with the collective ends, which alone have moral legitimacy. Second, when both democracy and freedom are treated as means, they lend themselves to different kinds of ends. It is not unnatural, though not necessary, to treat democracy as a means to collective ends, and this is indeed how democracy has been treated in China. Freedom, on the other hand, when treated as means, is most naturally, and primarily, taken as a means of realizing one's own projects and ambitions in the absence of unwarranted interference by the state. Thus the very desire and demand for freedom is symptomatic of alienation from collective goals and interests. In the very act of attaching importance to personal freedom, one shows oneself to be an individualist, with projects and ambitions that Mao Zedong in a famous article entitled "Combat Liberalism" described as "extremely harmful in a revolutionary collective"[15] and that are therefore not worthy of respect and still less of protection.

What is at stake in all this is the maximization of the freedom of the ruler and the minimization of the freedom of the ruled. Collectivism, with its rationale about freedom and democracy, does the job perfectly, giving the ruled the illusion of freedom and the ruler the trappings of democracy.

Collectivism is more concrete than communism, but altruism is more concrete still. Herein, and herein alone, lies the value of altruism. The primary function of morality in Mao's China was to distribute freedom and obligation, giving the former entirely to the ruler and the latter as much as possible to the ruled. For this function the combination of the code of belief and collectivism was already sufficient. Conceptually, altruism is both subordinate and redundant. This is reflected unmistakably in the communist insistence, reminiscent of Han Fei and contrary to the teachings of Confucius, that loyalty to the state must always override loyalty to family and friends. Altruism will be seen as misplaced, at best, if it asserts itself in opposition to collectivism. The subordination of altruism to collectivism is the subordination of the private to the public realm, of the individual to the social. This subordination is nowhere more manifest than in the belief that there is, and can be, no fundamental conflict of interest between individuals and the state in a socialist society. From this complete harmony of interests, it follows that no important conflict of interest is possible among the individuals who make up that collective called the state. For when all individuals have a complete commonality of interests with the collective, they will have exactly the same commonality of interests with each other, as members of the same collective. Thus, for the collectivist, nothing is left for altruism to do. In the process of subduing one's purely individual ambitions and interests in favor of collective goals, one achieves the feat of self-denial that altruism is designed to foster. Being either subordinate to collectivism in the case of conflict or redundant in the case of harmony, altruism has no place in Chinese morality as an independent principle.

But this is the case only conceptually. Psychologically,

altruism renders two indispensable services to collectivism. As a virtue that few would question, altruism conceals the sinister and potentially totalitarian character of collectivism. Unlike collectivism, which often has to promote fear and inculcate submissiveness openly and whose inevitable invocation of abstract ideas and distant goals can easily seem suspect, altruism appeals to the at once more tangible and more laudable instinct of sympathy for one's neighbor. Precisely because it is closer to the human heart and further from counterintuitive abstractions, and because, moreover, the relationship between individuals is more tangible than that between individuals and the state, altruism is, psychologically, the best training ground for the self-denial that collectivism conceptually enjoins. And once self-denial has been brought about through altruism, it can then be put to the service of the collective cause.

It is chiefly for this role that altruism finds a place in Chinese morality. Crucially symptomatic of this role is the specific meaning that altruism has in Chinese morality, namely, *wusi*, selflessness or complete altruism. "Altruism," as we have been using the term so far, is a convenient but inaccurate translation of a concept that may be more accurately rendered as "giving every weight to other people's interests and none to one's own." The opposite of altruism thus understood is complete egoism, which means putting one's interests above everyone and everything else. It is of profound significance that altruism and egoism are treated in Chinese moral discourse as contradictories rather than contraries, with no intermediate conceptual space between them. In theory though not quite to the same degree in practice, one is faced with the stark choice of utter selflessness or utter selfishness. There is no room for a position that gives approximately equal weight to one's own interests and those of others. This position, very revealingly, often goes under the name of altruism in the modern moral culture of the West, with its concomitant concept of supererogation,

Teleology as Morality 129

something that is totally absent from the Chinese moral consciousness. There are thus (at least) three possible positions to adopt with regard to the relative weight to be given the interests of the self and others. It is significant that whereas both Chinese and Western ethics have a ready term for the position called egoism, they should differ so radically in the prominence they give to the two remaining positions — so much so that what is understood in the West as altruism is in Chinese morality hardly conceptually distinguishable from egoism.

This profound difference reveals not the superiority of one moral culture over the other but rather the very different roles that altruism has been made to play in the two moral cultures. Altruism has meant limited altruism in the West because its function has been to regulate the relations, or more precisely the conflict of interests, among individuals, in the context of the simultaneous development of capitalism and individualism. As one solution to conflict of interests among individuals, limited altruism rests on the value judgment of private interests as morally legitimate objects of pursuit. It rests, further, on the assumption that the conflict of interests among individuals is unavoidable but reconcilable. From some such beliefs arises the Western concept of justice, which, through the concept of supererogation, requires of members of civic society not benevolence or self-denial, but fairness, such that one claims for oneself neither more nor less than what is one's due in a given system of justice.

The extreme character of altruism in Maoist morality is reason neither to praise its high purpose nor to condemn its hypocrisy, but rather to suspect that it serves a different cultural function. It takes only a moment's reflection to realize that complete altruism, as opposed to limited altruism, makes no sense as a principle for regulating the relations among individuals. For complete altruism, in enjoining everyone to take as one's sole duty the promotion of the interests of others, sets up a moral world in which no one has any interest for anyone else to promote. A world full of complete altruists requires at least one non-altruist to make their altruism meaningful, and they will be prepared to act as complete altruists only if the one non-altruist succeeds in disguising himself as the collective and the collective ideal. Mao Zedong did that perfectly. When everyone is an empty vessel for the sake of one's neighbor, all are empty vessels for the one who recognizes no neighbors.

Alongside the elaborate code of belief, the code of virtue and the code of conduct, insofar as they can be said to exist at all, boil down to little more than collectivism and altruism. If Maoist morality is so simple, it is because nothing more complex is required. The sole function of collectivism and altruism is to turn people into empty vessels, and they are willing to be so emptied, not knowing that they have been so emptied, only because they are filled with the code of belief. A less elaborate code of belief would not be able to induce and maintain that willingness; a more complex code of conduct would deprive the ruler of much of his freedom to make his people behave as would suit his changing needs and whims. From the point of view of the ruler, the mixture is just right.[16]

In such a belief-centered moral culture, however, disembodiment is a constant danger, because the code of belief is at the furthest remove from embodiment. And it is a danger that becomes actual whenever beliefs do not answer to needs that are genuinely felt. As we saw earlier, the top-heavy character of the Communist party's wartime morality did not lead to disembodiment because the code of belief answered to needs that were both real and continuing. The mind was drawn to communism because the body craved freedom from hunger and cold. In this sense we may describe the code of belief, in a brief formula, as moving from body to mind, that is, from needs to beliefs. What happened after 1949, by contrast, was a movement from mind to body; beliefs that had been developed in answer to genuinely felt needs on the part of the revolutionaries were imposed on the population at large, which was made to accept the beliefs without feeling the corresponding needs or feeling them to the same degree. Indeed, and this was always a sign of confidence on the part of those in power, people were made, often on pain of heavy punishment, not only to pronounce the correct political beliefs but also to act on them through the constant display of persecutory fervor in political campaigns and obedient diligence at work in more normal times.

Ironically, while the enforced embodiment of beliefs was being carried out by the population at large, those who had originally represented the voluntary embodiment of beliefs gradually showed signs that their beliefs, acquired under very special wartime conditions, were becoming disembodied under the more hospitable peacetime conditions. There thus occurred a reversal in the embodiment of beliefs, though not a reversal in power. Those who preached did not practice, and those who practiced did not have the power to preach. Eventually cynicism set in, and the whole project of embodiment was practically abandoned.

The clearest symptom of this change was that it gradually came to be enough only to pronounce certain beliefs; it was no longer necessary to act on them. The verbal expression of the correct beliefs, in the absence of actions that pointed unmistakably to the contrary, was hence looked upon as a sufficient and sometimes a necessary condition for the demonstration of belief. There was of course no guarantee here, as always with the use of words, of sincerity or conviction. But this did not matter greatly, since to say that one subscribed to certain beliefs was already to engage in an act of conformity. In the event, the institution of the political meeting survived the loss of genuine political belief. No longer a forum for inculcating belief, this remarkable institution, the only one where correct beliefs could be openly aired in a serious setting, was maintained for the purpose of fostering cowardice and passive conformity. What was demanded was not the embodiment of the code of belief but only a superficial conformity to it, a gesture of obedience to a political authority too weak to enforce embodiment.

Once the code of belief was disembodied, it was able to fulfill only one of its two most important functions. It could still make people passively obedient — and only because it was backed up by brute force — but it could no longer serve as a work ethic. It could still create conformity, but it could no longer generate energy or enthusiasm. There had never been moral reasons to behave morally. The reasons had always been political. Once the political reasons were discredited, there were no reasons to behave morally at all. Henceforth society could be kept together only by force, by convenience, by cowardice, by habit, and by what little had remained of simple humanity. Not a very happy state of affairs for those Chinese who survived Mao. But then the morality was not designed for their benefit in the first place.

With hindsight we can now see clearly the logic of a morality whose fragility became fully apparent only after the collapse of Mao's utopian project. The top-heavy structure of Maoist morality affords a great deal of flexibility, but it also carries a very high risk of disembodiment — disembodiment not only of the code of belief itself but of any commands coming from a ruler whose code of belief has lost credibility. The less independent the code of conduct (and the code of virtue), the greater the danger of disintegration of a moral order once the code of belief is significantly weakened. In the case of Maoist China moral conduct was made too dependent on belief. Belief was in turn made too heavily political, too closely linked with the stakes of a worldly political project whose success was in turn contingent, as we shall see in the next chapter, on the fulfillment of a hedonistic promise. There was scant regulation of narcissistic and aggressive impulses independent of the code of belief, little training in discipline that was not the precarious product of conscious sublimation. And so when the code of belief collapsed, the whole moral order collapsed with it. Mao's belief-centered society was able to last only a tiny fraction of the two millennia of the Confucian ritual-centered society. But if it took Mao Zedong many years to rid his new society of the Confucian code of conduct and code of virtue, it may take as long for the more pragmatic social order now emerging to fill the vacuum left by the collapse of Mao's morality.

CHAPTER FOUR

The Ascetic Pursuit of Hedonism

Since 1949 China has been governed, in practice no less than in theory, under a philosophy whose predominant feature is materialism. In this philosophy, hedonism, though not explicitly invoked, is to materialism what ethics is to ontology. Despite their complexities at a theoretical level, materialism and hedonism have combined to form a practical outlook[1] that means nothing more abstruse than viewing and organizing social life for the satisfaction of what Marx calls human "sensuous needs."[2] It is no accident that these important features of China's guiding philosophy are shared by the hedonist philosopher Epicurus, whom Marx regarded as "the greatest Greek representative of the Enlightenment."[3] Indeed, as will become clear in the following discussion, Mao Zedong's utopianism was nothing but hedonism sublimated and postponed.

For some, hedonism may evoke an image of single-minded pleasure-seeking in disregard of the all-around well-being of oneself and others. This, although perhaps true of some extreme exemplars of hedonism, does not capture the essence of hedonism as a considered philosophy of life. And it certainly does not apply to Epicurus (Nietzsche was much closer to the mark when he said: "A little garden, figs, little cheeses and in addition three or four good friends—these were the sensual pleasures of Epicurus").[4] The modesty of

The Ascetic Pursuit of Hedonism 135

Epicurean hedonism is a function of wisdom or, as Kierkegaard put it, of abstraction: "All worldly wisdom is indeed abstraction, and only the most mediocre eudaemonism has no abstraction whatever but is the enjoyment of the moment. To the same degree that eudaemonism is sagacious, it has abstraction; the more sagacity, the more abstraction."[5] The degree of abstraction, indeed, can be such that the underlying eudaemonism—Kierkegaard did not use the term in its strictly Aristotelian sense but to all intents and purposes equated it with hedonism—is submerged under the appearance of morality and even, as we shall see, the opposite of hedonism, asceticism. It is thus by virtue of abstraction that eudaemonism (hedonism) "acquires a fleeting resemblance to the ethical and the ethical-religious, and momentarily it can seem as if they could walk together."[6] But if we take care to peel away the abstraction, as we shall presently do with Mao's utopian project, we shall not fail to see the hedonistic core.

At this core is the view, based on a materialist ontology and an empiricist epistemology, that happiness consists in the satisfaction of the senses (as well as the intellectual faculties) and the pleasure consequent upon such satisfaction.[7] Within this broad outlook, which of the senses (and faculties), if any, has a greater claim to satisfaction, how such satisfaction is to be achieved, and what degree of satisfaction is deemed appropriate or prudent, may vary from person to person. Hedonism is opposed to any truly transcendental or otherworldly outlook on the one hand and to a materialist outlook such as Nietzsche's Dionysianism on the other. But hedonism is broad enough to encompass not only Mao Zedong's utopianism but also, as Nietzsche shrewdly pointed out, the attitude of a certain kind of "Christian, who is, in fact, only a kind of Epicurean, and, with his 'faith makes blessed,' follows the principle of hedonism as far as possible."[8]

At its core, as I will try to show, Mao Zedong's utopian

project was inspired by a vision that was essentially hedonistic and materialistic. This materialist-hedonist outlook had no room for the otherworldly or the transcendental. It is only because this materialist outlook was pursued with utopian zeal that Mao Zedong's China has sometimes been described in terms of idealism, apparently the opposite of materialism and, by implication, the opposite of hedonism. But this so-called idealism (*lixiang zhuyi* rather than *weixin zhuyi*) is not to be taken in an ontological sense, in which idealism is opposed to materialism. It had nothing to do with the nature or content of the utopia that was pursued, which was materialist through and through, but only with the "abstraction" that raised hedonism to the level of utopianism.

By virtue of its thoroughness this "abstraction" made the hedonistic character of the utopian project so oblique that at times it submerged it altogether. The abstraction was in turn dictated, not by any non-hedonistic or anti-hedonistic principle, but by material circumstances, foremost among which was China's poverty. It was in great measure the high degree of abstraction necessitated by poverty that made the hedonism of Mao's utopian project take the submerged and sublimated form it often did. Hedonism came fully into the open (and degenerated into pure hedonism, or hedonism without "abstraction") only *after* the pain of abstraction had failed eventually either to deliver the promised happiness or to justify continuing abstraction. If it was poverty that made possible for Mao's utopian project what Kierkegaard calls the "simulated transition . . . from eudaemonism to the ethical within eudaemonism,"[9] it was, as we shall see, the failure to remove poverty to the expected degree that eventually undid the transition and stripped hedonism of its sublimated encrustations.

The crucial role of poverty in converting hedonism into utopianism must not make us forget, however, that poverty

The Ascetic Pursuit of Hedonism 137

is not a sufficient condition of utopian consciousness. It is all the more necessary to demonstrate this since something close to the contrary view is found among both leaders of utopian projects and theorists of utopia.

In spring 1958, at the start of Mao's first full-scale utopian project, the Great Leap Forward, Mao Zedong singled out poverty as the chief source of utopian energy: "Apart from their other characteristics, China's 600 million people have two remarkable peculiarities; they are, first of all, poor, and secondly, blank. That may seem like a bad thing, but it is really a good thing. Poor people want change, want to do things, want revolution."[10] Here Mao saw a straightforward logic leading from poverty to the desire for revolution. In this context, however, Mao meant by revolution a struggle not against enemies but against backwardness, an all-out effort to bring about, as a Great Leap Forward slogan put it, a thousand years of happiness.

Mao Zedong is not alone in perceiving a psychological link between poverty and utopianism. E. M. Cioran, who shares neither Mao's enthusiasm for utopia nor Mao's confidence in achieving it, nevertheless sees the same psychological link.

Poverty is in fact the utopianist's great auxiliary, it is the matter he works in, the substance on which he feeds his thoughts, the providence of his obsessions. Without poverty he would be empty . . . the more destitute you are, the more time and energy you will spend in reforming everything, in thinking—in other words, in vain. . . . The delirium of the poor is the generator of events, the source of history: a throng of hysterics who want another world, here and now. It is they who inspire utopias, it is for them that utopias are written.[11]

Rhetorical simplification aside, both Mao Zedong and Cioran have assigned too big and too exclusive a role to poverty in the generation of utopian consciousness. Poverty does not by itself create utopian consciousness; it only causes a certain susceptibility to utopianism, a certain psychological readiness to respond. For the vast majority of those attracted to it, utopianism comes not from themselves but from a tradition of thought ready to hand as a more or less articulate vehicle for their otherwise vague aspirations.[12] Even this susceptibility to utopianism is not, as we shall see, a function of poverty alone. Other psychological conditions—hedonism above all—must also be present before poverty can make its own indispensable contribution to the emergence of utopian consciousness.

As a working definition, we may characterize utopian consciousness as the desire, based on a belief in the possibility of its realization, for rapid change from one extreme condition of life to its extreme opposite, which is seen as possessing as much value as the present condition does not. Thus a utopian project is at once a moving away from and a moving toward. The condition it moves toward is, as Adorno reminds us, always a totality. Adorno provides not an arbitrary stipulation but a fairly accurate description of the utopian mentality when he states that "what is essential about the concept of utopia is that it does not consist of a certain, single selected category that changes itself and from which everything constitutes itself."[13] Rather, as he points out earlier in the same discussion with Ernst Bloch, "Whatever utopia is, whatever can be imagined as utopia, this is the transformation of the totality."[14]

By the same token, the condition one is seeking to move away from is also a totality. However, this condition, in its psychological salience as the here-and-now, is necessarily felt in all its living specificity in a way that the condition one is seeking to move toward cannot be experienced. The present therefore is not perceived as a totality to the same degree as the future in the utopian vision but is likely to be marked by one or more salient features of actual experience, such as poverty. Poverty, by extension, can encompass spiritual, moral, or intellectual deprivation, so that the utopia envisioned in such conditions may also be one of spiritual, moral, or intellectual fulfillment. The rationale here is that one tends to long for the extreme opposite of one's actual negative condition: material abundance as opposed to dire poverty, everlasting peace as opposed to protracted war, social tranquillity as opposed to chaos, robust health as opposed to chronic illness, endless leisure as opposed to endless labor, moral purity as opposed to spiritlessness and corruption. It can perhaps happen, as Ernst Bloch observes, that "if [hunger] increases uninterrupted, satisfied by no certain bread, then it suddenly changes. The body-ego then becomes rebellious, does not go out in search of food merely within the old framework. It seeks to change the situation which has caused its empty stomach, its hanging head. The No to the bad situation which exists, the Yes to the better life that hovers ahead, is incorporated by the deprived into *revolutionary interest.*"[15] However, this does not happen as a matter of course. As Bloch goes on to remark, "Hunger transforms itself . . . into an explosive force against the prison of deprivation" only after "having been taught," and it is only "*enlightened* hunger" (my italics) that can give rise to "the decision to abolish all conditions in which man is an oppressed and long-lost being."[16]

Even after this transformation of hunger, since a utopian project moves from what is to what is not yet, psychologically it is more an act of negation (of the present) than an act of affirmation (of the future).[17] On the level of concrete lived experience the object of affirmation as pictured in the utopian imagination cannot but be informed by the object of negation as perceived in actual experience, even though on the level of thought and imagination the utopian ideal thus derived can then encompass much more than the opposite of the outstanding negative features of reality. It is above all on the second level that utopianism signifies what Adorno calls "the transformation of the totality." On the first level, however, every yearning for change, every act of negation and affirmation, receives from actual experience a certain focus corresponding to a certain pain, and this experiential focus not only informs but also drives every utopian project, however all-encompassing the latter may be in its intellectual conception.

This emerges most clearly in the practice, as opposed to the theory, of utopianism. Within some three decades of utopianist experimentation, Mao Zedong undertook two important and different full-scale utopian projects. The first of these, the Great Leap Forward of 1958–60, focused on material abundance and well-being. It was symptomatic of this focus that Mao, in the article quoted earlier, singled out poverty (that is, material deficiency) rather than, say, political oppression (moral deficiency), as he was later to do in the Cultural Revolution of 1966–76, as the lever for the utopian project. Unlike the Cultural Revolution, the Great Leap Forward was an earthy, though totally unrealistic, project, conceived and executed at a mundane level of utopian imagination. Material superabundance was the goal; on this were superimposed — in a manner riddled with tensions between creaturely hedonism and saintly self-denial — the soaring spirit of altruism and the ethos of complete communal sharing to give that materialist goal the semblance of an idealist totality called communism. For a utopian project like this one, where material abundance outweighed all other considerations, poverty was naturally the principal psychological lever. Accordingly, all that seemed to be needed to bring about utopia was, to borrow Bloch's expression, to enlighten poverty, to raise it to the level of political consciousness. From this enlightened poverty, it was believed, there would burst forth the utopian energy that would "change heaven and earth" (*gaitian huandi*). With the aid of that mixture of hedonism and idealism, a tremendous amount of energy was indeed called forth, but almost all of it was channeled into two tasks: to produce as much steel and as much food as possible. The road to communist paradise was to be paved with nothing more imaginative than limitless amounts of food and steel.[18]

For the emergence of this kind of utopian consciousness, whose focus, though not whose totality, is the unlimited satisfaction of sensuous needs, material deprivation is probably a necessary psychological condition. If, as Bloch seems to suggest, *all* utopian consciousness, whatever its focus, is marked by the transformation (through enlightenment) of the instinct of self-preservation under the threat of hunger into the much more radical aim of self-extension, then consciousness of material deprivation must count as a necessary psychological condition of utopian consciousness as such. Such material deprivation, moreover, need not always be one's own. Those who are not themselves living under the daily threat of hunger and poverty may nevertheless be moved by the spectacle of deprivation around them and see in this, as the deprived themselves do, the need for a total transformation of society.

Even for those whose experience of poverty is direct rather than vicarious, however, poverty is very far from a sufficient psychological condition of utopian consciousness. Poverty is not sufficient to cause the intense desire for material abundance, and every utopian consciousness whose focus is material abundance contains that desire in an intense form. Poverty, insofar as it threatens self-preservation, gives rise to the desire to remove poverty to the extent that it will no longer be life-threatening. But to desire to remove poverty *beyond* that extent, one must already have the desire for material abundance beyond self-preservation. In utopian consciousness we witness an intense form of this desire: the existing condition of poverty produces a longing for a future condition in which the principle of distribution will be, as Marx put it, "To each according to his needs."

It is instructive in this connection to look at a few figures in whose doctrine, if not necessarily in whose practice, we find no psychological link between poverty and the longing for material abundance and through it for utopia. For Confucius, creaturely comfort is simply not worth pursuing. "With coarse rise to eat, with water to drink, and with a bent arm for a pillow, there is still joy."[19] "The superior man seeks the Way and not a mere living. There may be starvation in farming, and there may be riches in the pursuit of studies. The superior man worries about the Way and not about poverty."[20] The classic Daoist text known as *Laozi* sees material abundance not only as not worth pursuing but as the source of trouble and unhappiness. "The five colors cause one's eyes to be blind. The five tones cause one's ears to be deaf. The five flavors cause one's palate to be spoiled. Racing and hunting cause one's mind to be mad. Goods that are hard to get injure one's activities."[21] "There is no calamity greater than lavish desires. There is no greater guilt than discontentment. And there is no greater disaster than greed. He who is contented with contentment is always contented."[22] It may well be the case that Confucius and Laozi were able to say this partly because they already had, to however limited a degree, what they dismissed as of no significance.[23] As Cioran would put it, they had not "tasted utter indigence."[24] Such a charge, however, is beside the point, since what we are trying to do here is not to assess the implementability of Confucius' and Laozi's doctrines or their sincerity but simply to see what we can learn about the logic of utopianism by comparing it with the logic (not the practice) of non-utopian doctrines.

In the outlook of Laozi and Confucius alike, no value is attached to creaturely comfort beyond the satisfaction of simple wants. But even the act of attaching value to material well-being is not sufficient to cause a susceptibility to utopianism. Such susceptibility depends on a conception of the good life in which material well-being occupies a high place. This conception we may describe as hedonism, or, as explained above, the idea and practice of pursuing material well-being as an important component of a good life. Here the case of Stoicism, in certain important respects the opposite of hedonism, is instructive. The Stoic, like the hedonist, prefers wealth to poverty, but he prefers the former only as a "natural advantage."[25] The Stoic, moreover, finds nothing wrong with trying to attain natural advantages, but he does not do so with zeal (zeal belongs to the pursuit of virtue, which alone has moral worth). As with Confucius and Laozi, it is not relevant here whether the Stoic acts on his belief, or even whether the Stoic's position is self-consistent. What is at issue is the logic of Stoicism as it contrasts with the logic of utopianism. Simply put, because of a lack of intense desire, though not the preference, for material well-being, the Stoic is not susceptible to the ineluctable hedonist component of utopianism, which would strike the Stoic as placing undue value on merely natural advantages.

Hedonism, then, is a necessary psychological condition for susceptibility to utopianism. The hedonistic character of a utopian project means that its appeal, at the level of ends, is to the desire for material well-being; the appeal to idealism and the inculcation of asceticism pertain, as we shall see, only to the level of means. The "pleasure principle" drives the utopian project. It is to the body that utopia appeals, and the advent of utopia, where material superabundance finally makes possible "to each according to his needs," will bring to a permanent end the history of the denial of the body, the history of what Marcuse aptly calls the "moralization of pleasure."[26] Hedonism — the body's need for sensuous satisfaction — is the bodily or material condition of utopian consciousness. This point is of crucial importance for understanding the trajectory of the Chinese utopian project. The role of hedonism as a necessary psychological condition of utopian consciousness helps, as we

The Ascetic Pursuit of Hedonism

shall see, explain the eventual failure of the utopian project and, as a significant part of that failure, the breakdown of asceticism.

The criterion for hedonism, however, is not the objectively measured extent of material well-being that one happens to seek—it is perfectly in keeping with Stoicism to want the greatest possible natural advantages—but rather the importance attached to material well-being in one's scheme of objectives. Corresponding to the importance one assigns to material well-being is the volitional intensity with which one pursues such well-being. Under certain circumstances, it is quite possible for the hedonist to pursue with zeal what objectively considered is only a moderate degree of material well-being. This was partly the case with Mao's utopian project. Let us characterize this pursuit and the mentality reflected in it as *rustic hedonism*, a description that fits the Chinese utopian consciousness particularly well.

Rustic hedonism may result from two different kinds of circumstance. A rustic hedonist may desire the greatest material abundance possible, but severe deprivation, or some other factor, may limit the degree and scope of material abundance that he imagines possible. Here the moderation of the rustic hedonist is such only by objective standards but not by the subjective terms of the hedonist's desire, which is for the greatest material abundance he considers possible. In other words, the moderation pertains to the imagination (as conditioned, say, by objective conditions of life), which is irrelevant here, but not to desire, which is decisive. It is possible, however, for the rustic hedonist to be content with less material abundance than he imagines possible, in the belief that the lesser amount is equally or more conducive to the greatest possible sensuous satisfaction. In this case it is the rustic hedonist's desire and not his imagination that is moderate. However, even here, the moderation pertains only to the degree of material abundance desired, but not to

The Ascetic Pursuit of Hedonism 145

the far from moderate volitional intensity with which what is wanted, moderate though it may be, is desired. In the final analysis, neither poverty of imagination nor modesty of ambition alters the defining feature of the rustic hedonist — a feature possessed by virtue of his hedonism and not his "rusticity" — namely, that he regards as a necessary condition of happiness a degree of material well-being beyond very plain living, which he accordingly desires intensely and pursues to the best of his ability. Poverty, by the same token, is for the hedonist undesirable in a stronger sense than it is for the Stoic.

This identification of hedonism as a central component of Maoist utopianism may seem to be contradicted, however, by certain more conspicuous features of Mao's utopian project. One such conspicuous feature was its egalitarian ethos (despite huge institutionalized inequalities in practice), with its emphasis on material equality. Egalitarianism, it seems, goes not with the practice of hedonism but with the practice of its very opposite, asceticism. This is indeed true — but only at the level of social practice and not necessarily at the level of social consciousness. Egalitarianism, let us remind ourselves, means equality not as such or in power but in wealth or material well-being. Thus the very nature of egalitarianism implies hedonism, since equality is sought only in what is considered highly desirable — in this case wealth and material well-being. This is not to say that egalitarianism follows from hedonism. Hedonism, typically self-regarding, leads to egalitarianism only when it is coupled with some form of collectivism. But once so combined, hedonism leads to egalitarianism in a way that, significantly, Stoicism would not — and this because, among other reasons, Stoicism does not attach enough importance to that which hedonism and egalitarianism alike find so deserving of equal distribution.

Yet another feature of Mao's utopian project, asceticism, seems to call into question the attribution of hedonism to

Maoist utopianism. But once again the contradiction is only apparent. For — and this is hardly a new discovery — asceticism invariably betrays hedonism. Since asceticism is aimed at curbing excessive desires for sensuous gratification, there must have been such desires and a consciousness of those desires in the first place. The rigor of an ascetic regime is only a measure of the strength of the desires to be conquered. One source of profound psychological tensions besetting Mao Zedong's utopian project was that it began by appealing to the desire for material well-being and then had to find a way of curbing that desire — often to the point of exterminating it.

Asceticism teaches duty, and the centrality of duty yields an ethical doctrine sometimes known as deontology. Hedonism, on the other hand, is clearly a form of consequentialism, as is utilitarianism. Not surprisingly, it is a short step from hedonism to utilitarianism, which also values pleasure and which differs from hedonism only in calculating pleasure from the point of view not of the individual but of society as a whole. It was no accident that Mao Zedong called his doctrine *revolutionary utilitarianism*, which differs from utilitarianism in enlarging the social emphasis in utilitarianism to embrace collectivism and egalitarianism.

It may well be the case that hedonism, though entirely compatible with collectivism, goes most naturally with some form of egoism, as the doctrines of Epicurus seem to suggest.[27] However, hedonism (as opposed to the purely prudential element of hedonism)[28] does not follow from egoism. An outstanding example of this is the proto-Daoist philosopher Yang Zhu (Yang Chu), whose prudence, more cautious even than that of Epicurus, made him advocate "despising things and valuing life" (*qingwu zhongsheng*), where the things to be despised were above all possessions and pleasure, in the same breath as he preached "each one for himself" (*weiwo*).[29] Given, however, the natural affinity between hedonism and egoism, each case in which the two

The Ascetic Pursuit of Hedonism 147

are not found together calls for explanation. In the case of Yang Zhu, prudence carried to the extreme severs the natural link between egoism and hedonism. In the case of Maoist utopianism, as we shall see, egoism is held in check by a combination of collectivism and asceticism.

I have emphasized hedonism as a necessary component of utopianism because the actual practice of Chinese utopianism was on the surface so ascetic and anti-hedonistic that it is easy to forget that without hedonism as an underlying driving force neither utopianism, of which hedonism is a part, nor asceticism, of which hedonism seems the exact opposite, would have made any sense. Although hedonism is only a necessary, but not a sufficient, psychological condition of utopianism, it is sufficient, in combination with poverty, to produce susceptibility to utopianism.

It was, however, purely by accident that the susceptibility to utopianism became articulated in twentieth-century China as full-blown utopianism. The conceptual vehicle for this articulation came ready-made from Marxism, and it was left to Mao to tailor utopianism to Chinese circumstances and to translate utopian consciousness into a utopian project. In discussing the Chinese utopian project, therefore, we need not inquire into the intellectual *origins* of utopianism. The soil — widespread and acute poverty — was indigenous, but the seeds were blown from Western Europe via the Soviet Union.

Marxism did not bring China either poverty or hedonism. Rather it brought the belief that poverty could be permanently eliminated and hedonism completely satisfied. China had been unable, with certain partial exceptions, to generate this belief on its own, because the dominant Confucian tradition did not have either the scientific rationality to engender confidence in material progress or the ideal of equality to make material prosperity for all a cultural goal. In the absence of confidence in material progress, Chinese hedonism aimed no higher than plain food and simple shelter for the majority and took on the tameness of prudence. In the absence of the ideal of equality, Chinese hedonism — in the sense of pleasure rather than mere prudence — became the legitimate province only of the privileged and hypocritical few.

All this changed through contact with the West. When Marxism came to China, the ground had already been prepared by the earlier arrival of scientific optimism and the egalitarian ideal, to both of which Marxism in its own way gave further impetus. Once Marxism had brought the optimistic belief that happiness lay in store for everyone, hedonism was able to separate itself from quietism and prudence — not for the first time to be sure but in a more convincing fashion than ever before. Hedonism as desire cannot exist without hedonism as belief. Without this belief there could be no full-blown utopianism in China, still less a utopian project. Poverty gives rise only to the desire for change. Hedonism, though it lends intensity to that desire and broadens it beyond the mere removal of poverty, is prone to subside to prudence. Even when it does not, it is sufficient only to engender susceptibility to utopianism, that is, to channel the desire for change in a potentially utopian direction. It is utopianism that gives articulation to that desire, and it does so by, among other things, creating the belief that utopia, the total satisfaction of hedonism, is possible, even inevitable.[30] Utopian energy springs from the combination of desire and belief. The desire comes from hedonism and is made all the stronger by poverty, but the belief can come only from an ideology such as communism.

The belief that the happiness envisioned in utopianism is feasible or, better still, inevitable bespeaks an optimism that contrasts sharply not only with the unsophisticated prudence of rustic hedonism but also with the reasoned resignation of Stoicism. What is resignation but the reasoned

The Ascetic Pursuit of Hedonism 149

cessation of effort or, with the benefit of foresight, cessation of the thought of effort even before the thought has been tested for its feasibility in action? Resignation is always preceded by effort or by the thought of effort, and effort in turn already signifies the pleasure principle. We see the pleasure principle unmistakably at work in the Stoic's preference for natural advantages over natural disadvantages. The hallmark of the Stoic is not the absence of desire for pleasure but the decision not to make one's happiness or true well-being depend upon pleasure. This decision comes not just from the ethically grounded belief that pleasure is not worthwhile as an end in itself but equally from the empirically grounded belief that pleasure is precarious and undependable. The second belief comes from experience; the first, while arguably independent, may nevertheless derive partly from the second belief; as in the Neo-Stoicism of Spinoza,[31] the vagaries of pleasure serve as data as it were for the process of reasoning that leads to the ethical belief. In an important sense, then, Stoicism is preceded by negative experience (direct or vicarious) — that is, by the failure to obtain natural advantages — and may be considered the wisdom that comes from that experience.[32]

It is not the wisdom of experience but the passion of the naïf that drives utopianism. Utopianism, though preceded by poverty, is not preceded by failure of effort, that is, by the only kind of effort that utopianism regards as adequate. The utopianist has tasted poverty but not the failure of a utopianism-inspired effort to overcome it.[33] In this sense, Stoicism is not opposed but posterior to utopianism, which may be understood here as encompassing all forms of optimism. Stoicism is one response to the failure of optimism. There must first be the expenditure or thought of effort, although the effort need not be strictly utopian in character. Stoicism and such other anticlimactic psychological formations as cynicism and de-sublimated hedonism follow only in the wake of the failure of some such effort. This, as we shall see, is borne out by the trajectory of the Chinese utopian project.

The idea of effort unites the otherwise diametrically opposed concepts of hedonism and asceticism. Their unity is a function of their being situated at different and fully compatible levels, hedonism at the level of ends and asceticism at the level of means. "Hedonism," says Marcuse, "is useless as ideology,"[34] but this is true only if hedonism is used, as it never is, as the whole rather than merely as a part of an ideology. Hedonism is dangerous on its own because, as Marcuse rightly says, "If [the hedonistic principle] were ever to take hold of the masses, they would scarcely tolerate unfreedom and would be made completely unsuited for heroic domestication."[35] However, as part of an ideology — asceticism now, hedonism later — hedonism can be immensely useful; so much so that, as in Mao's utopian project, it can serve precisely as the reason why the masses willingly accept asceticism and "heroic domestication." Since a utopian project is born of conditions of poverty and since it cannot be accomplished overnight, asceticism is required as a necessary means of carrying out a utopian project.[36]

No single expression sums up the Maoist spirit of asceticism better than the slogan daily invoked throughout the utopian project: "plain living and hard struggle" (*jianku fendou*). "Plain living," an extremely low level of consumption, was in Mao's China both an unavoidable fact of life and a necessary condition of investment. This ascetic accumulation of capital exhibited a mentality not unlike that found in the Protestant ethic.[37] "Hard struggle," the Maoist equivalent of "Work hard in your calling," served as the necessary work ethic for the realization of utopia, with "utopia" being something of an equivalent of the "glory of God." This work ethic was as antithetical to the traditional Chinese contempt for physical labor as it was identical with

Puritan asceticism.[38] What was called in Mao's China the "communist" attitude to labor was encapsulated in the popular catchphrase *bu laodong zhe bu deshi*, which reads as if it were a translation of Saint Paul's dictum "He who will not work shall not eat" (2 Thess 3:10). Thus in the ascetic pursuit of utopianism, labor and happiness, sharply separated in traditional Chinese thought, came conveniently together.

Much as in the Protestant ethic, where asceticism is a means to salvation, in the Chinese utopian project utopia was the end and asceticism only the means. If asceticism had been the end, there would have been no need for utopia. By the same token, the virtue of being poor lay not in poverty itself but in the desire to remove it. Indeed, poverty is a powerful motor of change because it generates the desire not only to remove poverty but also to achieve future abundance. Those who do not suffer from poverty have little incentive to sacrifice in the present. The ascetic virtues of plain living and hard struggle thus serve only to pave the way to utopia, but they are not an integral part of utopia. Once utopia is achieved, they cease to serve any purpose or to have any meaning. Ascetic virtues are virtues only in an impoverished world, and utopia is a world that knows no impoverishment.[39]

Asceticism in Mao's utopian project, therefore, was not the negation but only the postponement of pleasure. It differed from Stoicism in that it accepted natural disadvantages not with relative indifference but only in expectation of greater natural advantages to come. Thus asceticism, considered as a means rather than as an end in itself, is not at all incompatible with hedonism. Indeed, asceticism and hedonism are two sides of the same utopian coin. In Maoist utopianism, with its dual appeal to pleasure and sympathy (both natural inclinations), *present* asceticism is for the sake of *future* hedonism, and asceticism practiced on oneself is for the sake of the happiness of others. Nothing is more revealing of the psychology of the Great Leap Forward than

152 *The Ascetic Pursuit of Hedonism*

the contemporary popular slogan that enjoined three years of struggle in return for a thousand years of communist happiness.[40] This logic of utopianism, its fervent optimism aside, is not unlike that of hedonism displayed in Epicurus' remark, in expounding his philosophy of pleasure, that "we regard many pains as better than pleasures in cases when our endurance of pains is followed by a greater and long-lasting pleasure."[41] Every hedonist with a modicum of wisdom knows that present circumstances may well require a measure of asceticism after "calculation and consideration of advantages and disadvantages." Asceticism is the expression of hedonism under the pressure of the reality principle — the calculated decision, as Epicurus puts it, to "treat . . . the bad as good."[42] Utopianism is Epicureanism with both its asceticism and its hedonism pushed to the extreme.

This, then, is one sense in which utopianism is a form of exchange in which present asceticism is the price of future hedonism. When, as in Mao's China, a leader awakens the people's dormant hedonism with a utopian vision, utopianism is a form of exchange in the further sense that the leader promises hedonism in return for which members of the utopian community are prepared to practice asceticism for a more or less definite period of time. In fact, Mao launched the utopian project when the people, not yet emboldened with utopianism, would have been content with much less — sufficient food and a roof over their heads (*wenbao*, as the Chinese phrase has it). Given the second sense of exchange that characterizes a utopian project, we may speak of an implicit social contract — the utopian contract. This contract, not unlike the Hobbesian idea of the social contract in the Western political tradition, betrays a fundamental inequality of power between the two parties to the contract, the leader of the utopian community on the one hand and its members on the other.

Both senses of exchange apply to the members of the

utopian community. But the leader of the utopian community is party to the exchange only in the second sense. The leader is exempt from the first sense of exchange in that he does not have to practice asceticism, at least not nearly to the same extent. This exemption lends further proof and tangibility to the second sense in which a utopian project is a form of exchange.

The failure of a utopian project is a failure of exchange in both senses. The exchange character of a utopian project already contains the seeds of its failure. In a way Cioran is right when he says that "the more destitute you are, the more time and energy you will spend in reforming everything, in thinking."[43] But you have to be educated and "cultured" to raise, as Hegel said of Stoicism, your material condition to the level of thought. And it is on the level of thought that we find the idea of utopia. Is anyone educated and "cultured," however, likely to taste what Cioran calls "utter indigence"? To be sure, one can be educated and poor, as is all too common, but what are the chances of being so poor that one suffers from what Cioran calls "the delirium of the poor," which he sees as "the generator of events, the source of history"? Thus those who are educated enough are not poor enough, and those who are poor enough are not educated enough, to create the idea of utopia. Only when the two somehow come together does utopianism become a possibility both for thought and for action. And what brings them together is hedonism (among other things) on the part of the people and paternalism (among other things) on the part of the leader. In this light, Jesus is the archetypal builder of utopias, and every leader of a large-scale utopian project aspires to the status of Jesus, if not higher. In the figure of Jesus, we see writ large another inescapable mediation between poverty and utopianism, namely, the paternalism of those who design utopias. This paternalism can seem quite benign when it springs (partly, always only partly) from sympathy for the suffering of hu-

154 *The Ascetic Pursuit of Hedonism*

manity. But all too often paternalism has a way of shedding sympathy on its way to power, if only because the closer one is to power the more insulated one is from even the vicarious experience of suffering. So we should not be surprised when a utopianist, who is a paternalist to begin with, turns into a tyrant, any more than when we see a father tyrannize over his children.[44]

The leader, exempt (as we have seen) from the first form of utopian exchange, is in one sense not infrequently a hedonist satisfied, the lone inhabitant of a one-man utopia. But in another sense the leader may *not* be a hedonist at all, at least not in the same way as the common run of the utopian community. Here we confront a psychological trait of the small group of utopia builders not shared by the utopian community at large. The utopianist craves a future society whose freedom from toil and strife is in the nature of rest, the kind of rest found in the Garden of Eden. But to make eternal rest possible, the utopianist has to spend a lifetime not resting but striving. In order, in other words, to bring about an existence free of change, the utopianist finds himself committed to bringing about the greatest change yet contemplated by human beings. It thus turns out to be the utopianist's extraordinarily strong craving for rest, for freedom from change, that gives him the energy which sustains him in his striving, in his commitment to radical change.

This calls into question the relationship between the two outstanding attributes of the utopian mentality—the craving for rest and the willingness to strive—for the first is a conservative instinct and the second a revolutionary one. Anyone who craves rest will seize on any opportunity for rest that comes his or her way. One is willing to go out of one's way to strive only when, under conditions of utter deprivation, the only rest that may come one's way will come only after striving. Their "greed for happiness," as Cioran rather uncharitably calls it,[45] is such that they want perfect happiness only when they have no happiness at all.

The Ascetic Pursuit of Hedonism 155

This seems indeed to be the mentality with which most people — let us call them "conservative" utopianists or, in other words, deprived hedonists — throw themselves into a utopian project. But not everyone. For there are those — "revolutionary" utopianists — who enjoy a fair measure of rest but who always want more, and more perfect, rest, usually not only for themselves but also (ostensibly) for the entire humanity. To this end they are ready to spend every day in ceaseless striving — a whole lifetime without rest — in order to bring about a state of rest for posterity that they themselves will never live to enjoy. These are the real utopianists. But they are not really people who crave rest, at least not for themselves. Rather, they are filled with a craving for change, for striving, for activity, and for this craving the utopian project provides a direction and a teleology. This happens of course under definite historical conditions, which also make it possible for the tiny minority of revolutionary utopianists to convert, with the promise of hedonism, the vast majority of conservative utopianists to their cause. It is very revealing that in response to a question about his idea of happiness, Marx answered: "To fight."[46] Mao Zedong, a worthy successor to Marx in this regard if in no other, thoroughly relished the idea that the world would always contain contradictions and hence the permanent need for struggle.[47] Without revolutionary utopianists like Marx and Mao Zedong, there could be no utopian idea. Without the conservative utopianists in their sheer multitude, the utopian idea could not be translated into a utopian project. It takes both to set a utopian project in motion. But at some point they will part company, because the conservative utopianist craves rest much more than change and the revolutionary utopianist craves change more than anything else.[48]

The highly ambitious exchange that is constitutive of a utopian project has to be perceived as accomplishable, with hopeful signs all along the way, within the lifetime of members of the utopian community if it is to retain its tangible character and serve as a source of energy and motivation. But two insurmountable obstacles stand in the way, one objective, the other psychological. Objectively, one individual's or one generation's life — the largest wholly tangible length of human life — is all too short for a transformation of such gigantic material and mental proportions. Psychologically, the indispensable role of poverty in generating utopian energy, a role amply acknowledged by Mao Zedong, dictates that every step forward in a utopian project is simultaneously a setback. For the more favorable the *psychological* conditions for a utopian project, the less favorable the *material* conditions, and vice versa.

But this is, so to speak, the Stoic's wisdom. The utopianist does not believe any of this. Three years of struggle, a thousand years of communist happiness, as the Great Leap Forward catchphrase has it;[49] or as Fourier equally optimistically put it, "If I prophesy so unhesitatingly the universal harmony as an imminent phenomenon, it is because the organization of the societary state requires no more than two years."[50] Commenting on Fourier's confident prophecy, Cioran sees in this "naive avowal if ever there was one" nevertheless a "profound reality" — that is, a profound psychological reality.

Would we fling ourselves into even the flimsiest enterprise without the secret conviction that the absolute depends upon us, our ideas, our actions, and that we can guarantee their triumph in a short period of time? Any man who identifies himself completely with something behaves as if he were anticipating the advent of "the universal harmony," or considered himself its promoter. To act is to anchor in an imminent future, so imminent it becomes almost tangible; to act is to feel you are consubstantial with that future.[51]

There is yet another profound reason for haste. A utopian project, as long as it moves in the right direction, moves away from poverty, but in so doing it also moves

The Ascetic Pursuit of Hedonism 157

away from its very psychological condition. As poverty is reduced, so too is susceptibility to utopianism. The less poor you become, the closer you are materially to utopia. But, psychologically, the less poor you become, the weaker your longing for utopia and hence the lower your utopian energy. Therefore, unless you achieve utopia in one leap, you are never going to get there. If utopia is not achieved quickly, at some point the psychological link between poverty and utopianism is severed. Something like this was clearly recognized by Adorno: "What people have lost subjectively in regard to consciousness is very simply the capability to imagine the totality as something that could be completely different. That people are sworn to this world as it is and have this blocked consciousness vis-à-vis possibility, all this has a very deep cause, indeed, a cause that I would think is very much connected *exactly* to the proximity of utopia."[52] There can be no such thing as a gradual, voluntaristic movement toward utopia.

By the same token, poverty is important for utopia precisely because of its distance from it. Poverty is psychologically conducive to a utopian project both at the level of ends and at the level of means. At the level of ends, poverty promotes susceptibility to utopianism — that is, to the conception of utopian ends. At the level of means, poverty facilitates susceptibility to asceticism, if only because, given a minimal instrumental rationality, the desire for certain ends implies acceptance of the necessary means. Moreover, those already living in poverty find it relatively easy to accept asceticism, which does not constitute a change for the worse but gives meaning to a temporary continuation of an existing fact of life. In terms of purely material conditions of existence, a life of asceticism and a life of poverty are the same. It is only at the level of understanding that an ascetic life differs from an impoverished one. Asceticism makes poverty meaningful; communist asceticism, which treats itself as a means of bringing about utopia, makes poverty both meaningful and temporary — and hence all the more bearable.

Just as poverty is made meaningful by being denied its permanent continuation, hedonism is raised to the level of morality by being denied its *present* satisfaction. The hedonistic impulse, like many morally neutral impulses, undergoes a radical transformation — one might say sublimation — when its gratification is projected into a future that can be brought about only after struggle and sacrifice. There is a world of difference between pleasure immediately gratified and pleasure postponed into the distant future. Hedonism as the search for pleasure here and now would bespeak indulgence and dissipate creative energy. But poverty erects a barrier between the hedonistic impulse and its immediate fulfillment, and in so doing it transforms the hedonistic impulse into utopian energy and elevates hedonism to the level of an ideal.

In this process not only is hedonistic indulgence transformed into hedonistically inspired asceticism, but the very content of hedonism is elevated from the earthly plane of creature comfort to the ethereal one of spiritual fulfillment. At work in this moral idealization of pleasure is precisely the absence of pleasure, the postponement of gratification. Moreover, postponement makes for the moral idealization of pleasure in yet another way: it broadens the scope of hedonism to encompass the happiness of others, often to the point of placing others' happiness above one's own. The hedonistic impulse, ineluctably self-centered in and of itself and only slightly less so when tempered by sympathy for others, most easily assumes the character of altruism — pleasure for others — when both pleasure for oneself and pleasure for others are postponed to the distant future. It is relatively easy to practice self-denial when self-denial is a necessity imposed by circumstances, just as it is relatively easy to think of oneself as working for the welfare of others when that welfare, securely segregated in the future, does not take anything from oneself here and now. The correlation between pleasure sought for now and pleasure sought for oneself on the one hand and between happiness sought for the future and happiness sought for others on the other is more than accidental.

Hedonism, having undergone this twofold moral idealization through postponement, now means love of happiness in a very special sense, namely, happiness in the future and happiness for others. This new hedonism not only does not rule out but actually entails love of poverty for now and for oneself — or at least love of poverty for oneself for now. Hedonism retains its elevated status as an other-regarding moral ideal only as long as it is postponed. Poverty is hedonism's — that is, morally elevated hedonism's — very condition of existence. This is particularly true of the extreme poverty where not only is one constantly miserable but one also feels that he or she has nothing to lose — the condition that Marx and Engels saw as characteristic of the proletariat. Here bondage truly means freedom: the freedom to give up, because there is nothing to give up, and the freedom to build something new, because anything new is preferable to the nothing one now has. Given just a little moral enlightenment, poverty can do away with pettiness and turn its victims into moral saints. And it is such moral saints who make up a utopian community. They are comrades in poverty and hence comrades in utopianism. Altruism and collectivism represent the conscious recognition and practice of this solidarity, and in them self-denial is transformed from a fact of life into what is perceived as an act of positive self-affirmation. But when poverty shows signs of lessening, utopianism loses its appeal. As poverty shrinks, the moral saints it helps produce shrink back into everyday mortals.

In this instance as in many others, poverty has acquired a

moral value. This happens when, as is all too commonly done, a virtue is made of necessity and when, in the supposedly voluntary practice of asceticism, necessity is reinterpreted as freedom. But once asceticism becomes a virtue rather than something merely useful, a profound paradox appears. As a means (or instrumental virtue) asceticism is not an end in itself, whereas as a moral virtue that is precisely what it has to be. The two sides of the paradox answer, respectively, to two equally profound needs of the utopian project: on the one hand the need for a fresh motivation for asceticism through constant reminders of the hedonistic ends it serves, and on the other hand the need to impart to asceticism the kind of stoic patience that only the complete forgetting of the hedonistic ends can engender. In the progress of Mao Zedong's utopian project, however, we find a gradual shifting of emphasis — never complete, often interrupted, yet exhibiting an unmistakable general tendency — from the first side of the paradox to the second. At first, utopianism gives the ascetic virtues their logical and psychological ground. But once their raison d'être has been shown, the ascetic virtues can, through their proximity to action and to the present, acquire a psychological salience approaching the independence of ends, with their connection to utopianism taken for granted and hence receding into the background. Utopianism is first used to justify asceticism and is then displaced by it. With the utopian project failing, the ascetic pursuit of utopianism becomes the ascetic pursuit of asceticism itself.

It is thus yet another paradox that the ascendancy of ascetic virtues is the first sign of the corruption of the utopian spirit. For the leader, who is in the best position to see the handwriting on the wall, raising asceticism to the level of ends becomes a matter of political expediency. At this point in the utopian project, he will endeavor to promote the ascetic virtues without reiterating the utopian promise

The Ascetic Pursuit of Hedonism 161

in definite terms. This is indicative no longer of the importance he may once have attached to these virtues as means of achieving utopia but of his now paramount desire to tone down the exchange character of the utopian project and thereby to reduce his accountability. The more pronounced the exchange character of a utopian project, the easier it is to measure its failure, and in the case of failure the worse the political consequences for the leader of the utopian project. As long as asceticism feeds on the anticipation of pleasure, it is conditional, unstable, and even vengeful. Every contract, even a utopian contract, has a day of reckoning. When a utopian project comes to grief, the members of the utopian community may feel about the leader and the utopian vision much as they would feel about a crook who had broken a contract and abused their trust. And just as in the case of a contract, it is the deed—the honoring of the contract— rather than the intention that is decisive. The leader of the utopian project has only two alternatives—postponing the day of reckoning for the utopian contract or, better still, promoting asceticism as a virtue in itself so as to do away with the exchange character of the utopian project altogether. With the hedonistic element removed, however, the utopian project ceases to be a utopian project. When by this process asceticism completely eclipses hedonism in the utopian project, for the first time asceticism comes close to Stoicism in that virtue is made the object of pursuit for its own sake. For the leader's own reasons, which have nothing to do with virtue, the people's virtue becomes its own reward.

At this point, the utopian community becomes something that, much more than the Great Leap Forward, resembles what Max Weber calls a "charismatic community" devoid of definite economic goals. If the Great Leap Forward was an openly and straightforwardly hedonistic project pursued by ascetic means, the Cultural Revolution was hedonistic only in its anarchic negation of the status quo and the psychological release such negation afforded. Herein we find the most important difference between the Great Leap Forward and the Cultural Revolution, a difference that reflects the lessons Mao absorbed from the failure of the Great Leap Forward.

In fact, the lessons belong to a history that began much earlier, a history in which power and charisma were intertwined with hedonism and utopianism. In the years leading up to the communist victory in 1949, the Communist party and its army formed what may be quite accurately called a charismatic community. After 1949, as this community expanded to include the population at large, both its success and its expansion made it increasingly subject to the "routinization of charisma."[53] Weber might have been describing what happened after the communist victory in China when he wrote: "Every charisma is on the road from a turbulently emotional life that knows no economic rationality to a slow death by suffocation under the weight of material interests: every hour of its existence brings it nearer to this end."[54] What posed the greatest threat to Mao personally was the *depersonalization* of charisma.[55] By separating the charisma of office from personal charisma, depersonalization works in favor of bureaucratization at the expense of the charismatic leader. Once charisma becomes a function of office, the charismatic leader, who has up to now been the unique carrier of charisma, is dispensable. This is exactly what happened before the Great Leap Forward, as Mao was unobtrusively pushed aside not so much by political rivals as by the forces of depersonalization and routinization. Moreover, every step in the depersonalization of charisma is accompanied by an increase in economic stabilization, which in its own right works against the charisma of personality. At the hands of Mao's political rivals, the shift in focus from "revolution" to "production" marked a shift in the locus of power from Mao's person to the bureaucracy.

In 1958, while he still had enough charisma at his disposal, Mao struck back by launching the Great Leap Forward, which was in large measure a struggle against the routinization, and even more against the depersonalization, of charisma. But the new charismatic community that Mao created was ironically a utopian community whose overriding goal was economic and whose psychological basis was sublimated hedonism. It was thus a charismatic community only in its quasi-religious fervor and in its voluntarism. Without the freedom from definite economic goals that marks a charismatic community at its purest, Mao's utopian community could not even survive long enough for the gradual impact of the routinization of charisma; it lost its momentum as a charismatically inspired movement as soon as the economic miracles to which it was tied failed to materialize.

As a failure of the charismatic principle of social action, the miscarriage of the Great Leap Forward set in motion once again the routinization of charisma. The years that immediately followed, however, differed from the Great Leap Forward only in that the same, albeit less ambitious, hedonistic aims were pursued by other, more bureaucratic means. In the meantime Mao's own conception of utopianism changed profoundly, thanks to the insights the Great Leap Forward must have given him into the dangers of openly hedonistic utopianism. The result was the Cultural Revolution, launched by Mao in 1966 when the personality cult orchestrated by Lin Biao, then Mao's heir-apparent and closest ally, had restored Mao's personal charisma but not entirely his power. Like the Great Leap Forward, the Cultural Revolution was a struggle against the routinization and the depersonalization of charisma. The nature of this struggle was reflected, even more than during the Great Leap Forward, in an unprecedented cult of personality coupled with an unheard-of degrading of political office. This difference in degree was accompanied by a difference in kind. For the Cultural Revolution was more political than economic, more an act of negation of the actual non-utopian present than a premature act of affirmation, like the Great Leap Forward, of a possible utopian future. In at least one sense — as Adorno put it, "Insofar as we do not know what the correct thing would be, we know exactly, to be sure, what the false thing is" — the Cultural Revolution was more soberly utopian than the Great Leap Forward.[56] At the height of the Cultural Revolution almost the whole of China formed a gigantic "charismatic community," fully absorbed in the spectacle of the day, with little concern for the future and even less for economic interests.[57] Mao was the charismatic leader and everyone else who was not a "class enemy" was transformed, through political rituals, into what Guenther Roth, extending Weber's concept of a "religious virtuoso," calls an "ideological virtuoso."[58] Beyond subsistence, economic interests were temporarily forgotten.

Not long after the start of the Cultural Revolution, however, Mao, no doubt out of the same realism that had earlier made him downplay economic interests, began to show an increasing ambivalence regarding the place of economic interests in the charismatic community. Symptomatic of this ambivalence was the introduction of that seemingly simple yet profoundly enigmatic slogan "Grasp revolution, promote production" (*zhuageming cushengchan*), whose loose syntax and looser semantics made it conveniently unclear as to which was the end and which the means. As the carnivalesque energy that had sustained the Cultural Revolution began to flag, so the economic interests that had been forgotten started to reassert themselves. If Mao found it relatively easy to undo the depersonalization of charisma, he came to have a harder and harder time fighting against the routinization of charisma by economic interests. In the end,

Mao himself succumbed when he allowed the Four Modernizations — the all-around technological modernization of China — to be proclaimed the nation's supreme task, signaling thereby the end of the Cultural Revolution and the return of hedonism.

With the launching of the Four Modernizations and their continuation after Mao's death in Deng Xiaoping's program of reform, hedonism once again came to the fore, much as it had done in the Great Leap Forward some two decades before. The balance between hedonism and asceticism was, however, no longer what it had been. In the two decades or so after the "three years of struggle" of the Great Leap Forward failed to produce "a thousand years of happiness," hedonism had been etherealized or displaced, and asceticism raised to the status of an end in itself. In theory pleasure had been moralized and postponed, and in practice pleasure had been denied. In this twofold process lay the key to the survival of utopian consciousness. But utopian consciousness is what it is only because of its anticipation of pleasure, and pleasure — the most earthy and earthly of desires — does not long brook etherealization, postponement, or denial. As ideology — part of an ideology to be precise — hedonism can inspire effort, but by exactly the same token it makes everything done in its name conditional upon the eventual procurement of a tangible reward, a reward that may never materialize and that, when it does not, will, unlike the rewards of an otherworldly religion, be seen not to materialize. The lifespan of an ideology containing a pronounced hedonistic element is the length of the patience with which the postponement of pleasure is endured. And the moral authority of the regime based on that ideology is measured by its power to inspire asceticism with no immediate prospect of hedonism. Both the patience and the authority had begun to run out when first the Four Modernizations and then Deng's reform were set in motion after the futile attempt through the Cultural Revolution to keep hedonism — the "capitalist road" in the terminology of the day — at bay. Deng's reform, in particular, with its relaxation of moral and economic austerity, was an acknowledgment of a growing impatience that dragged hedonism from heaven to earth, from future to present. The new attitude toward asceticism relegated it to the status of mere means and necessity and would therefore tolerate as little of it as possible.

This ought to have come as no surprise, because the change occurred not in spite of but completely in accordance with the logic of utopianism. Hedonism was nothing new to utopianism; but only when utopianism broke down did hedonism's real place in the logic of utopianism fully reveal itself. Only then did it become clear that the marriage between asceticism and utopianism was one of convenience. But this was no mere intellectual revelation. The restoration of the original logic of utopianism represented a momentous change, because that logic, which had for all this while been submerged, had only now been allowed to come to the surface. This was the beginning of nothing less than a new balance of impulses, but paradoxically the new balance, with hedonism restored to its logical place, was no longer utopianism. Once hedonism came to the surface, it swept aside the asceticism, the altruism, and the collectivism that had, through etherealization and displacement, transformed hedonism into utopianism and without which utopianism would have degenerated into crude hedonism. So hedonism returned, and returned with a vengeance — in a world with neither enough pleasure to satisfy the newly released hedonism nor enough meaning to inspire the rapidly dying asceticism. Without asceticism, without altruism, without collectivism, hedonism knows no bounds except those imposed by reality, and these bounds do not dampen hedonism but only sour it. Sadly, but almost inevitably,

The Ascetic Pursuit of Hedonism

China's utopian project, which had begun as ideologically sweetened asceticism, ended as disenchanted hedonism. What is worse, those at the anticlimactic end of this failed journey could not find even the comfort that comes from the confident certainty of a noble beginning and the strength therein to begin anew.

CHAPTER FIVE

Meaning and Fatigue

When in 1949 Mao Zedong proclaimed on the rostrum of the old imperial Gate of Heavenly Peace (Tiananmen) the birth of a new society, he was doing so to a people who were exhausted yet jubilant, a people worn down by war and poverty but newly energized by the meaning and hope that the cause of communism had restored to their lives. From this new meaning and new hopefulness flowed the hidden resources that enabled a people who had known little but defeat and humiliation for more than a century to shake free of the exhaustion within a matter of years and to muster a concerted energy that promised to create a new heaven and a new earth. Some forty years later, with Mao dead and his utopian project buried with him, and with his successors' program of reform increasingly losing its idealistic underpinnings, the Chinese people once again found themselves under the weight of a paralyzing exhaustion—this time, however, mixed not with jubilation and meaningfulness but apathy and cynicism. If the earlier exhaustion was in large measure a function of physical fatigue that could be overcome by the injection of meaning, the new exhaustion resulted from the loss of meaning and innocence—from "the recognition of the long *waste* of strength, the agony of the 'in vain.'"[1] What had broken down was not the "human motor" but the search for meaning.[2]

Meaning and Fatigue 169

From this state of spiritual exhaustion, the nation awakened as it could have never done before to the spiritless call of hedonism. At least for the time being, there was no stomach for new ideals to fill the gaping void of meaning. The single-minded search for a better material life thus proved to be a twofold liberation: liberation from the oppressive rule of meaning, and liberation from — that is, compensation for — the pain of meaninglessness. No longer held back by idealism, nor troubled any longer by impoverishment of the spirit, an ideal-weary people found in their "human motor," much more robust now than it had been four decades earlier, a massive renewal of energy for the new pursuit of wealth and pleasure, each one for himself, for here and now.

In recounting the process that led to this outcome, I shall try to develop from it, as well as to bring to bear upon it, a theoretical understanding of the ebb and flow of social energy. But first I must briefly spell out a premise that lies at the center of this theoretical understanding, namely, the *duality of human energy*. Human energy, as distinct from purely mechanical energy, is a function of the interaction of the physical and the mental. In the exuberance as well as in the exhaustion of energy, body and mind invariably impinge upon each other and are in this sense, but only in this sense, one; neither can be reduced to the other. The readiness of human beings to exert energy is not just an epiphenomenon of physical health, of the measurable force of the "human motor." It is always bound up with a goal, with meaning, with memories of success and failure. That we feel energetic or lethargic is a statement not just about our physical condition but also, and often to a greater extent, about whether we have something to look forward to, some goal to achieve, and the innocence, born of memories of success or the ability to forget failures, to believe we can achieve it. States of mind, of elation and dejection, are closely linked to our physical condition, as anyone familiar with sickness or physical exercise can testify. But it is not always because we are in good physical health that we feel hopeful; hopefulness can actually contribute to physical health.

This view of the duality of human energy finds both its strongest support and its strongest rebuttal in Nietzsche's concept of will to power, which is the unity or juncture, if you will, of energy and meaning.[3] Indeed, my reasons for holding this dualist view will emerge more clearly from a brief consideration of the contradictions as well as the insights to be found in Nietzsche's position. Predating his concept of will to power is a highly illuminating distinction, one Nietzsche considered among his "most essential steps and advances." The importance of the distinction deserves a somewhat lengthy quotation from Nietzsche. "I have learned," Nietzsche wrote in *The Gay Science*,

to distinguish the cause of acting from the cause of acting in a particular way, in a particular direction, with a particular goal. The first kind of cause is a quantum of dammed-up energy that is waiting to be used somehow, for something, while the second kind is, compared to this energy, something quite insignificant, for the most part a little accident in accordance with which this quantum "discharges" itself in one particular way — a match versus a ton of powder. . . . The usual view is different: People are accustomed to consider the goal (purposes, vocations, etc.) as the *driving force*, in keeping with a very ancient error; but it is merely the *directing force* — one has mistaken the helmsman for the steam. And not even always the helmsman, the directing force.[4]

Nietzsche's choice of words (quantum, ton of powder, steam) betrays a mechanistic conception of human energy prevalent in nineteenth-century Europe, a conception that he elsewhere states more explicitly, going so far as to say that "our most sacred convictions, the unchanging elements in our supreme values, are judgements of our muscles."[5] However, when Nietzsche says that "the first kind of cause is a quantum of dammed-up energy that is waiting to be used *somehow, for something*" (my italics), this "for something"—the perception of meaning—already points to something specifically human.

Granted, for the sake of discussion, that "this world is the will to power—and nothing besides."[6] Granted also that *"every* animal . . . instinctively strives for an optimum of favorable conditions under which it can expend all its strength and achieve its maximal feeling of power"[7] (my italics). This all-inclusive conception of energy, of the will to power, still leaves something unsaid about the human animal. For the human animal is distinguished, as Nietzsche himself was often at pains to show, by "the basic fact of the human will, its *horror vacui: it needs a goal*—and it will rather will *nothingness* than *not* will."[8] The human being is an animal that needs meaning, that needs not only the achievement but also the consciousness of power (power, let me emphasize, as agency, not as domination).[9] These needs for meaning are so basic to human life that they form an important part of the "cause of acting" and underlie every "cause of acting in a particular way." In this light, "acting" does not entail "acting in a particular way," but it is not driven by a blind or indiscriminate force; it possesses instead a built-in logic of its own, one that seeks the maximum mastery of meaning as the specifically human manifestation of the will to power. The "cause of acting" is the will to power, and the human will to power, unlike the motor or even the animal, cannot do without meaning.

If the *horror vacui* is part of the will to power, of the "cause of acting," then that "people are accustomed to consider the goal (purposes, vocations, etc.) as the *driving force*" need not entirely be an "ancient error." It is not an error at all if the goal is understood as the generic need for goals as such rather than some specific goal. It may not be an error even when a particular goal is taken to be the driving force, since every particular goal partakes of the *horror vacui* that is part of the driving force. In his understanding of the "cause of acting" as "a quantum of dammed-up energy that is waiting to be used somehow, for something" Nietzsche only hints at, but fails to take full account of, this "basic fact of the human will, its *horror vacui*." Once we give due weight to this basic fact, the distinction between the driving force and the directing force is blurred and gives way to the distinction between *force*, the physical aspect of energy, and *directing*, the mental aspect of energy.

In fact, Nietzsche himself acknowledged: "Important as it may be to know the motives that actually prompted human conduct so far, it may be even more essential to know the fictitious and fanciful motives to which men ascribed their conduct. For their inner happiness and misery have come to men depending on their faith in this or that motive — *not* by virtue of the actual motives. The latter are of second-order interest."[10] By his own reasoning, then, Nietzsche is wrong when he says: "There exists neither 'spirit,' nor reason, nor thinking, nor consciousness, nor soul, nor will, nor truth: all are fictions that are of no use."[11] Fictions, yes — in an important sense. But "of no use"? Decidedly not, and according to Nietzsche himself, again quoted at length:

The meaninglessness of suffering, *not* suffering itself, was the curse that lay over mankind so far — *and the ascetic ideal offered man meaning!* It was the only meaning offered so far; any meaning is better than none at all; the ascetic ideal was in every sense the *"faute de mieux" par excellence* so far. In it, suffering was *interpreted*; the tremendous void seemed to have been filled; the door was closed to any kind of suicidal nihilism. This interpretation — there is no doubt of it — brought fresh suffering with it, deeper, more inward, more poisonous, more life-destructive suffering: it placed all suffering under the perspective of *guilt*.

But all this notwithstanding — man was *saved* thereby, he possessed a meaning, he was henceforth no longer a leaf in the wind, a plaything of nonsense — the "sense-less" — he could now *will* something; no matter to what end, why, with what he willed: *the will itself was saved.*[12]

Saved, that is, by meaning, by fictions, as only human beings can be saved and, indeed, as only human beings, with "the basic fact of the human will, its *horror vacui*," need to be saved in the first place.

We are not yet done with Nietzsche, for one fruitful way to think about the process leading from utopianism through nihilism to hedonism in China is, as I have found, to think *with* Nietzsche as he articulates the trajectory from original nihilism to "European" nihilism.[13] I will therefore pursue my narrative and analysis in intermittent dialogue with Nietzsche, mindful that Nietzsche was thinking about the European experience and we the Chinese, but not shy of discerning parallels that might illuminate and not shy even of using some of Nietzsche's terminology. Nor are we done with attempting to understand the ebb and flow of social energy theoretically. But I shall from now on leave that understanding to be enriched in the intermingling of narrative and analysis. For now, I resume the historical narrative, beginning, not with the utopian project itself, but with its antecedents.

What we need to look for in those antecedents are the mechanisms of that miraculous conservation of energy that more than anything else was to make the utopian project, with its enormous explosion of energy, possible. For every explosion of energy must be preceded by an equally extraordinary conservation of energy.[14] The implication is that the energy that explodes, so to speak, is not just what Nietzsche calls the ordinary "quantum of dammed-up energy that is waiting to be used somehow." Since that form of energy exists all the time, the explosion, as distinguished from ordinary expenditure, must be of energy that has somehow been conserved over and above the ordinary or stable quantum of energy.

The key to this accumulation of extra energy lies in four

outstanding features that marked the prehistory of the Maoist utopian project. First, the Chinese people had been suffering for a very long time. Second, their prolonged suffering had not produced a national religion of *ressentiment* or resignation. Third, there had been no major utopian project in recent Chinese history and no communist utopian project ever. And fourth, the utopian project was preceded by a successful revolution, itself largely inspired by the Marxist utopian vision, which had done much to boost national pride and confidence.

There is at least one sense in which prolonged suffering, the first feature of pre-communist China, may be said to help conserve energy. Suffering precludes the weakening of desire upon fulfillment and hence precludes the weakening of the energy that is part of the desire. As long as there is no fulfillment, there is no discharge.[15] As long as there is no discharge, there is tension, and tension produces energy. There is thus a related sense in which suffering may be said to generate, not just to conserve, energy, since the very experience of suffering is psychologically continuous with the desire-energy to remove the suffering.[16]

Such accumulation of energy, accumulation through suffering, is, according to Cioran, in the nature of a "biological advantage"; he describes the Russian people as "suffering without self-expenditure," which "allowed them to gain strength, to accumulate energy, to amass reserves, and to draw from their servitude the maximum of biological advantage."[17] To suffer without self-expenditure is to suffer without discharge. As we have seen, suffering can entail a certain conservation of energy, a certain absence of discharge. In this sense, it may seem that "without self-expenditure" is part of suffering. But this is not necessarily the case. Suffering, although it entails the absence of fulfillment (a *positive* discharge), is often accompanied by such negative feelings as fear, anger, and hatred, and these feelings produce a *negative* discharge. A negative discharge is a psychological

Meaning and Fatigue 175

event in which energy is discharged, not through removal of suffering and the satisfaction attendant upon this removal, but in negative affects, such as acute unhappiness, affects that result from believing simultaneously in the injustice of the suffering and in the impossibility of removing it.

It follows — and this brings us to the second feature of pre-communist China — that what prevents the dissipation of energy is not just suffering per se but a certain attitude toward suffering, an attitude that avoids negative affects. The Chinese people have often been commended, not least by themselves, for their ability to endure hardship (*chiku*), with the implication that they endure hardship with something approaching willingness and not just helpless resignation. This is just the kind of attitude that prevents negative discharge, an attitude which the Chinese people, not yet introduced to utopian expectations, exhibited to an extraordinary degree in pre-communist China. For a combination of reasons, among which were the overwhelmingly rural population and the high rate of illiteracy, suffering was, for the vast majority, barely raised to the level of consciousness, either in the form of *ressentiment* (as in Christianity, according to Nietzsche)[18] or in the form of *reflective* resignation (as in Buddhism or Stoicism). Elements of both *ressentiment* and resignation were undoubtedly present in the pre-communist Chinese consciousness, but neither developed into a full-blown system of belief that could have hindered the massive mobilization of energy for the utopian project. When the time came, resignation was swiftly swept aside by the example of a victorious communist army that had won a protracted series of wars and brought peace and unity to the land against overwhelming odds. And then, in the utopian project that soon followed, *ressentiment* was actively fostered in the interests of "class struggle" and repression of the self. As it turned out, there could have been no better way to conserve energy for the utopian project than the inaction of a patiently suffering people, who had not dissipated their energy either through positive or through negative discharge.

What is at work here is not biological but psychological advantage, the kind of psychological advantage that makes the best of biological disadvantage. Nietzsche had perhaps a deeper insight into the workings of such self-conservation than anybody else. Indeed, negative discharge is similar in its essential affects to what Nietzsche called *ressentiment*, and as Nietzsche said, in a metaphor with obvious reference to energy, "Nothing burns one up faster than the affects of *ressentiment*."[19] It was perhaps not by accident that Nietzsche, like Cioran, looked to Russia for "enlightenment about *ressentiment*,"[20] calling the enlightenment he found there "Russian fatalism." Nietzsche wrote in *Ecce Homo*, in a chapter entitled "Why I Am So Wise":

Against all this the sick person has only one remedy. I call it *Russian fatalism*, that fatalism without revolt which is exemplified by a Russian soldier who, finding a campaign too strenuous, finally lies down in the snow. No longer to accept anything at all, no longer to take anything, no longer to absorb anything — to cease reacting altogether.

This fatalism is not always merely the courage to die; it can also preserve life under the most perilous conditions by reducing the metabolism, slowing it down, as a kind of will to hibernate. Carrying this logic a few steps further, we arrive at the fakir who sleeps for weeks in a grave.

Because one would use oneself up too quickly if one reacted in *any* way, one does not react at all any more: this is the logic.[21]

If what makes the conservation of energy possible under such circumstances is the strength of instincts, what makes it so absolutely necessary, as the case of "Russian fatalism" reminds us, is physical weakness. The same can be said of pre-communist China. From a physiological point of view, China was anything but an energetic nation when Mao Zedong called forth so much energy for the utopian project. Material deprivation and malnutrition had not produced robust bodies; they never do. But the physical constitution is only that part of a person's or a nation's energy that is measurable. What is much less measurable, but potentially more explosive, is the readiness to use that energy for a cause — the energy, so to speak, to release energy. Moreover, this readiness to release energy need not be proportional to the amount of energy available for release. China, for example, is physically a much more robust nation now, but its readiness to expend energy for a cause is greatly reduced. In this light, the conservation of energy may be a matter as much of conserving the readiness to use energy as of conserving energy itself. The advantage that accrues to the first kind of conservation, in the case of Russia and pre-communist China alike, is not exactly what Cioran calls a "biological advantage" but more in the nature of a psychological advantage.

This psychological advantage, a function of the absence of negative discharge, was accompanied by yet another psychological advantage, of a different kind, which was attributable to the third feature of pre-communist China and which was conducive in particular to the conservation of *utopian* energy. The fact that recent Chinese history, particularly the stretch of history within living memory, had seen no major utopian project meant, in terms of the conservation of energy, that the "quantum of dammed-up energy" had not been used in this way. Since the participants in the utopian project had never spent their energy in any such project, they had experienced neither failure and frustration, which could have discouraged them from throwing themselves wholeheartedly into Mao's project, nor success and discharge, which would have reduced the need and desire for what was being offered them. The utopian project was so energizing because, having never been tried, it had no history — hence no memory, no inhibition. The unknown inspired effort but no fear, because it was supposed to be the unknown paradise. What is important here is not that the Chinese had not recently expended a great amount of energy, which is not true, but rather that they had not expended their energy in a particular way, that is, in a utopian project. This suggests, once again, that the conservation of energy is more a matter of energy not being used (or much used) in a particular way and thereby conserved for use in that particular way than a matter of the low expenditure of energy per se regardless of the purposes for which energy is mobilized. In pre-communist China, however much energy may have been expended, utopian energy — or more precisely, a susceptibility to utopianism — had been left untapped.

To be able to tap this potential utopian energy, however, one further psychological condition had to be fulfilled, and it could not have been better fulfilled than by the resounding victory of Mao's popularly supported revolution. This victory is the fourth outstanding feature of the prehistory of the utopian project; without it the launching of the utopian project would have been not only materially but also psychologically impossible. Suffering, although it may help to conserve and generate energy, can also, particularly if prolonged, reduce energy by reducing the belief that suffering can be overcome. What the victory of the communists did, as nothing else given the circumstances could have done with equal force, was to strengthen that belief. When the Communists swept to power in 1949, their victory was celebrated as one over tangible enemies. But much more important, it was a triumph over memory — painful memories that had crowded the Chinese mind for over a century. The burden of debilitating memories had been lifted. The slate had been wiped clean. A feat of national forgetting — not the forgetting of suffering but the forgetting of the near-impossibility of removing suffering — had been achieved. The nation was ready for a grand project. All this was very much in accordance with the inverse relationship of bad memory and bold action, which Nietzsche formulates as a "universal law," namely: "a living thing can be healthy, strong and fruitful only when bounded by a horizon," because "cheerfulness, the good conscience, the joyful deed, confidence in the future — all of them depend, in the case of the individual as of a nation, on the existence of a line dividing the bright and discernible from the unilluminable and dark; on one's being just as able to forget at the right time as to remember at the right time."[22] The Chinese people forgot at the right time, just before the launching of the utopian project.

Whatever we may wish to think of it, there is no denying that the Chinese utopian project was marked by a massive explosion of energy. But, as we have seen, the massiveness of an explosion of energy may be a function as much of the *explosiveness* of the energy — that is, the susceptibility to stimulus — as it is of the energy's sheer volume. Between these two factors there need be no proportionality. But when the explosion of energy is due more to the former than to the latter, as in the Chinese utopian project, the massiveness of the explosion is such only when measured not in terms of the separate amounts of energy expended by individuals but in terms of the total amount of energy expended by large numbers of people in a closely knit unit and channeled into a single collective project. The massiveness of the explosion of energy is here a function of the explosion of mass energy.

In such an explosion, one that is collectivist in its organization and in its aim, the individuals as such should not be given too much credit for the massiveness of the outburst. It cannot be inferred from the massiveness of the collective outburst of energy that the individual members of the collective possess the attribute of overflowing strength that the outburst bespeaks. We may indeed go further and suggest that the great collective strength of the Chinese utopian project came precisely from great *individual* weakness. The weakness of the Chinese people as individuals made the formation of the utopian community possible and even necessary. It would be impossible to understand the course of the Chinese utopian project and its aftermath without grasping this inverse relationship. Mao's profound intuitive grasp of this relationship was equaled only by Nietzsche's genealogy of Christianity. (The comparison between utopianism and Christianity that I will pursue presently is justified by their profound similarity in circumstance and psychology.)

When Mao Zedong repeatedly emphasized the importance of the collective spirit, it is clear not only from the context of his remarks but even more from his actual policies that he did so because of what he perceived as the weakness and insignificance of individuals. In an article written at the start of the Great Leap Forward in 1958, Mao characteristically extolled the advantages of sheer numbers. "The more people, the more views and suggestions, the more intense the fervor, and the greater the energy."[23] Thanks to this belief, coupled with his utopian projections for the Chinese economy, Mao turned a deaf ear to warnings about excessive population growth. Mao's rationale seems to be that since individuals are weak and insignificant, we need as many of them as possible to form one gigantic unit, which alone has real strength and significance. As Nietzsche put it, "Where there are herds, it is the instinct of weakness that has willed the herd."[24] Mao and Nietzsche, strange as this may sound, subscribed to the same logic; they differed only in what they made of it. Where Nietzsche saw in the strength of the herd the weakness of the individual, Mao saw in the weakness of the individual the strength of the herd.

When Nietzsche used the term *herd* in *On the Genealogy of Morals* — a term I will occasionally use for convenience but without Nietzsche's pejorative connotations — he meant by it something over and above the sense in which *every*

Meaning and Fatigue   181

human being can be called a herd animal, that is to say, a social being. This special, stronger sense of herd instinct, according to Nietzsche, is no more clearly at work than in the formation of Christianity.

When one looks for the beginnings of Christianity in the Roman world, one finds associations for mutual aid, associations for the poor, for the sick, for burial, evolved among the lowest strata of society, in which this major remedy for depression, petty pleasure produced by mutual helpfulness, was consciously employed. . . . The "will to mutual aid," to the formation of a herd, to "community," to "congregation," called up in this way is bound to lead to fresh and far more fundamental outbursts of that will to power which it has, even if only to a small extent, aroused: the *formation of a herd* is a significant victory and advance in the struggle against depression. With the growth of the community, a new interest grows for the individual, too, and often lifts him above the most personal element in his discontent, his aversion to *himself*. . . . All the sick and sickly instinctively strive after a herd organization as a means of shaking off their dull displeasure and feeling of weakness.[25]

Compare this with what Mao Zedong, in the same article quoted earlier, said about the Chinese people at the start of the Great Leap Forward. "Apart from their other characteristics, China's 600 million people have two remarkable peculiarities; they are, first of all, poor, and secondly, blank." This condition of being poor and blank and, as we shall see presently, hungry for activity and change is precisely what Nietzsche would call depression, depression not in a psychological-moral but in a physiological sense having to do with "a *feeling of physiological inhibition*."[26] For Mao, however, such a physiological state is "really a good thing," because it produces a psychological readiness to be mobilized for collective action, to be molded into a collective identity in which all individual claims are forgotten. As Mao immediately continued, "Poor people want change, want to do things, want revolution." In the eagerness with which Mao embraced this logic, Nietzsche would have detected the "prudence of the priest." To complete his logic, Mao ought to have added: Poor people want a leader. If "it is the instinct of weakness that has willed the herd," it is, as Nietzsche immediately went on to say, to complete his analysis of this logic, "the prudence of the priest that has organized it."[27]

Mao would have agreed not only with this comment but also with Nietzsche's remark that "the more general and unconditional the influence of an individual or the idea of an individual can be, the more homogeneous and the lower must the mass be that is influenced."[28] At the height of his power during the Cultural Revolution, when he could afford an honest confession, Mao told the American journalist Edgar Snow that he found the personality cult (the cult of Mao himself) "tiresome" (*taoxian*). At that moment Mao and Snow (at Mao's invitation) were watching an example of that cult being enacted in a mass spectacle from the rostrum of the Gate of Heavenly Peace. It is not in the least surprising that the only strong man in China found the weakness of his people as disagreeable as it was useful. This revealing conversation took place after the personality cult had already fulfilled its function in the early phase of the Cultural Revolution, but Mao must have known all along that it could not have been because they were strong, in any acceptable sense of the word, that the Chinese people had spent thirty years calling Mao Zedong their infallible leader and communism their unshakable faith. Firmness of faith in a doctrine, unswerving loyalty to a leader — these seeming tokens of strength betray needs that can spring only from weakness. For one seeks in an other what one does not have in oneself; or, as Nietzsche says of religion, "Faith is always coveted most and needed most urgently where will is lacking; for will, as the affect of command, is the decisive sign of sovereignty and strength. In other words, the less one knows how to command, the more urgently one covets someone who commands, who commands severely — a god, prince, class, physician, father confessor, dogma, or party conscience."[29]

In this as in many other respects, the psychology of Chinese communism resembles that of Christianity. This is so because, at the level of abstraction of this analysis, the circumstances that saw the birth of the Chinese utopian project—particularly if taken in its wider sense as beginning with the founding of the Chinese Communist party in 1921—are similar to those that led to the rise of Christianity. Indeed, this similarity is entirely in keeping with the Marxist commonplace that, as Engels put it, "The history of early Christianity has notable points in common with the modern working-class movement."[30] In conditions of prolonged hardship and distress, conditions that marked the beginnings of both Christianity and the Chinese utopian project, individuals find the locus of freedom not in their own separate activities but in a common cause, a common leader, a common faith. Because they feel powerless as individuals and powerlessness equals unfreedom, they seek freedom for themselves through freedom from themselves. This freedom they find in an Other—a crowd, a faith, a leader—an Other that is felt thereby as a new self. It is only from this identification with an Other that they can acquire a newfound sense of power and with it a modicum of self-identity. Since the Other is the source of one's own power and power is freedom, it is felt not as a paradox but as a profound truth that the crowd is freedom, the leader is freedom, the faith is freedom—alienation is freedom. In this light, what Nietzsche calls the will to the formation of the herd is an expression, under circumstances of extreme individual weakness, of the will to power, to freedom.[31]

Thus, a utopian community forms when individuals who have found unfreedom in themselves come together to remove the worldly causes of their unfreedom. However, insofar as a utopian project succeeds in ameliorating the conditions of hardship and distress, which is after all its goal, it succeeds to the same extent in destroying the psychological conditions of its own existence. Indeed, the very formation of a utopian community is, as Nietzsche says of the formation of closely knit groups in general, "a significant victory and advance in the struggle against depression."[32] In that very victory are contained the seeds of individual growth, and as these seeds sprout and grow, the collective ceases to be the only source of power and freedom. In proportion as the locus of freedom shifts from the collective to the individual, the collective may be felt more and more as a source of hindrance and even oppression. If the collective enterprise is to continue, another kind of prudence is required of the "priest," who must now devise artificial means of producing on the individual the same effects that have so far been produced by conditions of extraordinary hardship and distress but can no longer be sufficiently produced in this way thanks to the success of the collective enterprise.

There will in this way come a point at which individual growth poses such a threat to the continued existence of the utopian community that it can be held together only with the aid of repression. This is a function of a psychological precondition of utopian projects. Conditions of prolonged hardship and distress cause weakness of will, which in turn causes the "will to the herd," a psychological precondition of any utopian project. It follows from these causal relationships that a utopian community is in danger of disintegration as soon as the will of individuals gains significantly in strength. It follows further that if a utopian project is to last, individuals have to be kept in a state of weakness of will by repression. The "high achievements in the shape of abnegation, unselfishness, and devotion to an ideal" that Freud attributes to the positive aspect of group behavior are found in their spontaneous form only in circumstances of hardship and adversity.[33] In better times, such achievements have to be enforced.

We have two separate theses here, one concerns the pre-

Meaning and Fatigue 185

conditions for the launching of a utopian project, the other its continuation. The first thesis is that a utopian project requires for its implementation an existing condition of weakness of individual will. This is distinct from a second thesis, namely, that a utopian project requires for its continuation the repression of what might otherwise become strength of individual will. We now turn to the relationship between the continuation of a utopian project and the repression of individual power.

From the perspective of the leader of the utopian project, the increased need for repression is exactly proportional to the perceived growth of individual will. That there was such a perception on the part of Mao was reflected in the invention and gradual expansion of the institution of *dousi*, "combating selfishness" or simply "combating the self" — an institution whose origins in fact predated the success of the revolution. Elias Canetti speaks Mao's mind perhaps even better than Mao himself when he in one brief sentence describes the worst enemy of any collective enterprise: "Everyone belonging to such a crowd carries within himself a small traitor who wants to eat, drink, make love and be left alone."[34] This may not be the case at the start of a revolution or of a utopian project when there is little to eat or drink, nobody to make love with, and no decent roof under which to be left alone. But once conditions have significantly improved, the small traitor within looms large again, wanting not just to do the things Canetti half-facetiously mentions but also to think for himself and be his own conscience.

There is of course a profound difference between what is often thought of as selfishness on the one hand and strength of individual will on the other. If it is not, in our descriptive task, necessary to elaborate on this difference here, it is only because Mao himself chose not to recognize such a difference, preferring instead to place all manifestations of intellectual and moral independence in the deliberately oversimplified category of "selfishness." This enlargement of the concept of selfishness, one of Mao's chief weapons against the will to individual power, worked extremely well for some thirty years. Individuals were growing stronger, but their growth occurred more at the level of body and desire, where "the small traitor . . . wants to eat, drink, make love and be left alone," than at the level of consciousness and conscience. Although the small traitor inside rebelled from time to time, their conscious and conscientious selves still subscribed to the doctrines Mao had been feeding them. Among these was the belief that it is pure selfishness (or "bourgeois egoism," *zichan jieji geren zhuyi*) to want to pursue values and aims chosen by individuals themselves rather than decided for them by the all-knowing collective.

Nationwide "brainwashing" started at a time when the brain, agitated by the small traitor inside, needed to be washed, but also when the brain was still willing enough to be washed and when each individual still had enough doctrinal correctness to fight the small traitor inside. That the brain needs washing is a measure of individual power. But its willingness to be washed is a measure of individual weakness. The essence of *dousi* consists precisely in mobilizing individual weakness to fight individual power. The need for repression on the one hand and the success of repression on the other cast rather different, yet complementary, lights on the extent of individual power. The institution of repression was perceived as necessary because of the growth of individual power, but that same institution could be effectively maintained only because of the weakness of individual power compared with Mao's enormous moral authority as a charismatic leader. Together the two things are a measure of the growth of individual power: it was strong enough to be perceived by Mao as a threat to the utopian community but weak enough to yield to the charismatic authority of a single ruler.

Meaning and Fatigue 187

In this light, collective power cannot be seen as symptomatic of individual weakness alone. Whenever it is directly indicative of the repression of individual power, collective power is by the same token indirectly a sign of individual power itself. *Both* individual power and individual weakness are reflected in the institution of repression. It is all too easy to associate repression with individual weakness, but we will not understand the nature and mechanism of repression unless we pay at least equal attention to individual power. If it is individual weakness that makes repression possible, it is individual power that is repressed.

To know this is to realize that every effective repression, if it is to be long sustained, must be accompanied by an equally effective outlet, for what is repressed is power and power must express itself somehow. A new channel must be created for the discharge of energy whose original channel has been blocked. In the Chinese utopian project, the energy dammed up through the repression of individual power found an outlet in the exercise of greatly expanded collective power over nature or over other human beings. Collective power over nature took the form of "production campaigns," such as the Great Leap Forward; collective power over people took the form of "revolutionary campaigns," such as the Anti-Rightist movement of 1957. During the Cultural Revolution, the two kinds of campaign took turns in being the predominant expressions of collective power, both carried to the extreme. These collective enterprises testify to the thoroughness — as well as to the precariousness, as we shall see — with which individual power can be repressed and transformed into collective power. For a long time under Mao Zedong, the discharge of energy through collective channels was so satisfying that most people were completely unaware, or ceased to be aware, of the repression that had forcibly diverted individual energy into these channels, themselves created or expanded through repression. It was only when with the failure of the utopian project these channels of discharge were blocked that people became conscious of being repressed. And it was only in retrospect that they became conscious, moreover, of having been repressed earlier in a period that had in fact allowed the relatively successful discharge of energy and in so doing had prevented the conscious feeling of repression.

A simple yet highly effective mechanism is at work here. Every successful repression of individual power is almost at the same time a transformation of individual power. But once, and insofar as, individual power is so transformed, the object of repression (i.e., individual power) disappears and with it any feeling of repression. The most effective repression is that which immediately or even simultaneously does away with itself by transforming individual power into collective power and thereby transforming individual power, the ground of the feeling of repression, out of existence. The art of repression is the art of transformation. But there is always a residue of individual power that refuses to be so transformed, a residue that shows itself in the cries of the "small traitor" who refuses to go along. This residue, like the tip of an iceberg, stands as a chilling reminder of what has been transformed out of visibility. But much of this residue, still visible despite the transformation of suppressed individual power into collective power, will itself soon be rendered invisible. We see this further transformation at work when the residue of individual power, resisting transformation into collective power, is transformed under the pressure of collective power into power against the self. Fortunately, this further transformation has a repressive character that cannot be hidden.

This is not to say that individual power is inherently liberating and collective power inherently repressive. Repression is a function not of collective power as such but of the strength of that which is not allowed to express itself directly. Repression is exactly proportional to that strength. Where individual power is minimal, as in conditions of prolonged hardship and distress, the non-expression of individual power is not, nor is it felt to be, repression, even though the conditions of hardship and distress may have been caused by social oppression in the first place. For people with little (sense of) individual power, it is the lack of group solidarity rather than the lack of individual freedom that is felt to be repressive, and we choose not to call this feeling the product of repression only because, and insofar as, the lack of group solidarity is not overtly imposed by some political authority, coercion being a necessary feature of repression.[35] Even in the best of circumstances an individual cannot do entirely without collective power, for, as Aristotle said, "The individual, when isolated, is not self-sufficing."[36] He who is entirely self-sufficient, as Aristotle went on to say, "must be either a beast or a god." For those between the two extremes of a god and a weakling, collective power is felt both as liberation (from individual weakness and loneliness) and as repression (of individual power) — to degrees that reflect the strength of individual power. To the extent that a political order reflects and reproduces the strength of individual power, there will be little sense of political repression, even though collective power may far exceed individual power, as it does in most if not all societies.

Under Mao Zedong, however, the political order came gradually to fail so drastically to reflect the actual strength of individual power that a large portion of the repressed individual power could not be channeled into collective projects. It was politically necessary for this stubborn residue of individual power to be channeled inward, to be turned against itself, in order not only to prevent it from posing a threat to the collective project but also to sustain the very institution of repression. This political necessity also had psychology on its side. The institution of repression known as *dousi* was in the first instance imposed on individuals, against their will. Individual power, power for the self, could not have been turned into power against the self without initial coercion or pressure. But through regular participation in the institution of repression and gradual internalization of its rationale, repression became self-imposed, aided by rewards as well as by the opportunity to participate in the repression of others. Once self-imposed, repression of the will to individual power came to mean nothing other than self-hate, the hating of anything about the self that did not willingly merge into the collective, the collective ideal, and the collective's leader. Once self-hate had, through the repeated exercise of *dousi*, become second nature, the institution of *dousi* was perceived no longer as a source of repression but rather as a welcome source of relief, a ready means whereby one could unburden oneself and regain peace of mind, much as in the Christian practice of confession. Unlike most examples of Christian confession, however, *dousi* always took place in a public setting. By seeing the hateful self-image reflected in the equally hateful image of others, people learned to hate themselves with greater conviction and learned moreover the inverted golden rule "Hate others as you hate yourself."[37] In this way, they learned to help each other repress the will to individual power in the self-righteous belief that they were helping each other gain something morally valuable, namely, devotion to the collective. Then, too, there was the self-comforting though unspoken knowledge that they were making each other lose something precious, namely, mastery of one's own self, which they themselves had lost. If everyone else had lost it, whatever it was, then losing it was not so bad for oneself after all.

Having found out how hateful one was, one welcomed the opportunity to turn away from this hateful self and pour all one's energy into a collective project against nature (a "production campaign"), thereby both proving the depth of one's self-hate and relieving oneself of the burden of guilt. And how much more satisfying it was, in a collective project

Meaning and Fatigue 191

against fellow human beings (a "revolutionary campaign"), to suspend the inverted golden rule and, by persecuting others, to deflect and project one's self-hate away from oneself. In both cases, the sense of satisfaction and release came from energy's partial reversion to a more natural channel of discharge that had been forcibly bypassed or blocked. Nietzsche expressed a profound psychological insight when he observed that the discharge of the will to power outward in action is inherently more natural or primitive than its inward discharge as "bad conscience" and that, it follows, the will to other-directed aggressiveness (in the form of action) is inherently more natural than self-directed aggressiveness (again in the form of "bad conscience"). In *The Genealogy of Morals*, Nietzsche wrote:

All instincts that do not discharge themselves outwardly *turn inward* — this is what I call the *internalization* of man: thus it was that man first developed what was later called his "soul." The entire inner world, originally as thin as if it were stretched between two membranes, expanded and extended itself, acquired depth, breadth, and height, in the same measure as outward discharge was *inhibited*. Those fearful bulwarks with which the political organization protected itself against the old instincts of freedom — punishments belong among these bulwarks — brought about that all those instincts of wild, free, prowling man turned backward *against man himself*. Hostility, cruelty, joy in persecuting, in attacking, in change, in destruction — all this turned against the possessors of such instincts: *that* is the origin of the "bad conscience."[38]

It was the operation of this logic in reverse, that is, the removal of inhibitions against outward discharge, that restored the "joy in persecuting, in attacking, in change, in destruction," the kind of joy that was at once the reward and the driving force of Mao's "revolutionary campaigns." By a similar logic, the "production campaigns," which under normal circumstances would have been felt as partly repressive for their denial of individual initiative, were thanks to the inculcation of self-hate felt as liberating in that they meant the temporary cessation of the even more repressive regime of enforced soul-searching. In both cases, as the will to power was allowed temporarily to revert to its more natural, outwardly directed channel of discharge, the self-hate (bad conscience) that had resulted from the repression of that channel was suspended. Satisfaction naturally ensued — the kind of satisfaction that can come only from the lifting of the severest repression.

The transformation of individual power (power for itself) into power against itself, just as its transformation into collective power, depended on a goal whose legitimacy could provide the raison d'être for, and in so doing disguise, the twofold transformation. If it was a combination of the "instinct of weakness" and the "prudence of the priest" that brought the utopian community into being, it was the prospect of utopia, more than anything else, that held that community together despite the growth of individual power. Individuals could be made to practice self-denial only because self-denial had a meaning to which they could readily relate in each and every act of self-denial. That meaning lay in the realization of communism, from which every individual would benefit but for which in the meantime all individuals had to work together in total forgetfulness of the self — a forgetfulness that self-criticism was to bring about. Since self-denial was meant to be practiced for a collective goal in whose realization alone the individual would find personal happiness, those who internalized this kind of reasoning saw in self-denial the only means of self-affirmation. It was thus the enticing prospect of communism that made possible — but as we shall see, also made contingent — the remarkable feat of transforming, for such a large population and for so long, power for the self into power away from and against the self.

It was a prospect fashioned in significant respects on the model of Christian eschatology. This eschatological vision

Meaning and Fatigue 193

was combined with the spirit of world-mastery, also newly imported from the West via Marxism, to produce, in Mao's China as it had in Europe earlier, what Weber called "the economically eschatological faith of socialism" or what Cioran named a "modernized Parousia."[39] In the launching of socialism "the eschatological process [became] a political and social transformation of this world."[40] As long as this transformation seemed to be proceeding according to expectations, every useful expenditure of energy brought with it the satisfaction of discharge, because it had moved the prospect of communism that much closer to realization. But until the final goal was realized, every discharge was followed by a renewal of tension, a recharging of energy, because of the realization that much more remained to be done. From this optimal equilibrium of discharge and tension there flowed an abundance of human energy that seemed inexhaustible — until the goal was no longer to be seen without forced vision.

Just as for the early Christians the mood of euphoria arising from expectation of the Second Coming did not last long, so the energy generated from the expectation of a secular parousia in the form of communism soon found itself frustrated as the prospect of communist paradise receded from the realm of hope. This was followed by a series of attempts to tone down utopian expectations, to push utopia into the remote future without making it disappear altogether from the horizon. Once such attempts became necessary, it was only a matter of time before communism moved across — by subtle degrees, sometimes even back and then across again — the borderline separating what Mannheim usefully distinguished as utopia and ideology.[41] From this point on, the survival of communism depended on its transformation from a radical project into a conservative institution of political legitimation. But one thing was certain: the disappearance of the prospect of communism from the immediate horizon prevented the discharge of collective

194 *Meaning and Fatigue*

power. The collective was still there, but it was no longer an effective medium for the expression of collective power.

The severing of the psychological link between present effort and future goal destroyed the equilibrium of discharge and tension that had been the source of so much energy and so much energizing release. A massive and prolonged expenditure of energy is not felt to be exhausting only when there is both the satisfaction of discharge that comes from having accomplished part of a task and the energizing tension that comes from knowing there is more to be accomplished. In this equilibrium, energy successfully expends itself, thereby issuing in discharge, and is immediately replenished by rest and physical nourishment and by the return of tension sweetened by the preceding joy of discharge. Both discharge and tension depend on a goal, the one deriving from the sense of moving toward the goal, and the other from the sense of not yet being there. Once the goal is lost, energy can no longer replenish itself through the combination of discharge and tension, and a massive expenditure of energy is naturally followed by a sense of exhaustion.[42] "Duration 'in vain,' without end or aim" is indeed, as Nietzsche said, "the most paralysing idea."[43]

So once again the Chinese people were weak, weak from exhaustion, and exhausted from expending energy in vain. Worse still, this time the weakness followed rather than preceded the utopian project. And the faith that remained was no longer what it had once been. It was faith after rather than faith before hope, just as their new weakness was the weakness after rather than the weakness before striving.

But a people weakened by frustrated exertion could not find in themselves the strength immediately to discard the faith that had inspired them in their exertion, had given them their identity, in the first place. Their weakness made them need that faith as much as ever, and although the channel for the collective discharge of repressed individual energy was blocked, the psychological effects of the repression lingered on and, together with the effects of their weakness, made them cling to their faith in communism. But they kept their faith in communism as something to die for but no longer something to live for, since nobody then living, even according to official propaganda, would live to see its realization. Accordingly, as communism changed from a worldly political program into a functional equivalent of otherworldly religion, the will to power was forced to express itself in the will to nothingness, setting, in the spirit of Christian nihilism as Nietzsche described it, a paradisiac future of communism rationally known to be beyond human reach above a present doomed forever to be imperfect. But through this nihilistic version of communism, much as in Christianity, "the will itself was saved"[44] — under circumstances of a pervading weakness that might otherwise have caused paralysis of will.

This transformation of communism, once it reached a point of no return, was unmistakable, but the process occurred gradually and subtly. In its original, robust form, the collective pursuit of imminent communism was conceived as a worldly political project, although it was pursued with otherworldly zeal. It was this combination of a secular project and a quasi-apocalyptic vision that gave the project of socialism what Weber called its "quasi-religious" character.[45] But the lack of worldly success gradually pushed the Chinese utopian project in the direction of the otherworldly. This occurred through a subtle process during which the date for the realization of communism shifted between the foreseeable and the distant future, reflecting fluctuations of hope and enthusiasm, until one foreseeable future after another had passed with the promise unfulfilled. As the utopian project thus crossed and recrossed that hazy borderline separating worldly activism and otherworldly nihilism, now economic effectiveness, reflecting worldly activism, or now doctrinal purity, reflecting otherworldly nihilism, was in the forefront of the utopian agenda. But each time communism was postponed, it took a psychological step closer to its degeneration into a quasi-otherworldly ideal, until hopes in its worldly realization were completely lost and there was no longer any point even in speaking of postponement. When in this way the prospect of communism receded irrevocably from the immediate horizon but nevertheless remained as a matter of pure faith, a communistic form of nihilism set in, in which a future beyond human grasp was made both the basis for regulating earthly life and the sole source of comfort for those whose will to power was thwarted in the here and now. Henceforth, by a logic not unlike that which operated in the Christian Church, doctrinal correctness came to matter much more than economic effectiveness, and the struggle against the unfaithful rather than struggle for utopia became the chief goal for which to mobilize mass energy.

In theory, this new game could continue indefinitely, since the battleground had been shifted from the tangible world of promise and disappointment to the ethereal realm of self-invented devils and angels. Indeed, this phase of communistic nihilism, with its patient faith in an invisible future and with its internal struggles in the name of doctrinal purity, has a close parallel in the situation of the Christian Church after the radical revision of eschatology.[46] And just as God was kept alive despite the indefinite postponement of parousia, so for a time the idea of communism survived the indefinite delay of its realization. But only for a very short time. Mao Zedong either did not have the instinct, or did not find it possible, to diminish the present sufficiently to prevent it from naturally growing in importance while the future, in being deferred, was diminished. He seemed both too earthy and too proud — after all, he could be god only in this world — to take the decisive step of raising the future to the level of a full-fledged, all-important otherworldly goal. With the gradual shrinking of the future, hastened by the growth of individual power, and the lack of an adequate effort to artificially enlarge it, the present loomed larger and larger both in politics and in consciousness, until it came to be judged on its own merit without reference to an imagined future. Naturally it was found wanting, as it had almost always been purely in its own right. Thus whereas the Christian church kept its god alive for another two thousand years through the bureaucratization of the church[47] and through a "particular mastery of this business of delay,"[48] the would-be church of the Communist party, lacking those instincts and skills and perhaps operating under less propitious circumstances, failed to sustain and stabilize faith for long in the face of the receding prospect of communism. The communist god died not very long after the disappointment of these eschatological expectations. The miracle of the Christian church was not to be repeated, and the parallel with Christianity becomes apposite again only with the death of God — to the extent that god is dead — also in the Christian church.

With the collective god dead, each individual emerged as his or her own god. Just as the collective goal of communism had once furnished the political and psychological raison d'être of collective power, so now, with the failure of communism first as a worldly project and then also as a quasi-otherworldly ideal, that reason ceased to exist. Powerless now to bring about utopia, the utopian community still had power, however, over its members. But as soon as the second form of power was divorced from the first, it began to be felt as repression. For the loss of collective power's raison d'être undid the transformation of individual power into collective power, and the undoing of this transformation meant the return of individual power to its original form, that is, to raw individual power. With this individual power no longer suffering itself to be transformed into collective power and yet with few permissible channels for its discharge as individual power, the consciousness of repression emerged. This consciousness, moreover, in vengeful retrospect, saw repression not as coming into being only with consciousness of it but as having existed all along, even when the relatively successful transformation of individual power into collective power had prevented any acute consciousness of repression.

From this point on, if repression was to continue, individual power, the small traitor inside, had to be fought head on. Having attained consciousness of itself through consciousness of repression and seeing itself for the first time in a positive light, individual power would no longer allow itself to be transformed either into collective power or into power against the self. By now, the small traitor was neither small nor perceived by itself as a traitor. The traitor was rather the collective that had let its members down but refused to let go of its power. For the first time the collective took on the chilling visage of the enemy rather than of the provider of freedom, and accordingly the freedom more and more people began to demand was freedom from the collective, a form of negative freedom.

Originally the instinct of weakness and the search for positive freedom had launched the collective enterprise. Individuals had just emerged from years of oppression and hardship too weak to have, or to lay claim to, a distinct and separate selfhood, which is the psychological locus of negative freedom. Under such conditions, negative freedom — that is, freedom of the self from the power of the collective — made no sense, because the collective afforded the only sense of power and hence of freedom that individuals in their weakness could have. Later, even when they grew stronger, individuals continued to find positive freedom in the collective project as long as the collective could provide a meaningful goal and therein a channel for the expression of their will to power. That goal was the overcoming of positive unfreedom through the achievement of communism. The very striving for utopia was evidence of a consciousness of positive unfreedom, without which utopia would have made no sense. In the absence of a consciousness of negative unfreedom, however, the consciousness of positive unfreedom was not a source of division between leaders and members of the utopian community but rather a source of unity in the common pursuit of utopia. As a matter of subjectivity, unfreedom is nothing but the raising to political consciousness of experiences of frustration caused by the blocking of a channel for the meaningful discharge of energy. So long, therefore, as the utopian project was well and alive, all was well with freedom. Consciousness of negative unfreedom emerged only when the utopian project failed to fulfill expectations of positive freedom and could no longer provide for the meaningful discharge of collective energy. Without hopes of positive freedom to sustain the collectivist ideology in which the difference between leaders and the people was merely a division of labor in a common pursuit, negative freedom for the first time began to make sense. Soon collectivism came to be identified with repression and individualism with freedom.[49]

Accordingly, as post-Mao China moved gingerly from collectivism to individualism, as Deng Xiaoping's reform began to allow more room for the exercise of individual power, a significant reduction in repression occurred. This is not because as a cultural formation collectivism is inherently more repressive than individualism, but because having failed first as a worldly project and then as a quasi-otherworldly ideal, collectivism could no longer offer an effective outlet for the will to power. When individualism began at this point to replace collectivism, in ethos if not yet so much in practice, this was felt as liberating because individualism promised to provide a new channel for the meaningful expenditure of energy. Much as the collectivistic utopian project had earlier succeeded in mobilizing so much energy because energy had not been discharged in that fashion in living memory, so individualism, and for a time a new utopia—the utopia of negative freedom and "self-realization"—beckoned from the horizon.

When individual power returned, however, it returned socially and institutionally unembodied: collectivism had never allowed individual power to be expressed either in ideology or in institutions. Individual power returned as unrestrained selfishness rather than the regulated selfishness characteristic of individualism. Maoist collectivism had depended on a group ideal in the shape of communism and a group leader in the person of Mao Zedong. With the failure of the ideal and the demise of the leader, the group could no longer hold itself together. Solidarity, while it lasted, had acted as a brake on what Freud calls narcissistic self-love and drawn its cohesive strength from such restraint. Once solidarity was gone, narcissistic self-love returned, for, as Freud put it so well, "Love for oneself knows only one barrier—love for others."[50] With the voracity of newly liberated egoism compounded by the old habit of expecting quick and spectacular results, individual power returned as yet another utopian anticipation—this time the anticipation not of positive freedom but of negative freedom, not of communist heaven but of capitalist paradise. In its impatience and the enormity of its stakes, even in its content (now shorn of its old collectivism), the new individualism was a psychological carryover of the old utopianism.

With these not very promising characteristics, individual power soon found itself more frustrated than gratified. Individual power grew at a pace that far exceeded the gradual enlargement of channels for its expression. This frustration of individual power, particularly in its pursuit of material well-being, had a profound consequence: it raised individualism to the level of an inspiring goal, a grand ideology, a new source of meaning. By being denied immediate and ample satisfaction, individual power was sublimated, if only for a short while, into a new idealism of freedom and

Meaning and Fatigue 201

democracy, an idealism that forgot its origin in self-regarding projects and was ready for heroic sacrifice. It was this sublimated individual power that came into conflict with the still powerful holders of collective power, the cause of its coerced sublimation.

Not unlike manifestations of individual power under Mao Zedong, the new individual power, while strong enough to rebel, was too weak to resist suppression. For individual power was accompanied by a good deal of weakness, much of the old weakness that had allowed individual power to be transformed into collective power in the first place and a good deal of new weakness that had been fostered under collectivism. It was, let us not forget, the failure of the collective project more than the growth of individual power by itself that brought individual power, and its accompanying sense of unfreedom and repression, to the fore.

Unlike the tentative manifestations of individual power under Mao, however, the new individual power was suppressed but looked as if it could not be transformed. By virtue of this very refusal, energy was accumulating under suppression, but this was not in itself a hopeful sign. For energy can also dissipate under suppression. As long as the suppressed energy is voluminous enough to frustrate but not overwhelming enough to explode, it will be forced to turn inward and spend part of itself in ill-temper and cynicism—always a tempting and dangerous form of self-demoralization for the oppressed—unless it is charged with hope.

But how hard it was to be hopeful again after so much hope, so much effort, and yet so many failures! In the wake of the failure of the democracy movement, the will of China had all but collapsed under the combined weight of a threefold consciousness: of positive unfreedom, of negative unfreedom, and, worst of all, of the near-impossibility—for this was how the matter was perceived by individuals with limited life spans and limited willpower—of achieving either negative or positive freedom. The consciousness of unfreedom generates the energy to overcome unfreedom, but only if freedom is perceived as a genuine prospect. It is not out of a consciousness of unfreedom alone, but out of this *and* the hope for freedom, that creative energy is born. After so many setbacks in such rapid succession, the delicate balance between the consciousness of unfreedom (whether positive or negative) and the hope for freedom, it seemed, had finally been upset.

What little hope had survived was pinned on the resumption of the experiment with individualism. Whereas Maoist collectivism was thoroughly discredited because it had been allowed to run its course, individualism had yet to exhaust its potential because it was not properly born in the first place and then died a premature and artificial death. But the ideology of individualism, which had earlier called forth so much idealism and energy through the sublimation of individual power, was now, without being de-sublimated, losing its spell through familiarity and losing its momentum through loss of hope. Individualism, perhaps by nature, is not so much a goal as the aftermath of the loss of other goals, whether religious or utopian. And the loss of a goal is always worse than the loss of hope. After the failure of individualism, China's mood sunk to depths unprecedented since 1949 — not because there was anything special about the suppression of individualism but because all worthwhile goals seemed to have been tried and found to be either wanting or beyond reach. It felt as though the future was going to be an unbroken anticlimax. The will was left with no place to go but the self–torture chambers of cynicism and apathy. The more reflective became cynical, and the less reflective fell into apathy, with an enormous dissipation of innocence, belief, and energy. Authoritarianism was rendered lame, but even more so was its opposition.

Thus for the first time since 1949, there descended upon a depressed people the feeling that *everything* had been in vain[51] — a feeling made worse by the fact that it came after four decades of an extraordinary expenditure of energy. The Chinese people, in their weakness and in their search for power, responded to one stimulus after another until they were exhausted and there were no more stimuli to respond to.[52] Only at this point but not earlier, not even immediately after the death of Mao and the failure of the collective project, could it be said of recent Chinese history what Nietzsche said of "great men and ages," "The danger that lies in great men and ages is extraordinary; exhaustion of every kind, sterility, follow in their wake. The great man is a finale."[53] Looked at in a certain way, the reckless expenditure of power perhaps lends the Chinese communist experiment a certain greatness — more precisely a certain *spectacle* of greatness. But we must not forget that the power was born out of weakness, and perhaps we should not be surprised that it ended up as weakness.

With memories of the late 1980's democracy movement more and more overlaid with fears of chaos in a new global environment, this weakness once again manifested itself as the willingness of individual power to be transformed (in this case de-sublimated); it was a measure of the weakness of the regime that it could suppress individual power but no longer transform it into collective power. What was truly remarkable was the speed of the transformation, the almost obscene rapidity with which the same powers that had crushed the democracy movement were able to lift the hopelessness and cynicism and apathy. But apart from its speed, the transformation occurred in accordance with a logic that is easy to comprehend. If what had happened during the utopian project was the sublimation of individual power into collective power through the suspension of hedonism, what transpired after the suppression of the democracy movement — and for the first time in the history of communist-ruled China — was the de-sublimation of idealistic individualism into crude hedonism. Once again the art of repression proved to be the art of transformation.

By design, the period of straightforward repression after the democracy movement was soon followed by unprecedented opportunities for material and sensual gratification.[54] Under active official encouragement, business and consumerism flourished as never before. In a move whose ironic twists few would have thought possible, the country turned radically more laissez-faire *after* the suppression of the democracy movement. In this new atmosphere, the cynicism and apathy that had enveloped China immediately after the suppression of the democracy movement were soon suspended in the heady pursuit of wealthy and pleasure. From the ashes of burnt ideals, the intellectual ground of cynicism and apathy, there now rose a new species of thoughtless hopefulness kindled by prospects of material aggrandizement. In the pursuit of hedonism, no longer inhibited either by government policy or by ideology, the energy whose blockage under authoritarianism had been the physiological ground of cynicism and apathy was now allowed to flow freely.

In its own way, the mood of cynicism and apathy even cleared the way for hedonism. Alike in their detachment from idealism and things of the spirit and differing only in their ability to see through them, the cynical and the apathetic had no qualms about forgetting the days of ideals and struggle and responding avidly to the only stimulus left. In a poor country like China there had been few opportunities to see through wealth and pleasure. At a time when because of cynicism and apathy the national mood displayed the will not to believe and hence the will not to act meaningfully, the new hedonism encouraged a gainful pursuit in which the human spirit, the seat of belief and meaning, did not have to participate.

Apathy rather than cynicism, however, accounts for the

sheer volume of the energy that went into the new pursuit. For apathy lacks the urge or the ability to think, to see through (*kantou*). When thinking cannot but be futile, the ability not to think helps conserve energy for a future stimulus, energy that would be internally dissipated by cynicism because of its irresistible urge to reflect on what for the time being can only cause despair and ill-temper.[55] But in cynical consciousness at its most uncompromising thought is kept sharp, and the tension between what is and what ought to be is obliquely preserved. Little of such cynicism was in evidence when the tides of hedonism surged along. The cynics seemed to have either drowned or swum along with the current, such was the momentum of the newly released impulses.

When individual power had been sublimated before and during the democracy movement, it was a function of being forced from sensual into idealistic, from economic into political channels. By exactly the same logic in reverse, idealistic individualism underwent a thorough de-sublimation by being channeled away from idealism to hedonism, from political dissent to economic prosperity. For most people, it seemed, the pursuit of political objectives had lost its urgency, even its relevance — the more so as the regime found it increasingly unnecessary to resort to heavy-handed propaganda or coercion. Now that the underlying hedonism of individualism was amply satisfied, individualism could no longer serve as the soil for rebellious idealism. Once the body was free from want, the mind no longer wanted freedom. In the absence of sensual impoverishment, the idealistic aura that used to surround the individualistic values of freedom and democracy soon evaporated. Gratified individual power, as opposed to sublimated individual power, had no need of confrontation with the powers that be.

In hedonism, in the consequences of de-sublimated individualism, those who once faced each other on opposite sides of the political divide could now find a common ground, the only compromise that each side for its own reasons could regard as a victory for itself. Decisively, although only as long as opportunities for wealth and pleasure last, hedonism has replaced politics.

CHAPTER SIX

On the Far Side of the Future

The path traversed by Chinese consciousness in the past half-century is the path from utopianism to nihilism — a nihilism that retains all the implications of a profound loss of meaning even as it merges into hedonism. The way from the one to the other is marked above all by the loss of the most precious mental possession — belief in the future. On the calender of political events 1949 was the year the communists came to power, but, much more significantly, on the calender of consciousness it was the year the Chinese people were supposed to have come into possession of the future.

They came into possession of the future in consciousness and through heightened consciousness. But, some forty years later, the future that heightened consciousness envisioned has neither, in accordance with the secular utopian imagination, become reality nor, as in religion, purged itself of its links with reality. Having thus been unable to find a foothold either in this world or in the otherworldly, the future — that is, the future that was to be — has been irredeemably lost.

By purely material standards, however, reality has improved, but not by the standards of heightened, utopianized consciousness. Thus, not only has utopian consciousness been let down by reality, but equally reality has been betrayed and darkened by utopian consciousness. It is this mutual cancellation that has led from utopianism to nihilism—an impoverished spirit contemplating a reality it has itself helped to impoverish.

But this is not the end of utopianism, for half of utopianism is preserved in nihilism. Utopian consciousness, no longer utopian in its vital hopefulness but as utopian as ever in its exacting standards, has now neither the urge nor the strength to look forward to yet another future. Instead it casts a bitter look on the past and present, where by its exacting standards it can find no meaning. What it finds instead are new opportunities for hedonism, and in such opportunities, while they last, meaninglessness finds its own temporary oblivion.

But where meaninglessness is not thus buried in oblivion, the loss of meaning is seen not just as a cloud passing over the present, for in nihilistic consciousness the future is no longer seen as the transformation of the present but merely its extension. At long last, when it is too late for the generations now living to start conserving utopian consciousness, heightened consciousness of the future, which utopianism fed upon as if it were an inexhaustible source of meaning, has revealed itself, from the vantage point of nihilism, as the resource that is easiest to squander and hardest to replenish. The temporal infinitude of the future is not, for temporally finite individual human beings, equivalent to infinitude of meaning. Consciousness, too, whose accentuation has gone hand in hand with the stress on the future, has turned out to be not only the place where meaning is created but also the site where meaning can be destroyed. Once, in consciousness, there was no meaning; then there was the meaning derived from utopianism; then there was no meaning again. This time, however, unlike the first time, there was neither the innocence nor the strength to find meaning, but only the instinct of decadence to bury meaninglessness in hedonism.

Every raising of consciousness, every raising of hope for

the future, as this sad journey from utopianism to nihilism shows, is a raising of the stakes. When the wager is raised as high as it is in utopianism, the game acquires the proportions of a gamble with life and death stakes — a gamble with the meaning of life, with the spiritual ecology of a community — whose failure, quite fittingly, can mean nothing less than spiritual death. It was, in the Chinese case, a venture launched from an extremely complex mixture of motives and tensions — innocent optimism, exuberant energy, proud nationalism, personal ambition, outright ignorance, and irresponsibility. And it came to grief because of a logic that in retrospect seems to be inherent in certain attitudes toward the future and in certain practices of consciousness-raising characteristic of Chinese utopianism from the very beginning.

The conception of time as progress and of the future as the realm of perfect happiness may in large measure have been imported from Europe, but the Chinese eagerly embraced it because it answered to a real and profound need, a need that arose from a crisis in the emotional and intellectual relationship they had to their past and to their present. On this point, indeed, as on many other points in this account of China's trajectory from utopianism to nihilism, we can speak in terms that cover or can cover more than the Chinese experience.

Our sense of our relationship to the future — our hopes for it, our fears of it, even the degree of our consciousness of it — is a function of our sense and experience of our place in the world as it has been and as it is now. It is not necessarily true, contrary to what Hannah Arendt says in discussing Koyré on Hegel, that "the mind's attention is primarily directed toward the future."[1] For our mind's attention to be so directed is for us to envision change as possible and to will the future to be significantly different from the past and present, and we so will the future only when, and because, we are not contented with our existence. It is therefore far from being the case, as E. M. Cioran would have us believe, that "wisdom — fascinated by nothing — recommends an existing, a *given* happiness, which man rejects, and by this very rejection becomes a historical animal, a devotee of *imagined* happiness."[2] Rather, man becomes a devotee of imagined happiness because there is *no* given happiness, and what he rejects is not given happiness but given misery, out of which grows the yearning for happiness. There is no intrinsic reason why the as yet imagined happiness should always turn out to be purely imaginary, unless we subscribe to the metaphysical proposition, set forth by Schopenhauer among others, that this state of not being contented with existence is so inherent in the human condition that "happiness . . . *always* lies in the future" (my italics).[3] It follows from this proposition that insofar as our mind's attention is directed toward happiness, it is necessarily directed toward the future. Whether or not this is true at some rarefied level of consciousness, we know, as a matter of perceptible consciousness and at least relatively speaking, that not all of us are existentially and intellectually oriented toward the future to the same degree and that insofar as we are future-oriented, not all of us want, to the same degree, the future to be significantly different from our past and present. For some of us there may even be times when we will the future to be broadly the same as the past and present, and this would be a symptom and effect of our contentedness with our past and present. Indeed, for those fortunate enough to have been contented for a long time, willing the future to be broadly the same may even take the form of not consciously willing the future at all, of a certain lack of consciousness of the future and of time as such.

By contrast with this kind of relationship with the future, we may view our willing the future to be significantly different as a symptom of something amiss with our relationship to the past and to the present. Perhaps not only an acute consciousness of the future but even consciousness as such bespeak experience of unhappiness. "In all becoming-conscious," wrote Nietzsche in one of his most suggestive notes, "there is expressed a discomfiture of the organism; it has to try something new, nothing is sufficiently adapted for it, there is toil, tension, strain — all this *constitutes* becoming-conscious."[4] If "time finds its truth in the future since it is the future that will finish and accomplish Being,"[5] it is only because time finds no truth, no happiness, *now*. It is for this historically grounded, and not for some mysteriously metaphysical, reason that man " 'says *no* to his Now' and thus creates his own future."[6] Consciousness is thus inherently and primarily negative — negative, that is, in relation to what has been and what is. If this negativity stands all by itself, one's experience of life will be akin to the experience of (the moment before) death, for without hope for a better future hell now is hell forever. But the experience of misery itself creates the desire to remove it, and this built-in desire to remove misery already bespeaks a will to a different and better future — a positive, even optimistic, attitude in regard to what might be. Consciousness of the future is thus by nature both negative and positive, both sad and optimistic. It emerges from unhappiness with what has been and what is, and it looks forward to the happiness of what will be. To be conscious of the future is first and foremost to be conscious of the time ahead as a realm of difference and improvement. Under conditions of misery, to will at all is to will a better future. This intrinsic property of the will, which in being brought into existence by "toil, tension, strain" is already conscious, may be raised to a yet higher level of consciousness by an articulated belief that unhappiness can be removed, that is, by an ideology of the future. Such an articulated belief underlies all eschatological religions and all forms of utopianism.

All these ideologies of the future are alike in giving us a sense of power in conditions of utter powerlessness. They bring into being a well-articulated and hence stable realm — the realm of the projected future — where a thwarted and threatened will can find its home. Indeed to will at all is already to be conscious of one's power, although to will the future to be significantly different is also to be conscious of one's current powerlessness. Under conditions of unhappiness this sense of power comes specifically from our willing the future to be different — and better. But more generally, a sense of power accrues to every act of willing, whether under favorable or unfavorable circumstances. For the future alone is the object of willing, a realm where we can yet accomplish something, and hence the source of our sense of agency. We can will the past only in the sense that we can will the past to happen again in the future. In this sense, happiness does, as Schopenhauer says, always lie in the future. The past and the present can serve as a source of meaning and agency also, but they do so as the record of the successes or failures of our previous acts of willing. The more dismal that record is, the less secure the ground on which we feel able to will, but the more pressing the urge to do so. It is precisely this combination of circumstances that gives rise to eschatological religion and utopianism, which therefore exhibit at once weakness of will and the strength of the urge to exercise it.

This is but an extreme instance of a general truth. Our sense of the meaning of our life is a function of our sense of the relative values of our past, present, and future as these form a continuum of improvement or decline. We feel most at home in time when we face time to come with a hopefulness that is positively grounded in our experience of time past, that is, in experiences of successful willing that we have every hope of repeating, whether with the same or with a different content. But there are circumstances where we can meaningfully situate ourselves on one dimension of time alone. Meaning comes from the past alone, or principally from the past, as we reach old age, which, as Arendt puts it, "consists in the shrinkage of the future dimension" so that "man's death signifies less his disappearance from the world of appearances than his final loss of a future."[7] Here willing no longer brings much satisfaction, because the future will soon be no more. The past can comfort us, not because (as when we have a good portion of our lives yet to live) it serves as a record and reminder of good things that we can will to happen again, but only because it offers itself as the sole object for "the backward glance of the thinking ego [as opposed to the willing ego] in its search for meaning"[8] — meaning, however, that may not be there to be found.

Happiness in the present alone is perhaps the privilege of animals, but only because there is no other dimension of time on which they can feel either happiness or misery. If we humans occasionally approach the happiness of animals, it is only because we simultaneously approach their lack of consciousness. But for us, given the incorrigibly contemplative side of our nature, to be happy and not to be conscious of it — to be happy out of time — is not human happiness. It is our peculiarly human lot that when we are conscious of present happiness, it is either because we are happier now than before or because, having been less happy before, we fear we might be less happy once again. When we are consciously happy at present, the future may be a source not of meaning but of menace and dread. It is only when the present is filled with menace and dread that the future, under the pressure of our desperate need to will, *has* to appear to offer the prospect of happiness. The weight we place on the future is a precise measure of the weight of unhappiness under which we live here and now. We seek power and meaning from the future alone — the realm most out of reach — only when time within reach, time close at hand, offers us nothing but the certainty that it will pass. In the idea of the movement of time already lies the possibility of difference, the possibility of a change for the better, and hence the possibility of willing. Utopianism — at least fervent or desperate utopianism — arises when the future is the only source of meaning and power.

But the mental construction of a better future is only the beginning of a new problem. As an anticipated existence on one dimension of time alone, utopianism raises the stakes for the future to a dangerously high level — the more so because one day in some form the anticipated future will have to become the present. The anticipated future cannot forever remain just the future. This is true even for eschatological religions as well. Christianity, for example, began with the expectation of imminent parousia, whose advent those living could hope to live to see. When parousia failed to arrive at the anticipated hour, it was postponed. Almost at the same time, less naturally but more ingeniously, it was transformed from the falsifiable idea of a general resurrection into the unfalsifiable one of a heavenly afterlife for each and every worthy believer. In the course of time, what may be called the *strategy of postponement* gave way to the *strategy of separation* — separation of life and afterlife, this world and the Other World, Becoming and Being, appearance and essence, pain and ultimate fulfillment. Because the second of each pair is at once the realm of true value and the realm beyond experienceable time, willing takes the form of faith. Unlike temporal hope and anticipation, faith cannot fail — not only because the object of faith is beyond life and experienceable time, so that those who suffer are, as Nietzsche puts it, "sustained by a hope that can never be contradicted by any reality,"[9] but also because faith that fails is not true faith. Thus Christianity ingeniously and successfully solved the most difficult problem for utopias, the meeting of the future and the present. In the strategy of separation, the future and the present meet only in faith, but precisely because they meet only in faith, they cannot fail to meet.

When communism took over the eschatological aspect of

Christianity, it did not stoop to the Christian strategy of separation. This was the whole point of Marx and Engels's critique of religion. Marx said, "The abolition of religion as the *illusory* happiness of men is a demand for their *real* happiness," and Engels wrote, "Both Christianity and the workers' socialism preach forthcoming salvation from bondage and misery; Christianity places this salvation in a life beyond, after death, in heaven; socialism places it in this world, in a transformation of society."[10] This uncompromising stand against the strategy of separation clearly shows more honesty, an honesty that also betokens confidence. But historical determinism aside, this is not unlike the kind of confidence felt by Christians before their eschatological hopes were laid to rest. Unlike the Christians, however, Marx stipulated, before there was any chance of testing the eschatological promise, that the realization of this promise was to be sought only in this world. Without this condition, of course, Marxism would be little different from eschatological religion. But with it, Marx foreclosed the kind of transformation that Christianity underwent when the idea of parousia came to grief. In time the communist equivalent of parousia also came to grief, not long after practitioners of what they claimed to be Marxism came to power and then failed to deliver on their promise of utopia. But because they could not, without forfeiting their Marxist credentials, openly resort to the Christian strategy of separation (which would not have worked anyway, after all the education against it), they had recourse to the most awkward and unscrupulous use of the strategy of postponement. When postponement became indefinite—that is to say, infinite—it was not much different from the Christian strategy of separation.

Unable or unwilling to appeal to the idea of afterlife, with its natural clock that unfailingly strikes at the hour of death, communism has to set an artificial timetable for the realization of utopia. If "happiness . . . always lies in the future" for the Christian, it cannot do so for the communist, for the future ends with death. Without the idea of afterlife, the future, if it is to have the appeal of a concrete promise, has to have a fixed or at least an approximate date, to acquire the shape of a visible goal toward which we may hope to move closer and closer in life and not beyond life. A future that is both beyond life and beyond death is no future at all. But to promise a future in life is to hold the future, and those who make the promise for the future, accountable to the living, rather than much more simply to the dead. Mao Zedong made just such a promise, and in so doing he did not appeal directly to nihilism of the religious kind. Rather, he sowed the seeds of a later nihilism that would come to fruition on the soil where the future was appointed to meet the present. The future as such is always, we might say, before us. But when we fix a goal in the future, we make the future such that we can move, so to speak, beyond it, to its far side. If on the other side we find written "in vain," however, the meaning will be drained from our entire past. Unless we have enough spirit or foolhardiness to project another future, we shall find ourselves stranded in nihilism. The movement from utopianism to nihilism is the unsuccessful transit from one side of the future to the other.

Thus the overriding concern, when movement toward the future goal is not fast enough — as it never can be since a realistic goal is not inspiring — is to slow the movement to the other side of the future. Since the passage of time itself cannot be slowed, this can be done by moving the only thing about the future that is movable, namely, the future goal. When we fail to meet our timetable for the future, this is the only trick we can play: to move the future — that is to say the future goal — further forward into the future. But each time this trick is played, it shakes our faith in the future. Eventually the trick can work no more — not only because faith can be disappointed only so many times before it ceases to be faith, but also because the movable future will sooner or later run up against an immovable barrier: death. In regard both to the fragility of faith and to the inevitability of death, Christianity, in opting for the otherworldly, proved to be much more worldly-wise than communism. Christian eschatology permitted itself the luxury of only one fundamental revision, from the idea of a general resurrection in life to that of individual heaven after life. Faith was thereby preserved, and death was turned into the threshold to a happiness better than life itself. That the idea of heavenly afterlife worked is of course no proof that it is tenable, but then no more so is the Maoist utopian practice of placing the future goal in a time not beyond life but beyond the life of all now living. Insofar as there is an intelligible appeal in this practice, it is to the entirely selfless love of remote posterity, of whose very existence, not to mention happiness, we have no more guarantee than we have of our own afterlife and about whom, in their indefinite remoteness from us, we care even less.

In the end, the communist faith in the remote future degenerates into an embarrassing parody of the Christian faith in the afterlife, a contorted ideological acrobatics aimed at having the otherworldly masquerade as the thisworldly. Since the perfect happiness there will one day be is beyond my life (something the communist would readily concede), and since, furthermore, my life is the only life I have (something the communist would also readily concede in its non-moral aspect), the promised happiness is for me as good as beyond life as such. Since, moreover, I do not, unlike a Christian, believe in an afterlife, the promised happiness is beyond me completely, beyond both my life and my death. If the Christian in his misery is forced to will a realm of existence that is subjectively real but objectively nothingness, the communist in his despair does not even have the option of willing nothingness, because for him the nothingness is not even subjectively real and therefore cannot be an object of willing. There were indeed times in the heyday of Mao's reign when people appeared to draw inspiration from the oft-repeated vow that they would devote their entire lives to the achievement of communism, with the clear implication that they would not personally live to see the day. They could afford, however, to engage in this mindless ritual only because their daily life had been raised above unbearable misery and they no longer stood in desperate need of a tangible future. But then neither would they work so hard for that future—but for Mao Zedong's charismatic power, which bore the ravages of time somewhat better than the belief in the future he had fostered and manipulated.

If the communist utopian future is likely to result in disappointment, this is not just because communist utopianism will have nothing to do with the notion of an afterlife and more generally the strategy of separation. Communists feel the sting of disappointment so keenly because they believe they deserve otherwise. Unburdened by guilt or sin, they work not to discharge a debt but to secure a gain, not to earn salvation but to achieve tangible happiness, not to add to the glory of god but to give meaning to their own life. Unlike Christians, they do not work and wait; instead they work and demand, and the nature of the pursuit—tangible happiness here on earth—inspires an impatient activism, generally absent in Christianity and Confucianism alike, that makes disappointment all the more bitter after the expenditure of so much effort. However much communist utopianism may owe to Christianity, and however extensively Mao may have used ideas akin to Christian sin and guilt in manipulating the people, the communist idea of the future represents a fundamental reversal of the Christian conception of the relationship between man and god. The Christian can never be let down by the god that presides over his future, because god does not owe him anything. If Christians wait so patiently—"Even though he tarry, yet shall I wait for him," as the rabbinic saying, also representative of the Christian spirit, so aptly has it — it is because they know they have no right to demand. Nor is there any point in demanding, for, as Jesus, when asked when the kingdom of god would arrive, told the Pharisees, "the kingdom of God is *within* you" (Luke 17:20–21; my italics). The difference between communism and Christianity is not just between the this-worldly and the otherworldly but also between the outer-worldly and the inner-worldly. Insofar as Christianity is outer-worldly, it is the Christian who works for the glory of god and not god who works for the Christian's salvation. If the Christian fails to secure salvation (which would be known with certainty only in the afterlife), he has, because of the nature of his outer-worldly (insofar as it is outer-worldly) relationship to god and of the otherwise essentially inner-worldly character of his religion, only himself to blame. This is not unlike Confucius' comparison of the moral life to the art of archery: "When the archer misses the center of the target, he turns around and seeks for the cause of failure within himself."[11] The Christian stops believing in god, not because god has let him down but because he no longer needs god. Presiding over the future of the communist, of course, is not a god but a godlike Idea. The communist's faith in the Idea, however, is profoundly conditional. Despite all the rhetoric that raises the Idea above humanity much in the manner of Christianity, the real nature of the relationship unmistakably revealed itself in the almost universal disappointment in the Idea only three decades after the Idea was placed on the state pedestal.

When we bring communism and Christianity together in this way, we are comparing a doctrine that matured after the failure of its eschatological expectations and a doctrine that could draw lessons only from the rise and decline of Christianity but not yet from the failure of its own eschatological hopes. There is no more telling manifestation of Christianity's maturity than its building the profoundest hope upon the profoundest pessimism, with its elevation of death over life, of original sin over primeval goodness, and with its construction of heaven upon hell. This maturity lay not so much in Christianity's inner logic as in its proximity to (i.e., the extent to which it reflected) the actual conditions of life under which, and in response to which, it arose. This, rather than the intrinsic merits of the different religions, is precisely the point of Schopenhauer's remark "The power by virtue of which Christianity was able to overcome first Judaism, and then the heathenism of Greece and Rome, lies solely in its pessimism, in the confession that our state is both exceedingly wretched and sinful, while Judaism and heathenism were optimistic. That truth, profoundly and painfully felt by all, penetrated, and bore in its train the need of redemption."[12] Thus the burden of responsibility was decisively shifted onto the individual — now the individual sinner — and god, and hence the future, was thereby saved.

This Christian pessimism, contrary to what Schopenhauer thought, answered not to the human condition as such but only to the wretched conditions of the time. The way out of such conditions led, as we have seen, from the idea of parousia to the idea of the afterlife — in other words, from optimism to pessimism. In philosophical terms, the Christian search for salvation led from Becoming to Being. Marx's critique of religion was at once the rejection of Being and the resurrection of Becoming, wherein lay socialism's affinity with the eschatological phase of Christianity. But herein also lay a problem over which, had it not been transformed in time, eschatological Christianity, just like quasi-eschatological socialism, would have stumbled, namely, our possible failure to realize our hopes for the future is inherent in the nature of Becoming. After the disappointment of its eschatological expectations, Christianity sought refuge in the impregnable security of Being. Communism did not, either before or after the evaporation of similar eschatological hopes.

Utopia, unlike the Christian afterlife, is the temporal locus where the future and the present, hope and reality, are supposed to meet. It is the moment when Becoming successfully issues in Being. In this conception, unlike in the Platonic and the Christian conceptions, Being is continuous with Becoming, and the inherently certain state of Being can be reached only through the inherently uncertain process of Becoming. The failure of utopianism is the failure of Becoming to make contact with Being. It is a failure inherent in the very conception of Being as continuous with and conditional upon Becoming. Marxism, as we said, did not openly seek refuge in Being, but it devised an idea, historical determinism, whose function it was to impart to Becoming almost all the certainty of Being. The revisionist Eduard Bernstein, for his part, invented an equally ingenious solution when he sought to sever the link between Becoming and Being and make Becoming all-important: "To me that which is generally called the ultimate aim of socialism is nothing, but the movement is everything."[13] Marx's solution, if it had been tenable in practice, would perhaps have been more satisfactory, but since it was not, Bernstein's solution exhibited more realism and wisdom. If we cannot guarantee we will succeed, Bernstein seems to be saying, we can at least keep trying; if there is felt to be no point in trying without the certain prospect of success, let us make trying itself the point of it all. Mao Zedong, by the time he launched the Cultural Revolution in 1966, came close to this position, but he was even wiser than Bernstein because he made "movement" almost but not quite everything.

Historical determinism is not only communism's theoretical answer to the uncertainty of Becoming but also its practical answer to the problem of postponement. But this indispensable aid to the unavoidable strategy of postponement is caught in a paradox that progressively undermines both. Historical determinism is needed to maintain faith and morale in each case of postponement, but each postponement in turn undercuts belief in historical determinism. Eventually determinism, to be made intellectually defensible, has to be stretched so far into the future that it becomes emotionally ineffective. In its remoteness from experience and from now, determined Becoming secretly joins the company of Christian Being. The absurdity and hypocrisy of this practice are the price paid by the communist for considering himself wiser than religion.

These inventions, the communist's optimistic determinism and the Christian's heavenly afterlife, represent the enforced accentuation of the future in our experience of time, the anticipatory molding of the future into a definite shape and meaning long before the future is to arrive. The Christian becomes hostage to the future; the future becomes hostage to the communist. It is a sad comment on human history that we have either to abuse the future or to have the future abuse us, that this violence against time and against ourselves has become an imperative of consciousness. But humanity has not always and everywhere been like that; even those living in the midst of all this future-mongering can still from time to time feel a more "natural" sense of the future, which in its experiential aspect is almost unhistorical,[14] still less historically determined. This natural sense of the future is a cheerfulness, a lighthearted confidence, a "mysterious misty vapour,"[15] a rich yet vague feeling that there is going to be a future—in fact a feeling even vaguer than this—rather than the definite idea, as in Christianity or in communism, that the future is going to be like this or like that. But this natural sense of the future presupposes a correspondingly natural condition of human happiness; since happiness has been anything but a natural human condition, what I have pictured as the natural sense of the future is equally unnatural. This (ideal of a) natural sense of the future is invariably prevented or, having briefly existed, disrupted by conditions of severe unhappiness. Out of this unhappiness arises that ideological accentuation and concretization of the future we find in Christianity or utopianism. The accentuation of the future, we may say in the spirit of Marx, is the protest against an unbearable present. Marx said, "*Religious* suffering is at the same time the *expression* of a real suffering and also a *protest* against real suffering. Religion is the sigh of the oppressed creature, the sentiment of a heartless world, and the soul of soulless conditions. It is the *opium* of the people."[16] The same could be said of utopianism, except that before the disappointment of its eschatological hopes, it is more a protest and a program of action than an opiate or a sigh.

But after it showed signs of failing as a program of action, utopianism too became the opium of the people. The idea of the future, whose character as the not-yet makes it the realm par excellence of wish-fulfillment and ideology, gradually developed after (and indeed even before) the communists came to power first into a work ethic not unlike the Protestant ethic and then, when all the effort inspired by the work ethic had failed to produce the expected results, increasingly into what we may describe, borrowing a phrase from Habermas, as a "legitimation potential."[17] When the role of the future shifted more and more from a work ethic to a means of legitimation, this marked not only the failure of the utopian project but also the determination to hold on to power despite that failure. Those in power sought to keep possession of the present — that is, their present power and legitimacy — not in order to realize a vision of the future but in the name of the future. For those at the receiving end of this political sagacity, things were just the opposite. They had gained an imagined future — a future not so much imagined by them as for them — but had lost their present. The legitimation potential of communism is coextensive with belief in this ideologized future, and we call it ideologized future in the specific sense that it involves an unequal exchange where one side is powerful and in the know and the other powerless and in the dark. As long as the people believed in this imagined future, however vaguely or subconsciously, there was little that could not be done in its name. Social and political practices began to be felt as repression, brainwashing, forced labor, and so on only after there was no longer the belief in the future to impart a nobler meaning to them. The present is to the future what the means is to the end, and the means/present strikes the eye as ugly only when the end/future has lost its charm.

Before the spell of the future is lost, it can rub off, in the form of charisma, onto the leader who directs the onward march into the future. And the charismatic leader may even be able to return some of this magic power to the future when its spell is waning. There has never been a charismatic leader who did not have this special, two-way, relationship with the future. If the measure of charisma is its power to give (back) to the future, the art of charisma is its power to take from it. With every accentuation of the future goes an accentuation of the charismatic power of a prophet or leader. He who has it in him to lead the way to a heavenly future acquires from that power a charisma that partakes of all the mysterious appeal and boundless happiness that the future alone holds.

Indeed, it was the combined force of historical determinism and Mao's charisma that kept the game of postponement going for as long as it did. And as a variation on the theme of postponement, Mao's charisma, combined with historical determinism, was able to move for a time the locus of comparison between socialism and capitalism into the more or less distant future. When China became a self-proclaimed socialist state, its superiority to capitalism lay not so much in even its own perception of actuality as in its claim to the future, much as a child is sure of one day outstripping an adult in height. If the child's confidence is based knowingly or not quite knowingly on biological laws, the communist found encouragement in the impersonal power of historical determinism and the personal power of Mao's charisma. Even Mao did not say categorically that socialism as it was was already better than capitalism as it was. Only the future would make it so — by changing capitalism for the worse and socialism for the better. Before actual superiority arrived, a feeling of superiority could thrive only on historical determinism and Mao's charisma. Time was supposedly on communism's side, but time, alas, also put determinism and charisma to the test and found both wanting. When that happened, the locus of comparison shifted back from the future to the present. No wonder the occasional claim that socialism was already better than capitalism struck a note of desperation rather than confidence. It was an implicit acknowledgment that socialism had no future, that it might as well claim superiority to capitalism right now — or never.

When the present thus came to the fore, it was a sure sign that the future had come to grief, and the future came to grief not only on the rock of reality but also on that of consciousness. Utopianism meant the utopianization of *consciousness*, which, as the consciousness of a happy future, emerged from the consciousness of an unhappy present. The experience of pain — "discomfiture of the organism" — gives rise at once to an accentuated future and to heightened consciousness. In the Chinese revolution, the accentuation of the future was all along part of a more comprehensive accentuation of consciousness as a whole. Having charted the course and consequences of the accentuation of the future, we must now retrace what is essentially the same trajectory, but this time particularly as it took place in consciousness and as a result of the heightening of consciousness.

We must begin, however, not quite with consciousness

but with the body, that is, with material conditions. For utopianism arose in response to a crisis of the body, a crisis of material existence caused by war, hunger, and poverty. Utopian consciousness was the anticipation in consciousness of the transcendence of such unbearable material conditions. After that consciousness translated itself into a military victory in 1949, there began the attempted overcoming of the crisis of the body not only in consciousness but also in practice. The causes of the communist victory include more than just the energizing power and the legitimation potential of utopian consciousness, but there can be no question that the nature of the victory was much more than just military, much more even than just nationalistic. In terms of its long-term consequences, and not just psychological consequences, it was above all an ideological victory, even a religious victory — a victory of consciousness and in consciousness over a crisis of the body and of the old body politic. The importance of this feature of the Chinese revolution cannot be exaggerated, because for those imbued with utopian consciousness the military victory was not the end but only the beginning. Utopian consciousness, once aroused, had a momentum that would not rest content until its original basis, the crisis of the body, was overcome, until its hopes were either fulfilled or dashed.

Whatever combination of complex events and equally complex personal motives may have helped set in motion the three great utopian campaigns of post-1949 China — the Great Leap Forward of 1958–60, the Cultural Revolution of 1966–76, and finally Deng Xiaoping's reform in its early phase — none of them could have taken place without the engine of utopian consciousness. Hedonistic utopianism was the thrust of the Great Leap Forward; its decisive failure put an end to overt hedonism as an overriding aim of Mao's utopian project and thereby helped to change his whole conception of utopianism. Accordingly, the Cultural Revolution was primarily a moral crusade aimed at bringing about a utopia not so much free of want as free of "capitalist" and "feudalist" vices as represented by those supposedly taking the "capitalist road." The disastrous outcome of the Cultural Revolution signified the complete exhaustion of the ideological resources of communist utopianism, hedonistic or moral.

This was not, however, the exhaustion of utopian consciousness as such. For Deng's reform, launched with all the pomp and circumstance characteristic of Mao's voluntarism and wholesale mobilization, represented for a while the transference of utopian consciousness from communism to the market. It was a continuation of the pursuit of the utopian dream—the hedonistic, not the moral, utopia—by other means. Deng Xiaoping launched his ambitious reform program with the aid of the still powerful and prevalent utopian consciousness left over from the Maoist era. Paradoxically, Deng's reputation as a pragmatist, among other things, enabled him to tap the lingering utopian consciousness, igniting it once again into high hopes for the rapid all-around modernization of China. Once the old fanaticism, with its empty sloganeering and social disruptiveness, had been thoroughly discredited, Deng's style of pragmatism came to be regarded as a new source of hope, sober means for pursuing aims whose ambitiousness, not to mention the enthusiasm they initially aroused, as it soon became apparent, reeked of the old utopianism. Indeed, even the new pragmatic approach involved, particularly at the beginning, a good deal of intensive propaganda and national mobilization, yet another legacy of Mao's utopianism. It was only when Deng's reform failed to live up to expectations, which themselves were almost as utopian as those of Mao's utopian project, that utopian consciousness finally began to dissipate. There gradually occurred what may be described as the de-utopianization of reform; in its train came that natural combination of nihilism and hedonism.

Unlike utopianism, nihilism was a response not to a crisis

of the body but to a crisis of (utopian) consciousness, a new type of crisis that occurred under, and despite, much improved material conditions. Utopianism originated in a qualitative rise *in* consciousness precipitated by a crisis of the body, whose freedom from bondage was projected by utopian consciousness into the future, as well as in a qualitative rise *of* consciousness, in that utopian consciousness demanded much more than the mere solution of the original crisis of the body. Utopianism failed not because it had failed to solve the original crisis of the body (which had been effectively alleviated if not completely solved), but because it had failed to satisfy the utopian consciousness that derived from the original crisis of the body, the demand for wholesale emancipation. The failure of utopianism was experienced not as a return of the original crisis of the body but as a new crisis of the spirit, not as a threat to livelihood but as the loss of meaning — as nihilism.

What made matters even worse was that the crisis of consciousness was accompanied by a new crisis of the body. The utopian project, although it fell far short of its grand aims, did succeed in raising the vast majority of people above the old threshold of poverty and misery, but utopian consciousness succeeded no less in raising that very threshold. People were patient enough not to step over this new threshold only as long as they believed they would do so in the future. They were ready, in other words, to practice ascetic virtues and suppress their hedonistic urges in return for better things to come. But the more they practiced asceticism, the more they expected in return, and the more urgent and expansive became their hedonism. As it turned out, better things either did not arrive or came in quantities too small to appease the hugely expanded desires. When with one disappointment after another utopian consciousness finally evaporated, asceticism evaporated with it, for asceticism had all the while derived its solidity solely from the anticipation, however temporarily sublimated, of future returns. Hedonism, now thoroughly de-sublimated from utopianism, returned with a vengeance — in a world with neither enough pleasure to satisfy the newly unleashed hedonism nor enough meaning to inspire the rapidly dying asceticism. For the first time since 1949 there loomed a crisis of both body and consciousness, with neither enough pleasure for the one nor enough meaning for the other, a crisis that culminated in the great political upheaval of 1989. As the tumult subsided, however, so did the crisis of the body. Hedonism, up till then thwarted by both ideology and lack of opportunity, found itself in a new world, artificially created by a desperate regime, which offered ever-expanding opportunities for sensual gratification and imposed no ideological hindrances to such gratification. There remained only the crisis of consciousness, but most soon forgot even that crisis in their scramble for wealth and pleasure.

For those who cannot so easily forget, however, consciousness, under these circumstances, can move from utopianism to nihilism but no further. And once consciousness has traversed the path from utopianism to nihilism, it takes on the unique character of a doubly negative consciousness: consciousness at once of what is not and of what will not be. In its inherently negative character — its character as the experience of pain (Nietzsche), absence (Schopenhauer), or loss (Laozi) — consciousness is in the first instance an awareness of what *is* not. But although consciousness is inherently unhappy, its unhappiness is made bearable by a derivative consciousness, that is, consciousness of the future, which is positive and which takes the form of a belief in what will be. The doubly negative consciousness that we find at the end of the journey from utopianism to nihilism consists in the annihilation of the almost inherently positive character of derivative consciousness. Paradoxically, this violence to the positive character of future-consciousness (i.e., consciousness of the future) is committed not by purposely reducing its positive character but by intentionally raising it to its highest possible level, from which a fall is both more likely and more painful. It is indeed, as Schopenhauer says, "remarkable how, through the addition of thought which the animal lacks, so lofty and vast a structure of human happiness and unhappiness is raised on the same narrow basis of joys and sorrows which the animal also has."[18]

This is all the more true of utopian consciousness, where consciousness is raised to the level of a grand and precise teleology. In Hegel, as to some extent in Laozi and Zhuangzi on the one hand and in Vico, Adam Smith, and Kant on the other, this grand teleology, purpose, or design is the business of the Dao, Spirit, Reason, the invisible hand, or History and not of the individual human agent,[19] except when it falls to the philosopher to reflect on the operation of these impersonal agents after the event. In fact, something of the same distinction between subjective intention and objective teleology is present in Marxism, in the idea of false consciousness. Engels sounded remarkably like Hegel when he wrote: "The many individual wills active in history for the most part produce results quite other than those intended — often quite the opposite; *their motives, therefore, in relation to the total result are likewise of only secondary importance*. On the other hand, the further question arises: *what driving forces in turn stand behind these motives? What are the historical causes which transform themselves into these motives in the brain of the actors?*"[20] But everything is changed when the attempt is made to raise, through education, what Lukács calls the "psychological class consciousness" (class consciousness as it actually is) of the proletariat to the level of "imputed class consciousness"[21] (class consciousness as it objectively ought to be) — that is, to make the objective design (Spirit, Reason, History, or whatever) part of subjective consciousness and even subjective intention.

This undoing of the Hegelian distinction—we may also call this the correction of "false consciousness" or the subjective appropriation of the "cunning of reason"—is a courageous act on behalf of human dignity. But this places so much weight on human reason and goodness that human nature as it has evolved up to now cannot adequately support it. Thus what in the Hegelian conception is a disparity between Spirit and individual human consciousness becomes in Marxism a contradiction within human consciousness. The dignity Marxism imparts to human beings in effect turns them into gods, who then find the work of their human selves wanting. And they then become nihilistic and cynical, unable either to keep their godlike idealism or ever again to return to their human, all too human selves, which were devoid of great purposes but which were also spared great despair. Utopianism, not surprisingly, is the shortest route to nihilism. Thus it comes to pass that, whereas in Hegel (as in Vico, Adam Smith, and Kant), "in history an additional result is commonly produced by human actions beyond that which they aim at and obtain — that which they immediately recognize and desire"[22] (though perhaps not much beyond), in the consciousness and practice of Marxism results invariably fall below human aims. Sadly, the undoing of the Hegelian distinction has not reduced the distance between reality and ideal in practice but only in theory. And as long as reality and ideal fail to move closer in practice, the raising of the one to the level of the other in consciousness is not only theoretically untenable but also practically disastrous. When only human consciousness but not reality has been raised, both reality and consciousness will be experienced as so much the worse.

However, it is not much comfort to know that if we "gratify [our] own interest," "something further is thereby accomplished, latent in the actions in question, though not present to [our] consciousness, and not included in [our] design,"[23] that if we keep our subjective intention at a low enough level, the objective will always turn out to be better than the subjective. Not only does this not unfailingly happen; it is, moreover, to borrow a phrase from Max Weber, a stigma of our human dignity that we have to aim so low in our human pursuits in order not to miss miserably, that we accomplish good things despite ourselves.

No less is it a stigma of our human dignity that in the long run heightened consciousness and heightened belief in the future are enemies of optimism. Consciousness of Reason, History, as of meaning in general, is consciousness at once of a deficiency in the present and of belief in the power of Reason or History to make good the deficiency in the future. The present deficiency is the existential ground of the need for meaning, and belief in the future satisfies that need. A political order that keeps itself in existence as the sole provider of meaning is therefore caught in a paradox: to the extent that the deficiency is removed so is the need for meaning, but to the extent that the deficiency is not removed belief in the meaning is undermined. Either result can be experienced as consciousness of the loss or lack of meaning. Once deficiency and meaning are joined together in a worldly project, meaning—and the political order based on this meaning—is permanently under threat from one direction or the other.

Consciousness can fail not only to meet its goals in external reality but also to satisfy its own standards. The latter is a function of what we may call the *dialectic of indoctrination*, namely, that every attempt at indoctrination is, in its very act of setting the mind in motion, at once an intentional attempt at mental enslavement and an unwitting promotion of enlightenment. The potential for enlightenment lies in the dual character of indoctrination: as a content on the one hand and as an activity on the other. Every attempt at indoctrination involves the raising of consciousness as an activity at the same time as it is aimed at the lowering of consciousness as content. Indeed, consciousness, as activity, is raised in order that consciousness, as content, may be lowered. In a profound reversal of the more benign functions of learning and thinking, people are made to learn to be stupid, to think so as to end up not being able to think at all. Herein lies a paradox that must make us marvel at how often this process succeeds but that may also help to explain why every indoctrination eventually proves self-defeating. The temporary success of indoctrination is subject to the inexorable law that raised consciousness as activity, although it may successfully for a time bring about lowered consciousness as content, will sooner or later lead to raised consciousness as content.

In the course of our daily activity, we form opinions and impressions, many of which we never seriously take the trouble to call into question. We often fail to examine our prejudices because we form these prejudices in a way that bypasses conscious formulation; thoughts that bypass conscious formulation tend for that very reason also to bypass conscious criticism. This — the lowering of consciousness as content because of the lowering of consciousness as activity — is a natural force against enlightenment, to which indoctrination in its very character as organized mental enslavement can have no resort. For indoctrination is designed to make people accept consciously what they would not accept unconsciously, to make people believe under pressure what they would not believe of their own free will. Thus it is that every attempt at indoctrination involves the raising of consciousness as an activity at the same time as it is aimed at the lowering of consciousness as content. Indoctrination, for this reason, is always an uphill struggle against the mind, and always follows the path of most resistance.

It is in the nature of indoctrination that it must take the visible form of imposition. A visible idea is presented through a visible procedure for visible acceptance under the visible threat of sanction. Both the form and the content of indoctrination are conspicuously present to the raised consciousness. If this raised consciousness does not, however, immediately find the form conspicuously coercive and the content conspicuously stupid, it will in time. Sooner or later, by virtue of its ineluctable visibility indoctrination will invite resistance. In openly laying down doctrines for people to believe and to follow, indoctrination also sets up a visible, potential target for people not to believe and not to follow, to think against and to act against.

This potential target sooner or later becomes an actual target, because the very logic of indoctrination ensures that the need for indoctrination is in inverse proportion to the willingness to accept it. Because it always implies the existence of something to be indoctrinated against, indoctrination is always, at some level of consciousness of those subjected to it, a painful process, and where there is pain, there is the potential for thought and resistance.

What temporarily prevents this potential — and the logic of consciousness — from becoming active — what prevents enlightenment about indoctrination — is not the content or manner of indoctrination but what makes indoctrination possible in the first place, namely, the narcotization of consciousness under the charisma of a leader or the spell of an idea. It is only when consciousness is narcotized that it can be mobilized against itself, that it can be activated to be paralyzed, that it can be raised in order to be lowered. In indoctrination as in nowhere else, the raising of consciousness and its narcotization go hand in hand. The extent to which consciousness is raised is precisely a measure of the extent to which it is intended to be lowered. The forced raising of consciousness is nothing but the razing of unconscious resistance — resistance to ideas that have no intrinsic appeal. Since indoctrination raises consciousness in order to lower it, its appeal cannot lie in its own intelligence or even in its intelligibility. Indoctrination is always believed despite itself. But that indoctrination can be believed despite itself, that it can travel along the path of most resistance, and that it can wage an uphill struggle against the mind — this points to a force stronger than that of raised consciousness. This force lies in the charisma of a leader or the spell of a promise, which alone can perform the miracle of turning a profound contradiction — that consciousness is raised in order to be lowered — into a profound fact of political life. But for these narcotics of consciousness, raised consciousness as activity and lowered consciousness as content can never occur together, as they so miraculously do in the process of successful indoctrination.

By the same token, every awakening from these narcoses of consciousness will bring into direct contact the two components of indoctrination — raised consciousness as activity and lowered consciousness as content — that have been kept apart by the charisma of a leader or the spell of an idea. And wakefulness is bound to occur because our drugged consciousness cannot sleep peacefully when we are in pain. Once sleep ends, raised consciousness takes revenge — not only against lowered consciousness as content but also against the narcotics of consciousness. The effects of indoctrination are undone by its own logic when raised consciousness as activity, now free of its narcotics, sees through lowered consciousness as content and refuses to believe it any longer. Indoctrination, which has until now worked despite its logic, now fails because of that very logic. Paradoxically, the road from enslavement to enlightenment is paved with indoctrination.

Much of this enlightenment, or half enlightenment, however, takes place within the framework of indoctrination, since it is the only framework that has been allowed to exist. Within this framework one portion of the content of indoctrination may be turned against another, as when science was enlisted in the intellectual discrediting of sinified Marxism. The accentuation of consciousness in Mao's China involved not only the utopianization of consciousness but also, in large part because utopianism needed to be dressed up as science, the scientization of consciousness. Eventually, scientific consciousness, or the scientific conscience, carried to its logical limits, helped to discredit utopian consciousness and sinified Marxism. It did this by applying standards cultivated as part of the intellectual orthodoxy. The victory in this case, however, was rather ambiguous. For the rather dogmatic standards of science, as they had been inculcated within the framework of indoctrination, seldom if ever were questioned, least of all the scientism that had been an important part of this indoctrination. Following the disenchantment with utopianism, scientism, now purged of political fanaticism, came to flourish in a less politically charged but even more insidious form.

At work here is not so much enlightenment as the transferability of states of consciousness from one object to another, with Marxism made the object of a mode of consciousness — scientific consciousness — that was not meant to be applied to Marxism, whose scientific character was regarded as beyond question. The encouragement of scientific skepticism in regard to all other forms of thought finally turned into skepticism against sinified Marxism itself. What happened here on the intellectual level can also happen on the level of emotion and temperament. For years the government had, through its program of indoctrination, fostered hatred and resentment against all sorts of enemies, raising these negative feelings to a pitch and pervasiveness almost unknown in Chinese history, only to find itself the object of such sentiments once the political climate changed. But the transfer of states of consciousness, themselves fostered within the framework of indoctrination, from one object to another, whether on the emotional or on the intellectual level, is not yet enlightenment, even if it is carried out against forces that stand in the way of emancipation.

Just as unavoidably as it works against itself, indoctrination takes its toll. To the extent that enlightenment follows indoctrination as the fulfillment of the latter's logic, it cannot but bear traces of its journey. The resulting enlightenment is, in the first instance, enlightenment only about the visible manifestations of indoctrination. More destructive than generative, it is the revenge of raised consciousness, itself having been brought into play by indoctrination, against the visible content and the visible perpetrator of indoctrination. But enlightenment about and from indoctrination is not yet enlightenment into truth or goodness, which requires more than the mere negation of indoctrination. Nor, even, does enlightenment about indoctrination lead to complete emancipation from mental enslavement by the old order. Wakefulness from indoctrination is always only a partial wakefulness, because indoctrination is always only the tip of a huge iceberg that enslaves our body and soul beneath the surface of our consciousness. But the uncoupling of raised consciousness as activity from lowered consciousness as content is the first step out of the prison house of mental enslavement. Once raised consciousness is disenchanted, the body in pain will push it in the direction of enlightenment. Unfortunately, half-enlightenment, as a mere seeing through, can lead to mindless hedonism, and even genuine enlightenment, when it cannot be translated into practice, can turn into cynicism and mere cunning.

Conclusion

With the movement from utopianism to hedonism, the journey of Chinese communism has come full circle. In hedonism, utopianism returned to its pure, de-sublimated form, although de-sublimation occurred not entirely through fulfillment, as envisioned in utopianism, but only partly through fulfillment (that is, the improvement of material conditions) and partly through nihilism. There is yet another sense in which the circle has been completed. As long as utopianism existed as the idealistic form of hedonism, there was always the possibility that the idealistic form could, as during the Cultural Revolution, detach itself from its hedonistic content and become the vehicle of other ends. Now that utopianism has divested itself of its idealistic form, that possibility too has been removed. This means that the completion of the circle of utopianism and hedonism removes the spiritual resources for breaking out of it.

Thus as far as human volition, as opposed to material possibility, is concerned, hedonism is here to stay — the more so because utopianism itself was a training ground for hedonism. What little potential opposition to hedonism utopianism contained was merely a function of its idealistic form, and that idealistic form was in turn merely contingent upon temporary conditions of poverty and what turned out to be a passing faith in communism. Except for its contingent idealistic form, utopianism, itself merely hedonism sublimated, contained no resources for transcending hedonism. Once improved material conditions and nihilism had combined to divest utopianism of its idealistic form, what was left of utopianism was hedonism pure and simple. Not only did hedonism thus come to the fore, it did so with a vengeance, thanks to the simultaneous accumulation of desire and weakening of stamina caused by prolonged postponement of satisfaction and prolonged exertion in the utopian project. As the very essence of utopianism, hedonism could only be sublimated but could not be removed as long as one remains within the paradigm of utopianism itself. On the level of intellectual or spiritual resources, the negation of hedonism, as opposed to its temporary sublimation, presupposes a radically different conception of ends.

Some such conception of ends, originating in the Confucian tradition, survived into communist China. The intellectualism of the Confucian scholastic tradition, with its elevation of moral and intellectual values over material interests, had rested on the sharp division of mental and manual labor and on the prospect of official positions, with material advantages, through education. The fragments of Confucian intellectualism carried over into communist China, however, survived in an increasingly disembodied form, as the link between education and socioeconomic status became more and more tenuous, first under Mao Zedong and then, in a different way, after Mao's death. Under Mao Zedong, intellectual values were made subject, to a blatant degree, to political dictates and came, as values in their own right, under repeated criticism as remnants of Confucian elitism. In the gradual movement toward a market economy that occurred after Mao's death, intellectualism underwent yet another devaluation, but this time through the instrumentalization, as opposed to the politicization, of education. Whereas the old Confucian education hypocritically opposed hedonism directly and served hedonism indirectly, education in post-Mao China is valued directly, and unashamedly, for its potential to bring tangible material rewards. With the almost complete removal, at long last, of Confucian intellectualism through its twofold devaluation, there no longer exist any significant indigenous cultural resources for the negation of hedonism.

In the absence of any intellectual or cultural forces in the way of hedonism, the fate of hedonism and, with it, the foreseeable future of China will depend not on the choice of values but on the technical management of human and material resources. On the battleground of values, hedonism has already carried the day. If hedonism fails, it will be a *practical* failure, a failure of technical management caused by human incompetence or unfavorable material circumstances. At this practical level, hedonism may even be derailed by political forces that are not opposed to hedonism but whose vested interests may conflict with the new distribution of power and pleasure caused by hedonism. In terms of its politics and economics, hedonism is embroiled in far too many imponderables to have a readily predictable future.

The chances are, however, that, barring major economic setbacks, hedonism will continue to flourish. This means that hedonism, now awkwardly accommodated by remnants of the old institutions of sublimation, will not only be increasingly promoted by hedonistic ideology but also be more and more embodied in institutions of consumerism. As long as the need for sublimation — the source of all politics — keeps being reduced, the problematic of Chinese society will shift more and more from political control to technical management. The role of normative considerations will, accordingly, shrink more and more, although it is likely that in due course traditional values from the precommunist past will be brought back, in a duly domesticated and nonsubversive form, for the sake of cultural pride and distinctiveness in an otherwise homogeneous global culture of hedonism. To be sure, this new China will have its own problems, perhaps not unlike those now encountered in Western societies, but these problems, short of drastically increasing the necessity of sublimation, will belong to the new problematic. Solutions to them will be sought technically, that is, within hedonism. It would take a significant rise in the necessity of sublimation for at least a sizable minority — that is, a management crisis of hedonism — for hedonism to be called into question. But even then it is highly unlikely that utopianism will make a comeback.

Once utopianism has been de-sublimated into hedonism, it is hard to see how hedonism can be sublimated again into utopianism. The sublimation of hedonism into utopianism, let us remind ourselves, was made necessary by poverty and made possible by faith in communism. Both conditions have now been lost or significantly weakened, the first through improvement in material conditions, the second through nihilism. While both conditions obtained, it was utopianism, that is, hedonism in its sublimated form, rather than hedonism itself that was the object of consciousness. Those whose hedonism had been sublimated into utopianism did not know their hedonism for what it was, since they had never experienced hedonism as actuality and even lacked the desire for hedonism inasmuch as they did not believe it to be feasible. Communism gave them that belief, but at the exact same moment the belief in communism made them conscious of their latent hedonism, it made that hedonism latent again by sublimating it into utopianism, under material conditions that necessitated sublimation anyway. Because hedonism was thus experienced only in the form of utopianism, utopianism was not experienced as an imposition, as the frustration or deprivation of a previously existing hedonism. Now that hedonism has come to the fore in a situation of nihilism and improved material conditions, however, it will take more than a worsening of material conditions to bring back utopianism. For although poverty rendered sublimation necessary, it was faith in communism that had made sublimation, and hence utopianism, possible. Now that nihilism has destroyed faith in communism, with no new faith likely to take its place, a change in material conditions for the worse will not sublimate hedonism but only frustrate and sour it.

As long as nihilism continues, with or without the material conditions that make its merging into hedonism possible, it will carry with it bad memories of utopianism. Indeed, nihilism takes the form of negative and inhibiting memories. As a living record of false hopes and disillusionment, of what has been tried and found wanting, nihilism — the collective negative memory of utopianism — will have the power to inhibit for a long time to come. What nihilism did to utopianism was to separate its spirit and its institutional form. Once the spirit of utopianism, that is, faith in communism, had died, what was left was only the institutional form of utopianism, which on its own was no different from, and came for the first time to be experienced as, enforced sublimation, as totalitarianism. It is this retrospective association of utopianism with totalitarianism that has, more than anything else, given utopianism a bad name as not only practically infeasible but also morally insupportable. As long as this association is retained in collective memory, utopianism can only be imposed. But what is imposed cannot be utopianism, which is above all spirit, but only the institutional form of utopianism.

Many of the old institutions of utopianism, now institutions of sheer authoritarianism in the absence of the utopian spirit, have indeed survived in one form or another, and one cannot rule out circumstances in which they may once again be enforced to the point of totalitarianism. But if it is impossible, from a logical point of view, to bring back utopianism in the absence of faith, it is almost impossible, from a practical point of view, to maintain totalitarianism for long without utopianism. For totalitarianism is hard to sustain once it is experienced as totalitarianism, as China's own experience shows. For the better part of Mao Zedong's rule, totalitarianism was made all but invisible—that is, subjectively invisible—through the internalization of utopianism. Now that utopianism itself has been discredited, it can no longer serve as a cover for totalitarianism, and except for patriotism, which would be a poor substitute except under conditions of war, there does not seem to be anything capable of taking its place. Until a suitable substitute can be found, totalitarianism, even if it could be maintained for a while, would be a far cry from the totalitarianism of the Mao era. Collective memory will see to that.

Insofar as we can make sense of the past, we are in a position to suggest what the past, as it resonates in collective memory, makes likely or improbable in the foreseeable future. As a living record of success and failure, of joy and pain, of what has been tried and what has not, memory has the power to motivate and to inhibit, and hence the power to make certain things likely in the future and other things improbable. Both for better and for worse, many of the things described in these pages will not happen again for a long time.

REFERENCE MATTER

Notes

Chinese names are spelled in accordance with the *pinyin* system, with the exception of names, such as Confucius, that are so well-established in some other form that difficulty of recognition would result from the *pinyin* rendering. In some borderline cases, for example, Wang Bi (Wang Pi), I have given the name in *pinyin* first and then in some other, perhaps more familiar form in brackets. For complete author names, titles, and publication data for works cited here in short form only, see the Works Cited, pp. 269–74.

Introduction

1. One popular catchphrase, though wildly hyperbolic and, for the sake of linguistic effect, not quite accurate about the total population figure, captures China's present ethos well. Out of a population of one billion, it goes, nine hundred million have set up shop as businessmen, and the remaining one hundred million are poised to follow suit (*shiyi renmin jiuyi shang, haiyou yiyi dai kaizhang*).

2. Unless otherwise indicated, explicitly or by context, the term *utopian project* or *utopianism* is used, throughout this book, to cover the *entire* period of Maoism (1949–76), although this period was not uniformly utopian in temper from beginning to end. The Great Leap Forward of 1958–60 and the Cultural Revolution of 1966–76 may have been, in different ways, the two most fanatically utopian periods of Chinese communism, but the history of Maoist China is recognizably utopian as a totality distinct both from what preceded it and from what was to follow.

3. Of the three basic categories used in this book, only utopian-

ism rings at all familiar in the Chinese context. The other two categories, nihilism and hedonism, sound alien, perhaps even farfetched, as they are applied to China. In a sense this is only to be expected, since nihilism and particularly hedonism, or their equivalents in Chinese, have seldom if ever been used as categories to encapsulate recent Chinese experience. But then the experience to which I apply the categories of nihilism and hedonism has itself seldom been made the object of theoretical reflection. There is an urgent need to remedy this situation, a need at once to reflect upon the experience and to find the most appropriate categories with which to do so. Nihilism and hedonism, more than any other categories I can think of, meet this need well, as long as we keep in mind that they are but a shorthand for experiences that need to be described, not just named.

4. If it is also true of the Chinese situation that nihilism affected different people and different groups to different degrees, this is attributable not to differences in their intellectual capacities but to variations in their enthusiasm for utopianism, the psychological antecedent of nihilism. And the response to utopianism was far from being primarily determined by one's trained capacity for informed reflection, a capacity intellectuals as a group may possess more than any other group. For intellectuals and non-intellectuals alike in a situation of nihilism, what has gone wrong is a whole way of life, of which intellectual reflection is only a small part.

Chapter 1

1. This statement touches on problems with the term *modern* as it applies to Chinese history, the nature and degree of the "Western impact," and the significance of the Opium War. On the question of the "Western impact," I would readily agree with Paul A. Cohen that "it would be safer and more productive to think in terms of Western-influenced responses to Western-influenced situations, the degree of Western influence at both ends varying from case to case" (p. 54). One does not, however, have to believe, if anybody ever did, that everything of moment that has happened in China since 1840 has been the result of the "Western impact" to recognize that this impact has profoundly altered the subsequent course of Chinese history. The matter is all the more beyond question if we include Marxism (as I will show we should) as part

(though not just part) of the "Western impact" and if we view the "Western impact" as an ongoing causal chain — direct or indirect, conscious or unconscious, immediate or long-term — whose further links time has yet to reveal. In this light, we can assign to the Opium War a retrospective significance that it would not have had by itself and that was little appreciated by the Chinese themselves until much later, until, that is, the Opium War could be seen in retrospect as the beginning of a prolonged process of enforced "modernization" or "modernization" under pressure — a process that is still unfolding. And once we view the Opium War in this light, it is not inappropriate to see the period of Chinese history that began with the Opium War as "modern," whatever moral and political evaluation we may then wish to attach to the term.

2. This distinction, in its genesis in a third-century A.D. commentary by Wang Bi (Wang Pi) on the *Dao de jing* and in its subsequent use in Buddhism and Neo-Confucianism, is *metaphysical* in character, and the customary translation of these terms as "substance" or "essence" on the one hand and "application" or "operation" or "function" on the other more or less adequately captures the metaphysical thrust of the distinction. However, when this metaphysical distinction became embedded, at the hands of certain nineteenth-century reformers, in the slogan *Zhongxue weiti, xixue weiyong* (coined by Zhang Zhidong, following an idea most forcefully advocated by Feng Guifen), it acquired a *political* meaning and exercised a *political* impact it had never had before. In this new context, the standard rendition of the old metaphysical distinction is no longer adequate, despite important continuities between the old distinction and the new, and terms such as value vs. technology, ends vs. means, may suggest something of the spirit of the new political use of the old metaphysical distinction. The comment that the integrity of the traditional Chinese order had never allowed room for the *ti-yong* distinction refers to the distinction in its political and pragmatic aspects. Beyond this brief clarification, it is neither my purpose nor to my purpose to give an account of the contexts and nuances of the *ti-yong* concept as it took on a new meaning and a new life in the nineteenth and early twentieth centuries. For one such account, see Li, pp. 311–41. For the present argument, the nineteenth-century version of *ti-yong* is significant as a symptom of a profound cultural crisis and a new crisis mentality, which in a different or not so different form are still with us. I

use the *ti-yong* concept as a symptom of, and sometimes as a shorthand for, this general crisis as it has developed from the mid-nineteenth century to our own time and epitomized the mentality of a people, many of whom have not themselves explicitly formulated the matter in this way.

3. Joseph R. Levenson, "The Past and Future of Nationalism in China," in idem, *Modern China*, p. 5.

4. In the eyes of many, however, what happened is what ought by rights to have happened. Ray Huang reflects the mood of many Chinese, on the mainland as well as overseas, when, making a glorious virtue of necessity, he writes: "In the closing decades of the twentieth century, when a one-world history is needed, we cannot see how the story of capitalism, synchronizing the establishment of banks in Venice, Amsterdam, and London with the rise of the Italian Renaissance, the Northern Renaissance, and the English Renaissance, can be divorced from the study of Chinese history. In a rather crude but quite straightforward manner, we can say that Chinese history since the Opium War is a series of continual efforts at readjustment to meet this challenge. The settlement that we have in mind is essentially a merger of China's cultural tradition, developed on a huge continent, with this oceanic influence" (p. 241).

5. Adorno, p. 18.

6. *Gangchang mingjiao* refers to the totality of Confucian morals and rituals governing the behavior of individuals and the relationships among them. Specifically, *gang*, of which there are three, lays down a relationship of subordination of subject to sovereign, son to father, and wife to husband. *Chang*, often coupled with *gang* in the formula *sangang wuchang* (three *gang* and five *chang*), refers to the five virtues of *ren* (benevolence), *yi* (righteousness), *li* (propriety), *zhi* (wisdom), and *xin* (faithfulness). Together the three *gang* and five *chang* make up the Confucian moral code, whose tenor, as shown in the phrase *mingjiao*, is one of hierarchical distinctions and ritual correctness.

7. I realize that the near-personification of China here and elsewhere and the reference to China as a single psychological entity are in danger of implying a homogeneity of consciousness that has never in fact existed. Although I would certainly wish to avoid this implication, my aim, in a study conducted at this degree of generality, is to sketch out the broad commonality of consciousness and

circumstance, insofar as it has existed in the period covered here, rather than to do justice to regional, social, and other variations.

8. When we speak of the place of the Chinese tradition in Chinese consciousness, we must be careful to distinguish between the tradition as an object of conscious appraisal and the tradition as an unconscious influence on behavior, perhaps (very loosely speaking) even as the collective cultural unconscious. As is to be expected, the tradition has exercised on the people of modern China an unconscious influence that far outlasts their conscious acceptance of the tradition. Indeed, their conscious rejection of the tradition may reflect not only their perception of its observable effects but also their instinctive resistance to its hold on their unconscious.

9. Compare Nietzsche's concepts of "monumental history" and "antiquarian history" in "On the Uses and Disadvantages of History for Life," in *Untimely Meditations*.

10. Lin, p. 47.

11. Compare Deleuze, p. 39: "In Nietzsche consciousness is always the consciousness of an inferior in relation to a superior to which he is subordinated or into which he is 'incorporated.' Consciousness is never self-consciousness, but the consciousness of an ego in relation to a self which is not itself conscious. It is not the master's consciousness but the slave's consciousness in relation to a master who is not himself conscious. 'Consciousness usually only appears when a whole wants to subordinate itself to a superior whole.... Consciousness is born in relation to a being of which we could be a function.'" Compare Hegel's account of the self-consciousness of the Bondsman in *Phenomenology of Spirit*, pp. 111–19.

12. Thus, for example, the "master" as Nietzsche conceives of him strives to make, or to keep, the "slave" as *different* as possible from himself. In contrast to this "master" mentality, the desire to make others like oneself would be seen by Nietzsche as betraying precisely a "slave" mentality. See *On the Genealogy of Morals*, "First Essay." I suspect that a "master" who appears to be trying to make the "slave" like himself really enjoys not the slave's becoming like the master but rather the slave's trying and failing to become like the master. In this way, the master has his superiority doubly confirmed: by the slave's desire to become like the master and by the slave's inability to do so.

252 Notes to Pages 47–52

13. Conceptually reaction is defined by contrast with action. But descriptively reaction need not be viewed as a response to action properly so called (say, in a Nietzschean sense); all it presupposes is a certain stimulus, with the status of a given, which may itself be a reaction to some other stimulus. But the stimulus, in its very power to constitute a significant and sustained focus in relation to which action (that is, reaction) is oriented (that is, reoriented), has to come from a stronger force, so that what counts as reaction is a function of a relationship of unequal power between two parties, of which the party inferior in the relevant respect of power is characterized in terms of reaction vis-à-vis the stronger party.

14. The history of communist China is a compelling counterexample to Samir Amin's overoptimistic generalization that "in societies that have successfully made a popular national revolution (usually termed a 'socialist revolution'), the dialectic of internal factors once again takes on a decisive role" (p. 143). In the case of China, a large part of the "dialectic of internal factors" was brought in by Marxism in the first place.

15. Compare Deleuze, p. 39.

16. For the concepts of world-mastery and world-adjustment, see Weber, *Religion of China*, p. 248.

17. In addition, with the paradigm-shift from world-adjustment to world-mastery, what Herbert Marcuse calls the "performance principle" and "surplus repression" — terms coined by Marcuse to designate those sociohistorical manifestations of Freud's "reality principle" and "repression" that apply specifically to capitalism — came to characterize China's practice of socialism no less aptly than they do capitalism. Under the performance principle, Marcuse argues, "Efficiency and repression converge: raising the productivity of labor is the sacrosanct ideal of both capitalist and Stalinist Stakhanovism" (*Eros and Civilization*, p. 156). This applies equally to Mao's rationale of "Grasp revolution, promote production" (*zhuageming, cushengchan*), which exhibits a symptomatic ambiguity as to which is the means and which the end.

18. See "Dogmatism, Reason, and Decision," in Habermas, *Theory and Practice*; and "Technology and Science as 'Ideology,'" in Habermas, *Toward a Rational Society*.

19. Wallerstein, p. 40.

20. "Science as a Vocation," in Weber, *From Max Weber*, p. 144.

21. During the Cultural Revolution, few people received the honor of "revolutionary role model" unless they were also role models in the field of "production." A few such super-production role models even ended up in the prestigious Central Committee of the Chinese Communist party.

22. This is not to say that the Cultural Revolution or similar events were purely, or even chiefly, aimed at the promotion of "production." If "revolution" and "production" were both ends up to a point, it certainly seems that they were made subservient to more important ends, which we may sum up by saying that Mao both wanted himself to be the center of China and wanted China to be the center of the world.

23. There is almost a pattern that runs through modern Chinese history. From the Self-Strengthening movement in 1860's and 1870's through the Hundred Days' Reform of 1898 to the May Fourth movement of 1919, China's attempt to imitate the West moved from surface to depth, from technology to institutions and values, *from means to ends*. Then almost the same cycle was repeated after 1949, a cycle that neither the Cultural Revolution nor even the 1989 crackdown on the democracy movement was able to halt for long. There is invariably a movement, propelled by the momentum issuing from the adoption of Western technology, toward the adoption of Western values, but each time just before or when the adoption of Western ends is seriously under way, entrenched interests intervene and try to take everything back to square one. But after the Tiananmen massacre, the entrenched interests were left with an alternative to Westernization that had been thoroughly discredited.

24. It is hard to see how a nation can shake off its spiritual exhaustion unless a future beckons—a future that, to serve as a goad to the effort required to rebuild China not only economically but also spiritually, has to be seen as at once approachable and open-ended. The only future that China's exhausted vision can now reach, however, is the *present* of the West. That future may be approachable, but it is anything but open-ended. The future is at once a temporal and a conceptual construct. Where the only urge is to make the self like the other, there is no conceptual future but only a temporal future, because the temporal future will at best

unfold a conceptual future that has already been realized, namely, as the present of the West. In the meantime, all you can do is to imitate, to make yourself like someone else. But there is one thing that cannot be imitated: creativity, and all that comes with it, the sense of excitement, of unpredictability, of making history. Which is why the copy is always poorer in spirit than the original, even though it may look as good or even better. There is an objective side as well as a subjective side to the performing of a deed. When the deed is one of imitation, there is a loss in subjective meaning that no amount of objective success can compensate for. This is also true of the imitation of cultures.

We are concerned here with cultural self-respect not only as a value but also as a motivating or enabling state of consciousness. If we grant that a certain degree of cultural pride is a necessary motivating or enabling factor in the growth of a culture, we may further suggest that cultural pride requires a certain degree of ignorance of other cultures. Granted both of these observations, too much knowledge of the West may well prove to be to China's disadvantage.

John Hall writes: "A society . . . usually operates with knowledge of the possibilities revealed by other societies" (p. 11), as if such knowledge is always an advantage! A society can equally operate with knowledge of the *impossibilities* (or what appear to be such) revealed by other societies. Worse still, a society can operate with a sense of the impossibility of realizing the possibilities revealed by other societies. The West is in the first category, with regard to the ideal of communism. Many "developing countries" may be in the second, with regard to the ideal of capitalism. Both are deprived of the "delight in blindness" (Nietzsche, *Gay Science*, aphorism 287). This is probably the worst possible outcome of the contest between socialism and capitalism.

25. Ray Huang writes in his "macro history" of China: "It would be judged lunatic if anyone had . . . dared to predict that *only to put monetary management into effect*, China was yet to see Chiang's five suppression campaigns against the Communists, the CCP's Long March, the Xi'an Incident, the war against Japan for eight years, another civil war that lasted more than four years, and then a decade of turmoil called the Great Proletarian Cultural Revolution" (p. 231; my italics). Lunatic indeed, yet this is precisely the trajectory that the "cunning of reason" has guided. For

these events taken together do exhibit a certain "logic" that seems to have got the better of the intentions of the historical actors. In this regard, Alexandre Kojève showed his foresight when, long before China's Cultural Revolution, he saw the handwriting on the wall: "Now, several voyages of comparison made (between 1948 and 1958) to the United States and the U.S.S.R. gave me the impression that if the Americans give the appearance of rich Sino-Soviets, it is because the Russians and the Chinese are only Americans who are still poor but are rapidly proceeding to get richer. I was led to conclude from this that the 'American way of life' was the type of life specific to the post-historical period, the actual presence of the United States in the world prefiguring the 'eternal present' future of all of humanity" (p. 161*n*). In this context also, Kojève's apparently farfetched remark that "the Chinese revolution is nothing but the introduction of the Napoleonic code into China" (cited in Lilla, p. 3) makes sense.

Chapter 2

1. Benjamin, p. 255.
2. This formulation is borrowed from B. J. Smith, p. 73.
3. See Connerton, p. 12: "The more total the aspirations of the new regime, the more imperiously will it seek to introduce an era of forced forgetting."
4. Nietzsche, *On the Genealogy of Morals*, II, 3. In keeping with common practice, Nietzsche is cited by section or aphorism number rather than page number, unless otherwise indicated.
5. Benjamin, p. 255.
6. See the still informative study by Lifton, pp. 379, 390–92. On this, as well as on the general theme of memory and amnesia in twentieth-century China, see the thought-provoking article by Schwarcz.
7. Douglas, p. 76.
8. Ibid., p. 69.
9. Nietzsche, *Twilight of the Idols*, III, 5.
10. Douglas, p. 72.
11. Halbwachs, p. 78.
12. Marcuse, *Eros and Civilization*, p. 37.
13. Vološinov, pp. 88–89.
14. See ibid., p. 89.

15. Santayana, 1: 22.
16. Vološinov, p. 89.
17. Compare Nietzsche, *On the Genealogy of Morals*, II, 16, 22.
18. See Vološinov, pp. 89–90.
19. See Žižek, pp. 146–47.
20. *Laozi*, chap. 20, in Chan, p. 149.
21. This use of history is not unlike what Nietzsche calls "monumental history." See Nietzsche, "On the Uses and Disadvantages of History for Life," in *Untimely Meditations*, p. 69: "Of what use, then, is the monumentalist conception of the past, engagement with the classic and rare of earlier times, to the man of the present? He learns from it that the greatness that once existed was in any event once *possible* and may thus be possible again; he goes his way with more cheerful step, for the doubt which assailed him in weaker moments, whether he was not perhaps desiring the impossible, has now been banished."
22. Ibid., p. 76.
23. Nietzsche, *On the Genealogy of Morals*, II, 15.
24. Nietzsche, *Thus Spoke Zarathustra*, p. 141.
25. Nietzsche, *On the Genealogy of Morals*, II, 15.
26. See Douglas, pp. 73–74.
27. See Shils, p. 167.
28. Connerton, p. 102.
29. Habermas, *Legitimation Crisis*, p. 43.
30. For the idea that certain memory-traces are "often most powerful and most enduring when the process which left them behind was one which never entered consciousness," see Freud, *Beyond the Pleasure Principle*, pp. 24–25.
31. For a view that regards Aristotle as intending a real conceptual distinction between the two Greek verbs for "to remember," see Krell, chap. 1.
32. The very apt phrase "unknown memories" is taken from ibid., p. 108.
33. Nietzsche, *On the Genealogy of Morals*, II, 1.
34. Breuer and Freud, p. 6. The passage cited is italicized in the original text by Breuer and Freud. See also Freud, "Remembering, Repeating and Working-Through."
35. Kierkegaard, *Either/Or*, 1: 242. It is seldom an entirely straightforward matter to quote without explanation from Kierke-

gaard's pseudonymous works, such as *Either/Or*. Problems may be compounded when it comes to quoting, as I am doing here as well as in the next paragraph of the text, from the aestheticist "A," whose outlook as a whole Kierkegaard rejects. In this particular case, however, I believe that the substance of what I am quoting from "A" fits in a perfectly straightforward manner into the context of this discussion, provided we take care to disregard the tone and purpose of his remarks.

36. Spinoza, *Ethics*, Part V, Prop. XLII, proof, p. 270. The analogy we are drawing here has to be understood in the context of Spinoza's identification of virtue with power (in his special sense of these terms) and his theory of the mind-body parallelism.

37. Santayana, 1: 184.

38. Freud, *Beyond the Pleasure Principle*.

39. Freud, "Remembering, Repeating and Working-Through," p. 151.

40. Kierkegaard, *Either/Or*, 1: 242. See note 35 to this chapter.

Chapter 3

1. For a fuller treatment of Dong Zhongshu's (Tung Chung-shu's) philosophy, see Fung, vol. 2, chap. 2. For an excellent concise account of the history of *sangang wuchang*, see Zhang, p. 5.

2. *Dao de jing*, chap. 38, in Chan, p. 158.

3. *Analects*, 2.3, in Chan, p. 22.

4. *Analects*, 2.3, in Chan, p. 22.

5. *Analects*, 12.1, in Chan, p. 38.

6. *Analects*, 1.12, in Chan, p. 21.

7. *Analects*, 4.5, in Chan, p. 26.

8. *Analects*, 7.29, in Chan, p. 33.

9. *Analects*, 8.9, in Chan, p. 33.

10. *Analects*, 12.19, in Chan, p. 40.

11. Before he became a committed revolutionary, Mao Zedong's moral outlook was dominated by individualism and realism. His belief in individualism, among other things, caused him to take up, successively or simultaneously, anarchism, romantic utopianism, and the idea of nonviolent yet radical change. At no point in his subsequent long career first as a rebel and then as a ruler did Mao show any evidence of giving up this early vision of individual-

ism *as it applied to himself*. But his realism, the twin of his individualism, did in due course lead him to abandon almost all the early manifestations and means of his individualism in favor of violent revolution with the aim of seizing power and establishing what he envisaged as the dictatorship of the proletariat. The needs and contingencies of that protracted revolution dictated the substance and form of the Communist party's wartime moral codes, of which Mao was the chief architect but which were a product more of the revolution than of Mao's personality. A good deal of useful information can be found in Liu; see esp. pp. 69, 129, 165–67, 174, 176.

12. Around communism as the code of belief there also gradually developed a meta-code: a meta-code because although it was made to carry a certain content, it also had the character of formal or theoretical constructions. No less than the code of conduct and the code of belief, this meta-code reflected the pressing needs of the revolution. A revolution needs a clear targeting of its enemies and friends: hence the morality of *antagonism*, which serves to distinguish good and bad people and prescribes love for the one and hate for the other. Enemies are defined not only in terms of "objective" social facts but, more important, for purposes of propaganda and the mobilization of antagonistic energy, in terms of intentions: hence the morality of *intentionalism*, with its postulation of evil intentions and evil personal traits in the enemy. On the other hand, since morality is designed to serve the purposes of revolution, results rather than intentions matter in the final analysis: hence the morality of *consequentialism*, or "revolutionary utilitarianism." The result is a combination of antagonism, intentionalism, and consequentialism (*wuchan jieji de dongji yu xiaoguo tongyilun*). The substance of these positions found its way into the code of belief, but their abstraction can also be seen to constitute a metacode.

13. Whatever the actual role of Marxism in the emergence of regimes that ruled in its name, there can be no question that the practice of what purports to be Marxism, in China and elsewhere, has done great violence and injustice to Marxism as it is contained in the writings of Marx himself. Nevertheless it remains a fact that these regimes, including the Chinese, refer to their doctrine as Marxism. Short of settling the extremely complicated question of the relationship between the theory and practice of Marxism, it

seems to me that the best policy, at least in the case of China, is to take a regime's description of itself as Marxist at face value, mindful that the regime's idea and practice of what it calls Marxism may relate to the Marxism of Marx himself in ways that range from relative fidelity to complete distortion or divergence.

14. See Liu, pp. 396–99, 402.

15. Mao, "Combat Liberalism," p. 32.

16. The authors of the most authoritative (that is, officially backed) recent textbook in ethics in China, predictably entitled *Makesi zhuyi lunlixue* (Marxist ethics), ed. Luo Guojie, deplore the lack of systematic Marxist ethics (p. 10) and emphasize the independence of ethics as a discipline (p. 9). In the absence of any evidence that the authors were trying indirectly to subvert the moral orthodoxy, this betrays a total misunderstanding of the nature and role of morality in communist China.

Chapter 4

1. From the point of view of such a practical outlook, the two modifiers commonly attached to materialism, namely dialectical and historical, have been of lesser consequence since they pertain for the most part to academic discourse.

2. Marx, *Economic and Philosophic Manuscripts of 1844*, p. 143. "All history," says Marx, "is the preparation for '*man*' to become the object of *sensuous* consciousness, and for the needs of 'man as man' to become [natural, sensuous] needs."

3. Introduction to ibid., p. 14.

4. Nietzsche, *Human, All Too Human*, vol. 2, pt. 2, 192. In keeping with common practice, Nietzsche is cited by section or aphorism number rather than page number unless otherwise indicated.

5. Kierkegaard, *Concluding Unscientific Postscript*, p. 426n.

6. Ibid.

7. The purposes of this inquiry do not require a full exposition of hedonism, within which we would need to distinguish, among other things, between hedonism as a theory of normative ethics and as a psychological theory of human motivation, between pleasure-oriented and prudence-oriented hedonism, and between self-regarding hedonism and the utilitarian version of hedonism that has the greatest happiness of the greatest number as its object.

8. Nietzsche, *Nietzsche Contra Wagner*, p. 670. A similar view is found at much greater length in Kierkegaard; see, e.g., *Concluding Scientific Postscript*, pp. 232–33, 422–23.

9. Kierkegaard, *Concluding Unscientific Postscript*, p. 423.

10. *Hongqi zazhi*, June 1, 1958, pp. 3–4; English translation in *Peking Review*, no. 15 (June 10, 1958), p. 6.

11. Cioran, pp. 81–82.

12. See Shils, pp. 41–42.

13. "Something's Missing: A Discussion Between Ernst Bloch and Theodor W. Adorno on the Contradictions of Utopian Longing," in Bloch, *Utopian Function*, p. 7.

14. Ibid., p. 3.

15. Bloch, *Principle of Hope*, p. 75.

16. Ibid., pp. 75–76.

17. See "Something's Missing," in Bloch, *Utopian Function*, p. 12.

18. Throughout this utopian project newspapers were filled with statistics on steel and food production by which progress toward utopia could be measured.

19. *Analects*, 7.15, in Chan, p. 32.

20. *Analects*, 15.31, in Chan, p. 44.

21. *Laozi*, chap. 12, in Chan, p. 145.

22. *Laozi*, chap. 46, in Chan, p. 162.

23. The question of the authorship of *Laozi* is completely immaterial here.

24. Cioran, p. 82.

25. According to Diogenes Laertius, the Stoics "say that some existing things are good, others bad, and others are neither of these. The virtues — prudence, justice, courage, moderation and the rest — are good. The opposites of these — foolishness, injustice and the rest — are bad. Everything which neither does benefit nor harms is neither of these: for instance, life, health, pleasure, beauty, strength, wealth, reputation, noble birth, and their opposites, death, disease, pain, ugliness, weakness, poverty, low repute, ignoble birth and the like.... For these things are not good but indifferents of the species 'preferred.'" (Long and Sedley, p. 354).

26. Marcuse, *Negations*, p. 178.

27. See Long, p. 69; Marcuse, *Negations*, pp. 167–68.

28. A distinction is sometimes drawn between Cyrenaic and Epicurean hedonism, with the latter setting great store by pru-

dence and thereby leading to a position aptly described by Marcuse (*Negations*, p. 170) as "negative hedonism."

29. See Fung, 1: 133–43.

30. Indeed, when utopia is believed to be a realistic prospect, it ceases to be thought of as utopian.

31. See Spinoza, *Improvement of the Understanding*. The term *Neo-Stoicism* is taken from Tillich, p. 20.

32. It thus stands to reason that in Hegel's mapping of the trajectory of self-consciousness the stage of Stoicism should come after the stage of Lordship and Bondage, which witnesses the supreme effort of a "life-and-death struggle" (in order to attain to "the truth of [the] recognition [of oneself] as an independent self-consciousness") (*Phenomenology of Spirit*, p. 114). Hegel's remark that "as a universal form of the World-Spirit, Stoicism could only appear on the scene in a time of universal fear and bondage, but also a time of universal culture which had raised itself to the level of thought" (ibid., p. 121) must be taken to be stating necessary but not sufficient conditions, for among the necessary conditions is, as we have seen, the expenditure and/or thought of effort.

33. In the case of China, the utopianist tasted, in the communist victory in 1949, the fruit of success of what may be called a pre-utopian project. The *changzheng*, the 12,500-kilometer Long March undertaken by the Red Army for strategic purposes in 1934–35, came to serve as an inspiring symbol both of the cost and of the invincibility of the utopian imagination.

34. Marcuse, *Negations*, p. 166.

35. Ibid., p. 168.

36. Indeed, "plain living," as well as "hard struggle," was already practiced before the utopian project proper in order to promote the more moderate goals of the First Five-Year Plan (1953–57).

37. See Weber, *Protestant Ethic*, pp. 172–73.

38. See ibid., pp. 158–59.

39. Even virtue as such, particularly the virtue of justice, is not part of utopia. Material abundance, which makes possible "To each according to his needs," thereby makes unnecessary the virtue of justice and renders obsolete Han Fei's as well as Hume's conception of the necessity of justice as deriving from the want of universally desired goods. The superabundance of virtue in utopia, the other side of the coin of communist utopia, makes virtue redundant (just as it makes the state redundant) and does away with

the very consciousness of virtue. Utopia is truly beyond good and evil, both in the Daoist and in the Nietzschean sense.

40. For an excellent discussion in English of the relationship between asceticism and utopian expectations, see Meisner, esp. chap. 4.

41. Epicurus, "Letter to Menoeceus," in Long and Sedley, p. 114.

42. Ibid.

43. For this and other references to Cioran in this paragraph, see Cioran, pp. 81–82.

44. Nor need we always cast doubt on the original sympathy of the utopianist because of the cold-bloodedness of the tyrant he later becomes. For if we do, we shall be guilty of reading backward when people in fact develop forward.

45. Cioran, p. 106.

46. "Confession," in Fromm, p. 257.

47. See Meisner, chap. 7.

48. The craving for change and the willingness to strive are characteristic not just of the radical utopian mentality with which we associate the communist project. In a broader context, the utopian mentality is shared by many with no attachment to communism. Mannheim distinguishes, in roughly chronological order, four historical manifestations of the utopian idea: the Chiliastic, the Liberal-Humanitarian, the Conservative, and the Socialist-Communist (see pp. 211–47). Of these, the Conservative idea of utopia is in fact a "counter-utopia" (p. 230), but the remaining three manifestations partake of the character of utopia as ordinarily understood. Bienkowsky (pp. 58–60) sees the opposition between utopia and counter-utopia in terms of what he calls the "law of economy" and the "law of petrification," where the law of economy, the striving for optimal happiness, is the one that underlies all varieties of utopianism.

If we view these tendencies—utopia and counter-utopia, economy and petrification—as carried and manifested by two different types of people, we arrive at Nietzsche's idea—found in *Human, All Too Human*, 1: 224—of "*Ennoblement through degeneration.* – History teaches that the branch of a nation that preserves itself best is the one in which most men have, as a consequence of sharing habitual and undiscussable principles, that is to say as a consequence of their common belief, a living sense of community. Here good, sound custom grows strong, here the subordination of the individual is learned and firmness imparted to character as a gift at birth and subsequently augmented. The danger facing these strong communities founded on similarly constituted, firm-charactered individuals is that of the gradually increasing inherited stupidity such as haunts all stability like its shadow. It is the more unfettered, uncertain and morally weaker individuals upon whom *spiritual progress* depends in such communities: it is the men who attempt new things and, in general, many things. . . . To this extent the celebrated struggle for existence does not seem to me to be the only theory by which the progress or strengthening of a man or a race can be explained. Two things, rather, must come together: firstly the augmentation of the stabilizing force through the union of minds in belief and communal feeling; then the possibility of the attainment of higher goals through the occurrence of degenerate natures and, as a consequence of them, partial weakenings and injurings of the stabilizing force; it is precisely the weaker nature, as the tenderer and more refined, that makes any progress possible at all." Nietzsche fails to realize that the strong (the conservative utopianists) and the degenerate (the revolutionary utopianists) may, under certain historical conditions, come together in a utopian project.

49. This innocent optimism is tempered by what we have just called the Stoic's wisdom, which is best reflected in Mao's article "The Foolish Old Man Who Removed the Mountains." See discussion in Meisner, pp. 118–20.

50. Cited in Cioran, pp. 104–5.
51. Ibid., p. 105.
52. "Something's Missing," in Bloch, *Utopian Function*, pp. 3–4.
53. See Weber, *Economy and Society*, p. 246.
54. Ibid., p. 1120; see also pp. 246, 252, 1121.
55. See ibid., p. 1141.
56. "Something's Missing," in Bloch, *Utopian Function*, p. 12.
57. See Weber, *Economy and Society*, p. 243.
58. Roth and Schluchter, p. 131.

Chapter 5

1. Nietzsche, *Will to Power*, 12. In keeping with common practice, Nietzsche is cited by section or aphorism number rather than page number, unless otherwise indicated.

2. For a study of the mechanical conception of human energy (in nineteenth-century Europe) relevant to this discussion, see Rabinbach.

3. I have found the following treatments of the will to power particularly illuminating: Warren, chap. 4; Schutte, chaps. 3 and 4; and Strong, chap. 8.

4. Nietzsche, *Gay Science*, 360.

5. Nietzsche, *Will to Power*, 314.

6. Nietzsche, *Will to Power*, 1067.

7. Nietzsche, *On the Genealogy of Morals*, III, 7.

8. Ibid., III, 1.

9. We could say that the will to power is a formal, not a substantive concept, in the specific sense that acting/agency (formal) does not entail acting in a particular way (substantive). Thus to construe the will to power as the will to what is usually understood by power (i.e., political power) is to commit a serious misunderstanding, for the will to political power implies acting in a particular way, although there is more than an accidental connection between the two (see ibid., II, 17, 18). Clearly, the will to power construed as the will to (political) domination belongs properly to the "cause of acting in a particular way."

10. Nietzsche, *Gay Science*, 44. See also *Twilight of the Idols*, "Preface," and "The Four Great Errors," 3 and 4.

11. Nietzsche, *Will to Power*, 480.

12. Nietzsche, *On the Genealogy of Morals*, III, 28.

13. On the original nihilism, see *On the Genealogy of Morals*; on "European nihilism," see *Will to Power*, bk. 1. For a succinct discussion of the trajectory from the original to "European" nihilism, see Warren, chap. 1.

14. Nietzsche writes suggestively in *Twilight of the Idols*: "Great men, like great ages, are explosives in which a tremendous force is stored up; their precondition is always, historically and physiologically, that for a long time much had been gathered, stored up, saved up, and conserved for them — that there had been no explosion for a long time" ("Skirmishes of an Untimely Man," 44). Since "great men" are here compared to "great ages," we may take it that what Nietzsche says about the former is meant to apply also to the latter.

15. I have taken the term *discharge* partly from Nietzsche, who in turn borrowed it from the language of physics. In addition to its

mechanistic implications, the term may evoke for some a "phallocentric" view of human energy. As I employ the term, however, it is interchangeable with the "expenditure" of human energy as the latter term is understood in a fairly commonsensical way. The uses to which I put the term will be clear from the context and do not require, beyond the view of the duality of human energy explained above, a commitment to any particular physical or physiological model of human energy.

16. See Nietzsche, *Will to Power*, 697, 702, 703.
17. Cioran, p. 26. Cioran's point was anticipated by Nietzsche (*Beyond Good and Evil*, 208).
18. See Nietzsche, *On the Genealogy of Morals*. For a criticism of Nietzsche's concept of *ressentiment* as the source of Christianity, see Weber, in *From Max Weber*, p. 190.
19. Nietzsche, *Ecce Homo*, p. 230.
20. Ibid., p. 229.
21. Ibid., p. 230.
22. Nietzsche, "On the Uses and Disadvantages of History for Life," in *Untimely Meditations*, p. 63.
23. *Hongqi zazhi*, June 1, 1958, pp. 3–4. English trans. in *Peking Review*, no. 15 (June 10, 1958), p. 6.
24. Nietzsche, *On the Genealogy of Morals*, III, 18.
25. Ibid., III, 18.
26. Ibid., III, 17.
27. Ibid., III, 18.
28. Nietzsche, *Gay Science*, 149.
29. Ibid., 347.
30. Engels, "On the History of Early Christianity," p. 275.
31. One could suggest a somewhat more complicated account. What is characteristic of conditions of prolonged hardship and distress, whether caused by natural forces or by social oppression, is a particularly acute conflict between desire, with its locus in the self, and reality, with its locus in the Other. Because of their different loci, the conflict between desire and reality is also a conflict between the self and the Other. Caught in this irreconcilable conflict, the will, which is itself partly both the product and the spokesman of the Other/reality, is forced either to identify with the self/desire and in so doing to suffer intolerable frustration or to identify with the Other/reality and in so doing to suffer equally intolerable alienation (through complete self-denial) — with various positions in be-

tween. Under such conditions, the individual will on its own is utterly helpless, because it cannot identify with the self and it does not want to (completely) identify with the Other. Forced by the Other/reality into a realization of its own helplessness, the will now hates its helplessness no longer just as the effect but as the cause of everything that is wrong. Henceforth the will seeks liberation from itself by dividing the Other/reality into a Malignant Other and a Benign Other and by identifying with the latter, the individual's chosen crowd. Only in the crowd does frustration become tolerable because there is now the prospect of overcoming it, and only in the crowd does alienation become tolerable because, through the change of locus from the Malignant Other to the Benign Other, alienation can be felt as freedom.

32. Nietzsche, *On the Genealogy of Morals*, III, 18.
33. Freud, *Group Psychology*, p. 79.
34. Canetti, p. 23.
35. The very idea of repression contains the implication that something — energy, the will to power, etc. — is prevented from expressing itself in the most natural manner and is forced to express itself in a manner that is less natural and hence in some sense painful. "Unnaturalness" and pain are thus two necessary features of repression. When we speak of repression in a political sense, we add a third necessary condition, namely, some degree of coercion by political authority. The reason why it seems to make sense to speak of the repression of individual power into collective power but not vice versa is that we tend to believe that individual power is in some fundamental sense more natural than, or prior to, collective power. I do not, however, want to insist on this belief. What can be said with greater certainty is that repression is proportional to the strength of that which, to put it neutrally, does not, or is not allowed to, directly express itself.
36. Aristotle, p. 4.
37. See Nietzsche, *Gay Science*, 290.
38. Nietzsche, *On the Genealogy of Morals*, II, 16.
39. Weber, *Economy and Society*, p. 515. Cioran, p. 81; see also p. 87.
40. Weber, *Economy and Society*, p. 519.
41. Mannheim.
42. See Nietzsche, *Will to Power*, 703.
43. Ibid., 55.

44. See Nietzsche, *On the Genealogy of Morals*, III, 28.
45. Weber, *Economy and Society*, p. 515.
46. See ibid., pp. 520, 528.
47. See Johnson, pp. 55–56.
48. Canetti, p. 41; see also p. 25.

49. We need to distinguish between the will to individual power and what is ordinarily understood as individualism. The will to individual power, as contrasted with the will to collective power, is a human-generic category, whereas individualism is a culture-specific formation. As such, individualism, not just collectivism, may repress the will to individual power to a more or less obtrusive degree and give expression to the will to collective power in such forms as patriotism. It is perhaps in this sense that we can understand Arthur Danto when he describes the cultures of both East and West as "two modes of antiindividualism, cognitive and vital, which are implied by their basic anthropologies" (p. 390). By the same token, we must not confuse the will to collective power with collectivism. It is on the level of specific cultural formations that we find the distinction between individualism and collectivism, these being different and culturally specific organizations of the will to power. However, although there is no exact and straightforward correspondence between the two levels of abstraction—that is, between individualism and the will to individual power on the one hand and between collectivism and the will to collective power on the other—it is nevertheless not a complete misnomer when we describe a cultural formation as individualistic or collectivistic. For although both cultural formations are marked by the preponderance of collective power over individual power, the overt emphasis is on the individual in the one case and on the collective in the other, and these different emphases translate into manifestly different balances of individual and collective power.

50. Freud, *Group Psychology*, p. 102.
51. See Nietzsche, *Will to Power*, 55.
52. See ibid., 703.
53. Nietzsche, *Twilight of the Idols*, "Skirmishes of an Untimely Man," 44.
54. Whether and for how long such opportunities can be sustained is uncertain, but while they last their impact on energy, memory, and morale is unmistakable.
55. See Nietzsche, *Will to Power*, 10.

Chapter 6

1. Arendt, 2: 41.
2. Cioran, p. 81.
3. Schopenhauer, *World as Will and Idea*, 3: 383.
4. Nietzsche, *Will to Power*, 440. In keeping with common practice, Nietzsche is cited by section or aphorism number rather than page number, unless otherwise indicated.
5. Koyré, *Etudes d'histoire de la pensée philosophique*; cited in Arendt, 2: 41.
6. Arendt, 2: 41.
7. Ibid., 2: 42.
8. Ibid.
9. Nietzsche, *The Antichrist*, 23.
10. Marx, *Contribution*, p. 44; Engels, p. 275.
11. *The Doctrine of the Mean*, chap. 14, in Chan, p. 102.
12. Schopenhauer, *World As Will and Idea*, 2: 372.
13. Bernstein, p. 202.
14. See Nietzsche, "On the Uses and Disadvantages of History for Life," in *Untimely Meditations*, pp. 63–64, 95, 97.
15. Ibid., p. 97.
16. Marx, *Contribution*, pp. 43–44.
17. Habermas, *Theory of Communicative Action*, 1: 194.
18. Schopenhauer, *Parerga and Paralipomena*, 2: 295.
19. See Hegel, *Philosophy of History*, pp. 22–28; *Laozi*, e.g., chaps. 23 and 25, in Chan; *Zhuangzi*, chap. 6, in Chan; Vico, 132, p. 62; A. Smith, 1: 421; Kant, "Perpetual Peace: A Philosophical Sketch," in Kant, pp. 112–13.
20. Cited in Lukács, p. 47.
21. Ibid., p. 51.
22. Hegel, *Philosophy of History*, p. 27.
23. Ibid.

Works Cited

Adorno, Theodor W. *Against Epistemology*. Trans. Willis Dimingo. Cambridge, Mass.: MIT Press, 1983.
Amin, Samir. *Eurocentrism*. Trans. Russell Moore. New York: Monthly Review Press, 1989.
Arendt, Hannah. *The Life of the Mind*. 2 vols. New York: Harcourt Brace Jovanovich, 1978.
Aristotle. *The Politics*. Ed. Stephen Everson. Cambridge, Eng.: Cambridge University Press, 1988.
Benjamin, Walter. *Illuminations*. Ed. Hannah Arendt. Trans. Harry Zohn. New York: Schocken Books, 1969.
Bernstein, Eduard. *Evolutionary Socialism: A Criticism and Affirmation*. Trans. Edith C. Harvey. New York: Schocken Books, 1961.
Bienkowsky, Wladyslaw. *Theory and Practice*. Trans. Jane Cave. London: Allison & Busby, 1981.
Bloch, Ernst. *The Principle of Hope*. 3 vols. Trans. Neville Plaice, Stephen Plaice, and Paul Knight. Cambridge, Mass.: MIT Press, 1986.
———. *The Utopian Function of Art and Literature*. Trans. Jack Zipes and Frank Mecklenburg. Cambridge, Mass.: MIT Press, 1988.
Breuer, Joseph, and Sigmund Freud. *Studies on Hysteria*. In Sigmund Freud, *The Complete Psychological Works, Standard Edition*, ed. James Strachey, vol. 2. London: Hogarth Press, 1955.
Canetti, Elias. *Crowds and Power*. Trans. Carol Steward. New York: Farrar Straus Giroux, 1984.
Chan, Wing-tsit. *A Source Book in Chinese Philosophy*. Princeton: Princeton University Press, 1963.

Cioran, E. M. *History and Utopia*. Trans. Richard Howard. New York: Seaver Books, 1987.
Cohen, Paul A. *Discovering History in China*. New York: Columbia University Press, 1984.
Connerton, Paul. *How Societies Remember*. Cambridge, Eng.: Cambridge University Press, 1989.
Danto, Arthur. "Postscript: Philosophical Individualism in Chinese and Western Thought." In *Individualism and Holism: Studies in Confucian and Taoist Values*. Ed. Donald Munro. Ann Arbor: University of Michigan, Center for Chinese Studies, 1985, pp. 385–94.
Deleuze, Gilles. *Nietzsche and Philosophy*. Trans. Hugh Tomlinson. New York: Columbia University Press, 1983.
Douglas, Mary. *How Institutions Think*. Syracuse, N.Y.: Syracuse University Press, 1986.
Engels, Friedrich. "On the Early History of Christianity." In *Marx/Engels on Religion*. Moscow: Progress Publishers, 1975.
Freud, Sigmund. *Beyond the Pleasure Principle*. In Sigmund Freud, *The Complete Psychological Works, Standard Edition*, ed. James Strachey, vol. 18. London: Hogarth Press, 1955.
———. *Group Psychology and the Analysis of the Ego*. In Sigmund Freud, *The Complete Psychological Works, Standard Edition*, ed. James Strachey, vol. 18. London: Hogarth Press, 1955.
———. "Remembering, Repeating and Working-Through." In Sigmund Freud, *The Complete Psychological Works, Standard Edition*, ed. James Strachey, vol. 12. London: Hogarth Press, 1958.
Fromm, Eric. *Marx's Concept of Man*. New York: Continuum, 1966.
Fung Yu-lan. *A History of Chinese Philosophy*. 2 vols. Trans. Derk Bodde. Princeton: Princeton University Press, 1952, 1953.
Habermas, Jürgen. *Legitimation Crisis*. Trans. Thomas McCarthy. Boston: Beacon Press, 1975.
———. *Theory and Practice*. Trans. John Viertel. Boston: Beacon Press, 1973.
———. *The Theory of Communicative Action*. 2 vols. Trans. Thomas McCarthy. Boston: Beacon Press, 1984.

———. *Toward a Rational Society*. Trans. Jeremy Shapiro. Boston: Beacon Press, 1970.

Halbwachs, Maurice. *The Collective Memory*. Trans. Francis J. Ditter, Jr., and Vida Yazdi Ditter. New York: Harper & Row, 1980.

Hall, John. *Powers and Liberties: The Causes and Consequences of the Rise of the West*. Berkeley: University of California Press, 1986.

Hegel, G. W. F. *Phenomenology of Spirit*. Trans. A. V. Miller. Oxford: Oxford University Press, 1977.

———. *The Philosophy of History*. Trans. J. Sibree. New York: Dover Publications, 1956.

Huang, Ray. *China: A Macro History*. New York: M. E. Sharpe, 1990.

Johnson, Paul. *A History of Christianity*. New York: Atheneum, 1976.

Kant, Immanuel. *Kant's Political Writings*. Ed. Hans Reiss. Trans. H. B. Nisbett. Cambridge, Eng.: Cambridge University Press, 1970.

Kierkegaard, Søren. *Concluding Unscientific Postscript to Philosophical Fragments*. Trans. Howard V. Hong and Edna H. Hong. Princeton: Princeton University Press, 1992.

———. *Either/Or*. Trans. David F. Swenson and Lillian Marvin Swenson. Princeton: Princeton University Press, 1944.

Kojève, Alexandre. *Introduction to the Reading of Hegel*. Ed. Allan Bloom. Trans. James H. Nicholas. Ithaca, N.Y.: Cornell University Press, 1980.

Krell, David Farrell. *Of Memory, Reminiscence, and Writing*. Bloomington: Indiana University Press, 1990.

Levenson, Joseph R., ed. *Modern China: An Interpretative Anthology*. London: Macmillan, 1971.

Li Zehou 李泽厚. *Zhongguo xiandai sixiangshi lun* 中国现代思想史论 (Essays on the history of modern Chinese thought). Beijing: Dongfang, 1987.

Lifton, Robert Jay. *Thought Reform and the Psychology of Totalism*. Chapel Hill: University of North Carolina Press, 1989.

Lilla, Mark. "The Two Lives of Alexandre Kojève." *Times Literary Supplement*, Apr. 5, 1991.

Lin Biao. *Long Live the Victory of People's War!* Beijing: Foreign Languages Press, 1965.

Liu Guangdong 刘广东. *Mao Zedong lunli sixiang jianlun* 毛泽东伦理思想简论 (An outline of Mao Zedong's ethical thought). Ji'nan: Shandong renmin chubanshe, 1987.

Long, A. A. *Hellenistic Philosophy*. Berkeley: University of California Press, 1986.

Long, A. A., and D. N. Sedley. *The Hellenistic Philosophers*, vol. 1, *Translations of the Principal Sources with Philosophic Commentary*. Cambridge, Eng.: Cambridge University Press, 1987.

Lukács, Georg. *History and Class Consciousness*. Trans. Rodney Livingstone. Cambridge, Mass.: MIT Press, 1971.

Luo Guojie 罗国杰, ed. *Makesi zhuyi lunlixue* 马克思主义伦理学 (Marxist ethics). Beijing: Renmin chubanshe, 1982.

Mannheim, Karl. *Ideology and Utopia*. Trans. Louis Wirth and Edward Shils. New York: Harcourt, Brace & World, 1936.

Mao Zedong. "Combat Liberalism." In Mao Zedong, *Selected Works*, vol. 2. Beijing: Foreign Languages Press, 1967.

———. "The Foolish Old Man Who Removed the Mountains." In Mao Zedong, *Selected Works*, vol. 3. Beijing: Foreign Languages Press, 1967.

Marcuse, Herbert. *Eros and Civilization*. Boston: Beacon Press, 1955.

———. *Negations*. Trans. Jeremy J. Shapiro. Boston: Beacon Press, 1968.

Marx, Karl. *Contribution to the Critique of Hegel's Philosophy of Right: Introduction*. In *Karl Marx: Early Writings*, trans. and ed. T. B. Bottomore. New York: McGraw-Hill, 1963.

———. *The Economic and Philosophic Manuscripts of 1844*. Ed. Dirk J. Struik. Trans. Martin Milligan. New York: International Publishers, 1964.

Meisner, Maurice. *Marxism, Maoism, and Utopianism*. Madison: University of Wisconsin Press, 1982.

Nietzsche, Friedrich. *The Antichrist*. In *The Portable Nietzsche*, ed. and trans. Walter Kaufmann. New York: Viking Press, 1954.

———. *Beyond Good and Evil*. Trans. Walter Kaufmann. New York: Random House, 1966.

———. *Ecce Homo* (together with *On the Genealogy of Morals*). Trans. Walter Kaufmann. New York: Random House, 1967.

———. *The Gay Science*. Trans. Walter Kaufmann. New York: Random House, 1974.
———. *Human, All Too Human*. Trans. R. J. Hollingdale. Cambridge, Eng.: Cambridge University Press, 1986.
———. *Nietzsche Contra Wagner*. In *The Portable Nietzsche*, ed. and trans. Walter Kaufmann. New York: Viking Press, 1954.
———. *On the Genealogy of Morals* (together with *Ecce Homo*). Trans. Walter Kaufmann and R. J. Hollingdale. New York: Random House, 1967.
———. *The Will to Power*. Ed. Walter Kaufmann. Trans. W. Kaufmann and R. J. Hollingdale. New York: Random House, 1967.
———. *Thus Spoke Zarathustra*. In *The Portable Nietzsche*, ed. and trans. Walter Kaufmann. New York: Viking Press, 1954.
———. *Twilight of the Idols*. In *The Portable Nietzsche*, ed. and trans. Walter Kaufmann. New York: Viking Press, 1954.
———. *Untimely Meditations*. Trans. R. J. Hollingdale. Cambridge, Eng.: Cambridge University Press, 1983.
Rabinbach, Anson. *The Human Motor: Energy, Fatigue, and the Origins of Modernity*. New York: Basic Books, 1990.
Roth, Guenther, and Wolfgang Schluchter. *Max Weber's Vision of History*. Berkeley: University of California Press, 1979.
Santayana, George. *The Life of Reason*. 5 vols. New York: Collier Books, 1962.
Schopenhauer, Arthur. *Parerga and Paralipomena*. Trans. E. F. J. Payne. Oxford: Clarendon Press, 1974.
———. *The World as Will and Idea*. 3 vols. Trans. R. B. Haldane and J. Kemp. London: Routledge & Kegan Paul, 1883.
Schutte, Ofelia. *Beyond Nihilism: Nietzsche Without Masks*. Chicago: University of Chicago Press, 1984.
Schwarcz, Vera. "No Solace from Lethe: History, Memory, and Cultural Identity in Twentieth-Century China." *Daedalus*, 120, no. 2 (Spring 1991): 85–112.
Shils, Edward. *Tradition*. Chicago: University of Chicago Press, 1981.
Smith, Adam. *An Inquiry into the Nature and Causes of the Wealth of Nations*. 2 vols. London: Methuen, 1904.
Smith, B. J. *Politics and Remembrance*. Princeton: Princeton University Press, 1985.

Works Cited

Spinoza, Benedict. *Ethics*. In *Works of Spinoza*, vol. 2, trans. R. H. M. Elwes. New York: Dover, 1955.

———. *On the Improvement of the Understanding*. In *Works of Spinoza*, vol. 2, trans. R. H. M. Elwes. New York: Dover, 1955.

Strong, Tracy B. *Friedrich Nietzsche and the Politics of Transfiguration*. Berkeley: University of California Press, 1988.

Tillich, Paul. *The Courage to Be*. New Haven: Yale University Press, 1952.

Vico, Giambattista. *The New Science*. Rev. trans. T. G. Bergin and M. H. Fisch. Ithaca, N.Y.: Cornell University Press, 1968.

Vološinov, V. N. *Freudianism*. Trans. I. R. Titunik. Bloomington: Indiana University Press, 1987.

Wallerstein, Immanuel. *Historical Capitalism*. New York: Routledge, Chapman & Hall, 1983.

Warren, Mark. *Nietzsche and Political Thought*. Cambridge, Mass.: MIT Press, 1988.

Weber, Max. *Economy and Society*. 2 vols. Ed. Guenther Roth and Claus Wittich. Berkeley: University of California Press, 1978.

———. *From Max Weber*. Ed. and trans. H. H. Gerth and C. Wright Mills. New York: Oxford University Press, 1946.

———. *The Protestant Ethic and the Spirit of Capitalism*. Trans. Talcott Parsons. London: Unwin Hyman, 1930.

———. *The Religion of China*. Trans. Hans H. Gerth. New York: Free Press, 1951.

Zhang Dainian 张岱年. *Zhongguo lunli sixiang yanjiu* 中国伦理思想研究 (Studies in Chinese ethical thought). Shanghai: Shanghai renmin chubanshe, 1989.

Žižek, Slavoj. *The Sublime Object of Ideology*. London: Verso, 1989.

Character List

baihua 白话
Baihu tongyi 白虎通义
bu laodong zhe bu deshi
　不劳动者不得食
changzheng 长征
Cheng Hao 程颢
Cheng Yi 程颐
chiku 吃苦
Chunqiu fanlu 春秋繁露
dao 道
Dao de jing 道德经
di-xiu-fan 帝修反
Dong Zhongshu 董仲舒
dousi 斗私
fa 法
Feng Guifen 冯桂芬
fengjian yidu 封建遗毒
gaitian huandi 改天换地
gang 纲
gangchang mingjiao 纲常名教
geming 革命
guwen 古文
Han Fei 韩非
jianku fendou 艰苦奋斗
kantou 看透
Laozi 老子
Lei Feng 雷锋
li 礼
Lin Biao 林彪

linghun shenchu naogeming
　灵魂深处闹革命
lishi guilü 历史规律
lixiang zhuyi 理想主义
pixiu 批修
qingwu zhongsheng 轻物重生
Qin Shihuang 秦始皇
quqi jinghua, quqi zaopo
　取其精华，去其糟粕
ren (benevolence) 仁
ren (human being) 人
renmin de qinwuyuan
　人民的勤务员
sanda jilü baxiang zhuyi
　三大纪律八项注意
sangang wuchang 三纲五常
Shang Yang 商鞅
shengchan 生产
shiyi renmin jiuyi shang,
　haiyou yiyi dai kaizhang
　十亿人民九亿商，还有一亿待开张
shunying ziran 顺应自然
siduan 四端
Tao te ching 道德经
taoxian 讨嫌
ti 体
ti-yong 体用
tian 天
Wang Bi 王弼

Wang Chong 王充
weiwo 为我
weixin zhuyi 唯心主义
wenbao 温饱
wenyanwen 文言文
wu 五
wuchan jieji de dongji yu xiaoguo tongyilun 无产阶级的动机与效果统一论
wusi 无私
xin 信
Xunzi 荀子
yang wei zhong yong 洋为中用
Yang Zhu 扬朱
yi 义
yiku sitian 忆苦思甜
yong 用
Zhang Zai 张载
Zhang Zhidong 张之洞
zhi 智
zhongguo 中国
Zhongxue weiti, xixue weiyong 中学为体,西学为用
zhuageming, cushengchan 抓革命,促生产
Zhuangzi 庄子
zichan jieji geren zhuyi 资产阶级个人主义
ziran 自然

Index

In this index an "f" after a number indicates a separate reference on the next page, and an "ff" indicates separate references on the next two pages. A continuous discussion over two or more pages is indicated by a span of page numbers, e.g., "57–59." *Passim* is used for a cluster of references in close but not consecutive sequence. Entries are alphabetized letter by letter, ignoring word breaks, hyphens, and accents.

Adorno, Theodor, 29, 138, 157, 164
Alienated labor, 78
Altruism, 78, 102, 112, 122, 127–30, 140, 158f, 166
Amin, Samir, 252
Anti-intellectualism, 72
Anti-Rightist movement, 79, 81, 187
Anti-traditionalism, 38
Arendt, Hannah, 209, 212–13
Aristotle, 98, 189
Asceticism, 3, 10, 13f, 143–47 *passim*, 150–52, 157–58, 159–61, 165–67, 228
Asiatic mode of production (Marx), 29

Becoming, 214, 220–21
Being, 214, 220–21
Benjamin, Walter, 68
Bernstein, Eduard, 221
Bienkowsky, Wladyslaw, 262
Bloch, Ernst, 139, 141
Breuer, Josef, 99

Canetti, Elias, 185
Capitalism, 25f, 28–29, 49, 51–52, 58f
Center mentality, China's, 33–34, 36–37, 40–48 *passim*, 57, 60
Charisma, 161–65, 224–25, 234–35
Charismatic community, 161–65
Christianity, 180f, 183, 192–93, 196–97, 214f; and communism, 214–23
Cioran, E. M., 137, 153, 156, 174, 193, 210
Classical Chinese, 69–70
Cohen, Paul A., 248
Collectivism, 78, 102, 122–30 *passim*, 159, 199, 267
Collective power, 187–89, 267
Communism: as morality, 116–17; nihilistic phase of, 195–96; and Christianity, 214–23
Confessions, *see Dousi*
Confucianists, Song and Ming, 50, 106
Confucius, 104–10 *passim*, 127, 142, 219

Index

Connerton, Paul, 97, 255
Consciousness: heightened, 4f, 207f, 225–32; moral, 108; negative aspect of, 211, 229; positive aspect of, 211, 229–30
Consumerism, 7, 10, 204, 241
Cultural crisis, psychological adjustment to, 30f, 36, 45
Cultural Revolution, 77–81, 161–65, 182, 187, 221, 226–27
Cultural self-identity, 25, 33–38, 40f, 46f, 49, 56–60, 61
Cultural superiority/inferiority, 27, 29–30, 34
Cynicism, 5f, 91, 96, 201ff, 204–5

Danto, Arthur, 267
Dao de jing, 105f. *See also Laozi*
Deleuze, Gilles, 251
Democracy, 8, 36, 122, 123–27, 205
Democracy movement, 2, 76, 201, 203f; and hedonism, 7–12, 203–5; collective amnesia of, 10f, 203
Democratic centralism, 123f
Deng, Xiaoping, 6–7, 94, 165f, 199, 226–27
Dialectic, 16, 232
Dong Zhongshu, 78, 94, 103–5
Douglas, Mary, 72
Dousi, 80, 90–91, 185f, 189–90

Egalitarianism, 78, 145f
Egoism, 146–47
Ends and means, 26, 28, 31, 51, 54–56, 61, 114, 119, 224
Energy, human: duality of, 169–73; and memory, 169, 177, 178–79; conservation of, 173–79; and suffering, 174–75, 178; discharge of, 174–76, 264–65
Engels, Friedrich, 183, 215, 230
Enlightenment, European, 49
Epicurus, 12, 134, 146, 152
Eschatology (communist or Christian), 192–93, 196–97, 211f, 214–15, 219

Ethnocentrism, 37, 40
Eurocentrism, 35

False consciousness, 230
Feudalism, 29, 93
Forgetting: forced, 64–65, 67f, 74f, 77; cognitive, 65–68; affective, 65–68, 81; indirect (unconscious), 69, 73f, 98. *See also* Memory
Four fundamental principles, 115f
Four Modernizations, 165
Fourier, Charles, 156
Freedom, 8, 78, 122, 123–27, 183–84, 198–99, 200–5 *passim*, 265–66
Freud, Sigmund, 79, 99f, 184, 200
Future: (heightened) consciousness of, 4, 208, 209–25; and will(ing), 209–14; ideology of, 211–12, 214–25; conceptual vs. temporal, 253–54*n*24

Gangchang mingjiao, 33f, 250
Great Leap Forward, 55, 137, 140, 151, 161–63, 180f, 226

Habermas, Jürgen, 97
Halbwachs, Maurice, 76
Hall, John, 254
Han Fei, 108, 127
Hedonism, 2–3, 5f, 12–19 *passim*, 102, 134–36, 140–52 *passim*, 158–59, 228–29, 239–40, 259, 260–61*n*28; and nihilism, 5ff, 168–69, 204, 208; and democracy movement, 7–12, 203–5; and asceticism, 145f, 150–52, 165–67; as ideology, 150, 165; triumph of, 206, 241. *See also under* Utopianism
Hegel, Georg Wilhelm Friedrich, 209, 230f, 261
Historical agency, 230–31
Historical determinism, 82, 88, 221–22, 224–25
Historiography, official, 82–89

Huang, Ray, 250, 254

Idealism, 14, 51, 136, 140, 239
Imperial China, 31f, 43
Individual power, 185–92, 267; repression of, 185–88; transformation of, 188, 192, 197–98; sublimation of, 200–201, 202, 205
Individualism, 95, 125, 129, 199–200, 203–5
Indoctrination, 76, 93, 186, 224, 232–37
Inferiority complex, China's, 43, 46f
Instrumental rationality, 51f, 56, 102
Intellectualism (Confucian), 240–41
Intellectuals, 96, 248
Internationalism, 40, 42

Kant, Immanuel, 230
Kierkegaard, Søren, 100f, 135f, 256–57
Kojève, Alexandre, 255

Language, state's control of, 71–73
Laozi, 110, 230
Laozi, 84, 142
Legalism, 94, 108
Lei Feng, 114
Lenin, Vladimir, 93
Li (ritual), 103–10
Lin Biao, 43, 163
Linguistic reification, 71–74
Long March, 86
Lukács, Georg, 230

Mannheim, Karl, 193, 262
Mao Zedong, 42, 47ff, 53ff, 62–65, 79–80, 94, 114, 120, 126, 130, 137, 140, 155, 162–65, 185f, 257–58; and Nietzsche, 180–84
Mao Zedong Thought, 63, 116

Maoist Chinese (language), 71–73, 74
Marcuse, Herbert, 143, 150, 252
Marx, Karl, 12f, 51, 53, 134, 141, 155, 215, 220f
Marxism, 38–40, 41f, 51–53, 117–19, 147–48, 231; as China's self-identity, 38–40, 56–60; as ideology, 117–19; use and abuse of, as label, 258–59
Materialism, 13f, 134ff, 259
May Fourth movement, 112
Means and ends, *see* Ends and means
Memory: and utopianism, 3, 243–44; and language, 69–74; as part of social order, 73–74, 75; as subversion, 75–77; role of official historiography in shaping, 82–89; and punishment, 89–92, 95–97; and nihilism, 98–100, 243; unconscious, 98–101
Mencius, 104ff
Middle Kingdom (*zhongguo*), 35, 42
Modern China, concept of, 26, 248–49
Modern Chinese, 69, 71f
Moral codes of communism: on conduct, 111, 113, 119–22, 130, 132; on belief, 111–12, 113, 115, 119–22, 130–33; on virtue, 112f, 119–20, 130, 132
Moral codes of Confucianism: on conduct, 104–10, 119–20; on belief, 104–7, 119–20; on virtue, 104–10, 119–20
Moral consciousness, 108
Morality, rationale/structure of: Confucian, 103–10, 119–20; communist, 110–13, 119–22, 130, 132–33, 258

Nationalism, 38, 42
Nature, traditional conception of, 50
New Culture movement, 69

Nietzsche, Friedrich, 74, 87, 91, 99, 134f, 170–79 *passim*, 191, 194, 203, 211, 214, 262–63
Nihilism, 2–3, 5–7, 8–15 *passim*, 98f, 207–9, 227ff, 248. *See also under* Hedonism; Utopianism
Nihilistic phase of communism, 195–96

Obsession with difference (from West), 43–49, 60
Opium War, 25f, 33, 39–47 *passim*, 54, 248–49

Paternalism, 153–54
Patriotism, 87
Periphery mentality, China's, 35–37, 39, 43f, 47, 60
Persecution, 89–91
Personality cult, 163, 182
Politicization of morality, 113–16, 132–33
Protestant ethic, 150–51, 223

Reactive mentality (reaction), 47–48, 60, 252
Reform, Deng Xiaoping's, and utopianism, 226–27
Remembering: affective, 65, 68, 81; cognitive, 66–68. *See also* Memory
Ren (benevolence), 103–10
Repression, 184–92, 266; consciousnesss of, 188, 197–98, 224
Ressentiment (resentment), 174, 175–76, 236
Revisionism, 48, 94
Revolution and production, 54–55, 164
Roth, Guenther, 164

Sangang wuchang, 103, 107, 250
Santayana, George, 79, 100
Schopenhauer, Arthur, 210, 212, 220, 230
Scientism, 112, 117, 236

Self-identity, cultural, *see* Cultural self-identity
Shang Yang, 108
Smith, Adam, 230
Snow, Edgar, 182
Soviet Union, 11, 39f, 147
Spinoza, Benedict, 100, 149
Stoicism, 143ff, 148–49, 151, 153, 260f
Sublimation (of hedonism), 8f, 14, 102, 121, 158–59, 200–201, 241, 242–43

Teleology, 13, 16, 42, 51–54, 56, 88, 111
Tian (heaven), 103–7
Ti-yong, 26–28, 30–37 *passim*, 45, 47, 54, 61, 249–50
Totalitarianism, and utopianism, 243–44
Tradition, Confucian, 31–42 *passim*, 66, 69, 147–48, 240–41; unconscious relationship with, 63, 70, 251

Unconscious, role of the, in Cultural Revolution, 77–81
Universalism, 36, 41, 49
Utilitarianism, 146, 258
Utopianism, 3–5, 19, 136–43, 148–49, 153–57 *passim*, 226ff, 247, 262–63; and hedonism, 2–3, 9, 12–15, 134, 166, 239–40, 242; and nihilism, 2, 9, 12, 15, 98, 207–9, 231, 243; de-sublimation of, 14, 102, 229, 242; and poverty, 136–43, 147–53 *passim*, 156–60; susceptibility to, 137, 142, 147f, 157, 178; as social contract, 152–55, 161
Utopian project: antecedents of, 173–79; and weakness of individuals, 179–85, 203; as gamble, 209, 214

Vico, Giambattista, 230
Vološinov, V. N., 79

Voluntarism, 4, 53–54, 88, 227

Wallerstein, Immanuel, 51–52
Wang Bi, 249
Weber, Max, 49, 52, 161f, 164, 193, 195, 232
West, imitation of, 25, 36, 55–56, 60–61, 254
Western impact, 25, 248–49
Western morality, modern, 128–29
Work ethic, 47, 132, 150, 223

World-adjustment, 29, 49–50
World-mastery, 16, 29, 49–50, 52–53, 193

Xenophobia, 38, 87

Yang Zhu, 146–47

Zhongxue weiti, xixue weiyong, 26, 249
Zhuangzi, 230

Library of Congress Cataloging-in-Publication Data
Ci, Jiwei, 1955–
 Dialetic of the Chinese revolution : from utopianism to hedonism / Jiwei Ci.
   p. cm.
 Includes bibliographical references and index.
 ISBN 0-8047-2354-0 (alk. paper) :
 ISBN 0-8047-2373-7 (pbk: alk. paper):
 1. China — Social conditions — 1976–   2. Social psychology — China.   3. China — Politics and government — 1976–   I. Title.
 HN733.5.C6 1994
 306'.0951 — dc20   94-2558
                                                             CIP
                                                             REV.